THE GUPTA EMPIRE

Mathurā standing Buddha Image showing halo decorated with elaborated lotus and geese, and stylised drapery of Gandhāra design, and, on the pedestal, a Sanskrit inscription in Gupta script of 6th Century A. D., recording that it was the religious gift of a Sākya-Bhikshu named Yaśadinna.

THE
GUPTA EMPIRE

RADHA KUMUD MOOKERJI

MOTILAL BANARSIDASS
Delhi Varanasi Patna Bangalore Madras

Fifth Edition : 1973
Reprint : Delhi, 1989

MOTILAL BANARSIDASS
Bungalow Road, Jawahar Nagar, Delhi 110 007

Branches
Chowk, Varanasi 221 001
Ashok Rajpath, Patna 800 004
24 Race Course Road, Bangalore 560 001
120 Royapettah High Road, Mylapore, Madras 600 004

ISBN: 81-208-0089-3 (Cloth)
ISBN: 81-208-0440-6 (Paper)

PRINTED IN INDIA
BY JAINENDRA PRAKASH JAIN AT SHRI JAINENDRA PRESS, A-45 NARAINA INDUSTRIAL AREA, PHASE I, NEW DELHI 110 028 AND PUBLISHED BY NARENDRA PRAKASH JAIN FOR MOTILAL BANARSIDASS, DELHI 110 007.

To My Grandsons

Kṛishṇa Kumud

and

Pradīpta Kumud

PREFACE TO FIRST EDITION

This work was written in the last days of my teaching at the Lucknow University and suggested by its needs. Its title indicates its scope and limits. It deals only with imperial Gupta history, and not with that of the later Guptas. It seeks to bring together in a concise and condensed form all the facts and data which are derivable from different sources, literary, epigraphic or numismatic, but are treated in separate specialised works. It will thus be found useful to both students and teachers of its subject, who will find in one handy volume all its materials collected and utilised. A special feature of the work is its account of the moral and material progress of the country achieved in the spacious times of the Gupta Emperors, and of the various institutions, social, economic, and administrative in which that progress was embodied. It gives a picture of India's civilization in some of her best days, the days of national freedom and planning, of the beginnings of her expansion, and intercourse with Indonesia and China. It is hoped that it will thus have a larger and more general appeal beyond the narrow circle of academic students of history. Another special feature of the work is its Illustrations, some of which, especially those of coins, are based on line-drawings to bring out more clearly their details which are somewhat obscure or defaced in the originals. The Illustrations will thus serve as useful aids to the study of the coins. Some of the line-drawings I owe to the distinguished Artists, Messrs. Nanda Lal Bose, Asit Kumar Haldar, and P. Neogy, to whom I am grateful. There have been at places repetitions of the same material where it had to be presented from different points of view, and in its various aspects. Such repetitions have not been ruled out.

The method of transliteration adopted in the work is shown in the following examples: *Kṛishṇa, Vaṃśa, Lichchhavi*.

The publication has been delayed by the prevailing difficulties of printing, and by my deputation by Government to an FAO Conference at Washington (U.S.A.) in October 1946.

I owe acknowledgements to my following pupils who helped me in copying out my MS for the press: Abinas Srivastava, M.A., M. C. Joshi, M.A., Dina Nath Tandon, M.A., and B. Subba Rao, M.A. My thanks are due to Mr. Raja Ram Jayasval, M.A., for the Index.

PREFACE

I am grateful to my friend, Dr. Benjamin Schwartz, Ph.D., of the Indic Section of the Library of Congress at Washington, D.C., U.S.A., for his kind help in correcting the final proofs of the work at Washington.

June, 1947. RADHA RUMUD MOOKERJI

★

PREFACE TO SECOND EDITION

It is gratifying to the Author to find that a work which is somewhat technical in its character with its necessary documentation, literary, epigraphic and numismatic, should call for a second edition in such a short time. Some necessary additions have been made on the basis of new numismatic material derived from the Bayana hoard of Imperial Gupta gold coins recently found in Bharatpur State.

The Author is greatly indebted to the line drawings and other suggestions made by Sri Sivaramamurti, M.A., Superintendent of Archaeology, Indian Museum, Calcutta, in the preparation of the addendum.

The Author records his deep sorrow at the sad and untimely death of his old pupil Sri Raja Ram Jayaswal, M.A., who prepared the Index which remains unchanged in the Second Edition.

39 Ekdalia Road, Calcutta,
April, 1952.

RADHA KUMUD MOOKERJI
(Member of Parliament)

PREFACE TO THIRD EDITION

That a third edition of the work has been called for is gratifying to the author. My thanks are due to the Publishers for their readiness to meet the demand and for the improved get-up which will now make the book more attractive to its readers.

39 Ekdalia Road,
Calcutta 19;
July 1959

RADHA KUMUD MOOKERJI

CONTENTS

CONTENTS

CHAPTER XIII

VAINYA GUPTA

CHAPTER XIV

KUMĀRA GUPTA III

CHAPTER XV

LOCAL KINGS OF EASTERN INDIA

CHAPTER XVI

MATERIAL AND MORAL PROGRESS

CHAPTER I

BEGINNINGS

Sources. The sources of imperial Gupta history are of four classes: literary works, inscriptions, coins and monuments.

The literary works include: (1) the *Purāṇas*; (2) the play called *Kaumudī-Mahotsava* composed by a lady called Vijjākā; (3) the play called *Devī-Chandraguptam* composed by Viśākhadatta (probably same as author of *Mudrārākshasa*, but traced only in citations contained in the rhetorical work *Nāṭya-Darpaṇa*, the hero of the play being Chandra Gupta II); (4) Bāṇa's *Harshacharita*; (5) the Mahāyāna Buddhist chronicle, *Ārya-Mañjuśrī Mūlakalpa*, dealing with imperial dynasties from 700 B.C. to A.D. 750. To these may be added the records of travel of the two Chinese pilgrims, Fa-Hien and Hiuen-Tsang who visited India in the fifth and seventh century A.D. respectively.

The inscriptions are sources of much important and reliable history for the Guptas. They are incised on stone, and metal, as in the case of copper-plates, or in that of the Meherauli Iron Pillar inscription. Some inscriptions are chronicles of events, as is the Allahabad Pillar inscription of Samudra Gupta or the Mandasor Pillar inscription of Yaśodharman. Others are records of religious endowments or secular donations. The donative inscriptions are more in number.

The Gupta coins throw light on both general and numismatic history. They present a wide variety of types as shown in their legends, symbols, standard or weight, and fabric. They show the progressive evolution of indigenous Indian coinage and of its emancipation from the prevailing foreign and Kushān models.

Monuments are also a source of both artistic and religious history. They illustrate different schools of art and architecture. Three different Schools of Art are distinguished as (1) Mathurā, (2) Vārāṇaśī, and (3) Nālandā. As in the case of coinage, Gupta art set the standard for Indian art free of foreign influences which are seen in Gandhāra and Kushān art. The image of the seated Buddha at Sarnath Museum is taken as the masterpiece of Indian art, and of its Vārāṇaśī School, though by origin it is descended from the images of the Buddha and the Bodhisattva fashioned by the earlier Mathurā School. Examples of what may be called the Nālandā School of Art are seen at their best at Nālandā and at Kurkihar from which typical specimens are gathered at the Patna Museum. As regards architecture, evolution of its different styles is seen in the various temples of the times.

These temples throw light on religious history. They represent the main religions of the times and their deities of worship—Vishṇu, Śiva, Durgā, Buddha or Bodhisattva, and Jain Tīrthaṅkaras. The worship of Vishṇu is seen in the temples at Udayagiri in Gwalior and at Pathāri. An Udayagiri temple is dated as early as A.D. 401 and shows the emergence of Gaṅgā and Yamunā as goddesses. The famous temple at Deogarh in Jhansi district is dedicated to the worship of both Śiva and Vishṇu or Kṛishṇa. It is of the sixth century A.D. We may next note the Durgā temple at Aihole of the fifth century and the fine sculptures of the Bādāmi caves.

Background. We may briefly consider the political environment in which the Guptas emerged into power and prominence and became a new factor in Indian history.

History after the Mauryas. The imperial tradition of the Mauryas did not long survive them. They were able to achieve the Vedic political ideal as defined in the *Aitareya Brāhmaṇa* that a king should make himself the king of kings and establish his authority as the sole sovereign (*Ekarāṭ*) 'of the entire country up to the seas.' It was, however, difficult to organize the whole of India as a political unit. The country is much too large for that. The unity of the history of India as a whole has been very often lost in the diversity of separate provincial and local histories. The Maurya Empire which had ruled over a Greater India extending approximately from Persia to Mysore was split up soon after Aśoka, after a period of about 100 years, into a number of small States or kingdoms. The frontier provinces had already become a separate political entity under king Sophagasenus (Saubhāgyasena) before 206 B.C. if we may believe in Polybius. He as 'King of the Indians' confronted Antiochus III of Syria when the latter 'descended into India' but had to 'renew his friendship' with him. According to the Kashmir tradition, Aśoka's own son named Jalauka set up an independent kingdom in Kashmir and even extended its territory by conquests. In the interior, the Mauryas were succeeded about 185 B.C. by the Śuṅgas (of Baiṁbika family, according to Kālidāsa in his drama *Mālavikāgnimitram*), and, later, by the Kāṇvas. The Kāṇvas ruled for 45 years, and were overthrown in about 28 B.C. by a king of the Śātavāhana dynasty known as the Āndhra dynasty. Kalinga also which was annexed to the Maurya Empire by Aśoka became now a powerful kingdom under the Cheṭas whose heroic king Khāravela was a menace to Magadha, to the Śātavāhanas and even to the South. India was thus in a state of great political unrest marked by struggles between different States and Powers for supremacy.

Foreign Invasions : Greek. In the North-West, the situation was beyond control. It invited foreign invasions. The first of these invaders were the Bactrian Greeks led by Demetrius and Menander (king Milinda of the Buddhist work *Milinda-Pañho*) who, according to Patañjali, besieged Madhyamikā (near Chitor) and Sāketa (Oudh) and, according to the *Gārgī Saṁhitā*, occupied Pañchāla and Mathurā, and even menaced Kusumadhvaja or Pāṭaliputra. The tide of this invasion was for a time stemmed by the Śuṅga emperor Pushyamitra whose grandson Vasumitra defeated the Yavanas on the south bank of the Sindhu (Indus ?), as related by Kālidāsa in his *Mālavikāgnimitram*. But this reverse did not prevent the Greek conquest of the Punjab where Menander began to rule, with his capital at Sākala (Sialkot). The extent of Greek authority and influence in India is indicated by the fact that the coins of Apollodotus and Menander were in circulation in the bazaars of Barygaza (Broach) in the first century A.D., as stated in the *Periplus*. The Greek power in India, however, did not make much headway, as it was handicapped by factions led by the two rival Houses of Eukratides and Euthydemos. Of the former House, the king named Antialkidas has some Indian interest. He deputed from his capital at Taxila his ambassador named Heliodorus to the Indian king Kāśīputra Bhāgabhadra of Vidiśā (Bhilsa) where Heliodorus as a '*Bhāgavata*' erected a Garuḍa pillar in honour of god Vāsudeva, as recorded in his inscription on the pillar at Besnagar. King Bhāgabhadra may be taken to be the fifth Śuṅga king named Bhāga in the *Purāṇas*. To the House of Euthydemos belonged Apollodotus and Menander.

Śaka-Pahlava. Both the Greek Houses were overwhelmed by Śaka-Pahlava irruptions in the first century B.C. There were in those days extensive race-movements from Central Asia. The Hiung-nu drove before them the Yueh-chis who in their turn drove the Śakas (Scythians) out of Bactria and other settlements. The displaced Śakas and their kinsmen, the Pahlavas (Parthians), found their way into India through the lower Indus valley from their settlements in Gedrosia, Arachosia, Seistan and Bactria. Thus Greek rule in India was supplanted by Śaka-Pahlava rule represented by some powerful kings like Maues, Vonones and Gondophernes.

Kushān. By the first century A.D., the Śakas and Pahlavas had in their turn to give way to the Yueh-chis led by the section called Kushāns who under their leaders Kadphises I (called Kujala on his coins) and Kadphises II (called Vima on his coins) established the Kushān Empire which was further consolidated by Kanishka I about A.D. 78, the commencement of the Śaka era. His empire in India included Kāpiśa, Gandhāra and Kāśmīra and extended in the east up to Vārāṇaśī and beyond. The eastern part was governed in the year 3 = A.D. 81 by his satraps, Mahā-Kshatrapa Kharapallāna and Kshatrapa Vanashpara[1] [*E.I.* VIII, 176, 179] and the northern by his general Lala, and satraps Vespasi and Liaka. The great Kushāns are taken to be (1) Kanishka I with his Viceroy Vāsishka; (2) Huvishka (*c.* A.D. 106-138) who had as his Viceroy Kanishka II; and (3) Vāsudeva I (*c.* A.D. 152-176). After Vāsudeva I, the Kushān Empire broke up into a number of small States whose rulers imitated the coins of Kanishka I and Vāsudeva I, and reigned in the third and fourth century A.D. and gradually disappeared before the advance of the Sassanians in the west and north, and of the Guptas in India.

Little Kushāns. The Kushān Empire was already shrinking in the time of Vāsudeva whose inscriptions are all found in the Mathurā region, showing that his hold on the west was weakening. In the third century A.D., we know of four small Kushān States ruling in (1) Ta-hia (Oxus region), (2) Ki-pin (Kāpiśa), (3) Kabul, and (4) the Indian borderland. The Sassanian king Varhān II (A.D. 276-293) conquered Śakasthāna and parts of north-west India. A Kushān king gave his daughter in marriage to his Sassanian overlord, Hormisdas (or Hormizd) II (A.D. 301-309), while the Sassanian Shāpūr II, when besieging Amida in A.D. 350, made use of Indian elephants given to him by his Kushān feudatories. Very soon, this Sassanian supremacy was replaced by that of the Guptas, as will be seen later. The Allahabad Pillar inscription of Samudra Gupta refers to the precious presents sent to him in recognition of his suzerainty by these Kushān kings who are aptly described by the title, *Daivaputra Shāhi Shāhānushāhi*. We also know from their coins that in the fifth century Kushān kings known as Kidāra Kushāns were ruling in Gandhāra and Kāśmira.

Just as the Punjab and the North-West were the scene of so many political vicissitudes through these centuries, the rest of India fared no better for want of a political equilibrium.

Śaka Satrapies. While the Śakas and Pahlavas were swept away by the Kushāns, the dynasties of their satraps survived them at Mathurā and in the Western India. The Mathurā Lion-capital is covered with inscriptions giving the genealogy of the satraps of Mathurā among whom may be mentioned as more famous Rājūla (whose coins call him Rājūla and Rañjuvula) and his son Śoḍāśa

1. The name Vanashpara suggests its connexcion with the Banaphar Rajputs of the third century A.D. whose home is located by Sir George Grierson in eastern India at Buxar(×Baghaar×Vyāghrasarah/ (*JBORS*, 1920, p. 150/. Visvasphāni of this family is stated in the *Purāṇas* to have established by his prowess (*mahāviryah*, his supremacy in Magadha and status as an emperor by overthrowing the older Kshatriya ruling families, posting his own followers as kings in different regions (*sthāpayishyati rājāno nānā desesbu*, 'and inaugurating a new Kshatriya order. The rise of this family is to be traced to its early patronage by emperor Kanishka I.

who was at first a mere Kshatrapa under Patika Kusuluka of Taxila as the Mahā-Kshatrapa, but himself became a Mahā-Kshatrapa in the year 72.

Kshaharātas. In Western India, these satraps established two independent ruling families, one of which had more than 300 years of history which was ended by the Gupta emperor Chandra Gupta II, as we shall see later. The other family had a much shorter history. Its founder was Bhūmaka who issued coins on the model of those of Maues, Azes, and Spalirises, by keeping on their reverse the arrow, the thunderbolt and discus. He was succeeded by his son Nahapāna in the first century A.D. He also showed loyalty to Śaka traditions by having his bust on the obverse of his coins after the coins of Strato I. Their family name is Kshaharāta which itself is derived from the Chhaharas and Chukshas mentioned in the Patika inscription of Liaka Kusūlaka, their chief of Taxila. Nahapāna had a daughter of Indian name, Dakshamitrā, who was married to Ushavadāta (Ṛishabhadatta) known from his charities recorded in his inscriptions at Nasik. One of these relates his victory achieved with his allies, the Uttamabhadras, over the Mālavas, and another shows that Nahapāna ruled over an extensive territory around the Gulf of Cambay, some of which was acquired from the Āndhras. This led to Āndhra-Kshaharāta conflict which ended in the extermination of this Śaka power by the Āndhras whose king Gautamīputra states in his inscription to have destroyed the Śakas, Yavanas and Pahlavas, and, more precisely, 'exterminated the race of Kshaharātas.' The inscriptions of Ushavadāta are dated to years 41-46 of an era which may be taken to be Śaka era, in which case A.D. 124 would be a date in Nahapāna's reign. The *Periplus* of the first century A.D. calls Nahapāna as Mambanos and his capital as Minnagara = Minpolis of Isidore of Charax, which is not identified but probably corresponded to an old form of Junnar near the coast.

The Kshaharāta conquest of Āndhra territory was thus shortlived. Nanapāna lost it as early as the year 18 of the reign of the Āndhra king Gautamīputra Śrī Śātakarṇi. This is the date of his Nasik inscription which he issued from his victorious camp at Vejayanti (= Banavāsī) and addressed to his Amātya ruling at Govardhana (Nasik). As Nahapāna had reigned up to at least A.D. 124, the eighteenth year of Gautamīputra's reign should be earlier than A.D. 124, so that he reigned from A.D. 106. The later Nasik inscription issued by his mother Bālaśrī in the nineteenth year of her grandson Pulumāvi (Vāśishṭhīputra Śrī-Pulumāvi) fully details the conquests of her son, which in their turn were again lost by the Āndhras to Rudradāman I, the western Kshatrapa king. Gautamīputra's overthrow of Nahapāna is further proved by coins. A hoard of over 13,000 silver coins was found at Jogaltembhi in

Nasik district, of which 4,000 were of Nahapāna and the remainder restruck by his conqueror, Gautamīputra, who called in the local currency and countermarked it with his own types. His son Pulumāyi was probably the Śātakarṇi whom the Kanheri inscription mentions as the son-in-law of 'Mahākshatrapa Ru' (dra)=Rudradāman. That is why his life was spared by Rudradāman who 'twice in fair fight completely defeated him' and regained much of the land conquered by Gautamīputra.

Śaka Kingdom of Ujjain. The end of the Kshaharāta dynasty did not mean the end of the Śaka satraps. Their other family, as already stated, had a more successful career. It was founded at Ujjain by Chashṭana whose time is supposed to be A.D. 78-110.[1] His son Jayadāman (c. A.D. 110-120) calls himself only a Kshatrapa, as the Āndhras must have diminished his dominion. Tables were, however, turned by his successor Rudradāman by his victories over the Āndhras. In his Girinagara (Girnar) inscription dated 72=A.D. 150, Rudradāman speaks of his victories over the Yaudheyas of the north, Śātakarṇi 'Dakshiṇā-patha-pati' (lord of Deccan), who married his son to Rudradāman's daughter, and of his ruling over Cutch and Kāthiāwar, Sind, eastern and western Malwa, and portions of Rajputana.[2] In his province of Surāshṭra, he appointed as his Amātya or Governor a Pahlava named Suviśākha, son of Kulaipa. He was succeeded by his son Dāmaghsāda=Dāmajada who was succeeded by Jīvadāman. Their later history for about 200 years is not known. Chashṭana's line came to an end with the death of Viśvasena, son of Bhartṛidāman in A.D. 304. Rudrasiṁha II and Rudrasiṁha III were the last of the dynasty, though not in its direct line. The latter's coins are dated 312=A.D. 390. He was killed by Chandra Gupta II during his conquest of western India.

Nāgas. We shall now follow the fortunes of other powers

1. The Āndhau inscriptions of the year 52=A.D. 130 refer to 'king Rudradāman, son of Jayadāman, son of king Chashṭana, son of Yśāmotika'. Though it is not expressly stated, king Rudradāman may be taken to be the grandson of Chashṭana.

2. The places mentioned in the inscription are: (1) Ākara=eastern Mālwā (capital Vidiśā); (2) Avanti=western Mālwā (capital Ujjain); (3) Anupa-nivrit (region)=Valley of Upper Narmadā with its capital Māhishmatī=Māndhāta or Maheśvara in Nimad district; (4) Ānarta=north Kathiawad with its capital Ānartapura=Ānandapura=modern Vadnagor in Baroda State (or capital Dvārakā ?); (5) Surāshṭra=south Kathiawad (capital Girinagara); (6) Śvabhra, the tract on the Śvabhramatī=Sābarmatī; (7) Maru (Marwar); (8) Kachchha=Cutch; (9) Sindhu=west of Lower Indus; (10) Sauvīra=east of Lower Indus; (11) Kukura (between Sind and Pāriyātra or Aravalli mountain as stated in the *Bṛihat Saṁhitā*); (12) Aparānta=north Konkaṇa with capital Sūrpāraka; (13) Nishāda, between Vinaśana and Pāriyātra=western Vindhya and Aravalli.

before the rise of the Guptas. The Andhra dynasty of 30 kings ruled for about 460 years and came to an end after the third century A.D. Meanwhile, in the north, the place of the Kushāns at Mathurā and other adjoining regions was taken over by a new people known as the Nāgas who, according to the *Purāṇas*, ruled in the third and fourth century A.D. King Maheśvara Nāga, son of Nāgabhaṭṭa, is mentioned in a Lahore Copper Seal inscription of the fourth century A.D. [Fleet, *EI*, Vol. III, p. 283].

Bhāraśivas. Several Vākāṭaka inscriptions mention Bhavanāga, sovereign of the dynasty known as the Bhāraśivas who were so powerful that they had to their credit the performance of as many as ten *Aśvamedha* sacrifices following their conquests 'along the Bhāgirathī (Ganges)'. According to the *Purāṇas*, these Nāgas had several centres of their authority such as Vidiśā, Padmāvatī, Kāntipurī and Mathurā and counted another powerful king named Chandrāṁśa who is taken by some to be king Chandra named in the Delhi Iron Pillar inscription. The political status attained by the Nāgas will be evident from the fact that the Gupta emperor Chandra Gupta II married a Nāga princess by way of an alliance, while a Nāga governor was ruling in the Gangetic Doab even in the time of Skanda Gupta.

Vākāṭakas. With the Nāgas and Bhāraśivas are to be counted the Vākāṭakas as their rivals for supremacy in northern India. The *Purāṇas* tell of their first kings, Vindhyaśakti and Pravīra=Pravarasena I succeeded by his grandson Rudrasena I followed by his son Pṛithivīsheṇa I whose son Rudrasena II was a contemporary of Chandra Gupta II. The Bhāraśiva king Mahārājā Bhavanāga had his daughter married to Gautamīputra, a son of Pravarasena I, just as Chandra Gupta II had his daughter Prabhāvatiguptā married to Rudrasena II. Vākāṭaka power was at its zenith in the time of Pṛithivīsheṇa I whose authority was acknowledged in the territory extending from Nachne-kī-talāī and Ganj in Bundelkhand up to Kuntala or Kanarese country of which he is described as the lord in an Ajaṇṭā inscription. The tracts in Bundelkhand were directly ruled by his vassal Vyāghra-deva. After Pṛithivīsheṇa, Vākāṭaka supremacy in Central India was replaced by Gupta under Samudra Gupta and Chandra Gupta II. Western Deccan was ruled by Pṛithivīsheṇa I, but eastern Deccan which was under his vassal Vyāghra was conquered by Samudra Gupta, as stated in his Eran inscription, while his Allahabad Pillar inscription states that he 'uprooted' the rule of Vyāghra-rāja whom it is reasonable to identify with the Vākāṭaka feudatory Vyāghra. The Vākāṭakas now took their place as a southern Power.

Maukharis. We may also note here the supposed connexion

with Magadha of certain other peoples. A clay seal bearing the legend *Mokhaliṇam* points to Maukhari rule in the Gayā region. Maukhari power is also testified to by three inscriptions discovered at Beḍvā in the Kotah State [*EI*. XXIII] recording erection of sacrificial pillars by Maukhari *Mahāsenāpatis* in the third century A.D. The *Kaumudī-Mahotsava* mentions the Magadha king Sundaravarman defending Pāṭaliputra against the Lichchhavis in the time of the Bhāraśivas. This Sundaravarman is taken by Pires to be a Maukhari. To this is to be added the evidence of the Chandravalli inscription of Mayūraśarman indicating that the Maukharis were ruling in Magadha in the time of the early Kadambas, i.e., about the fourth century A.D.

Lichchhavis. There is again some evidence of Lichchhavi rule in Magadha. According to the Nepal inscription of Jayadeva II Lichchhavi, his ancestor Supushpa was born at Pāṭaliputra about the first century A.D. The Lichchhavis might have been ruling in Magadha since then and acknowledged Kushān suzerainty when Kanishka's minister Vanashpara marched against Magadha.

Lichchhavi power in Magadha may explain the alliance of Chandra Gupta I with the Lichchhavis.

We have now set the stage for the emergence of the Gupta power in Indian history.

NOTE TO CHAPTER I

Along with the Bhāraśivas, Nāgas or Vākāṭakas, the *Purāṇas* mention another people named Devarakshitas as one of the ruling powers at the time of the rise of the Guptas. Their territories included Pauṇḍra (northern Bengal?), Kośala (Oudh), Oḍra (Orissa) and Tāmralipta up to the sea (*Tāmraliptān sasāgarān*). As they thus had their sway in eastern India and Bengal, they may be connected with king Chandra of Meherauli Pillar inscription with its reference to his victory against a coalition of the Bengal powers (Vaṅgas) and with the other king named Chandravarmā of Susunia Rock inscription describing him as ruler of Pushkaraṇā (=village Pushkaraṇā near Susunia hill in Bankura district). The Susunia inscription describes Chandravarmā as son of Siṁhavarmā. The Mandasor inscription of Mālava year 461=A.D. 404 also mentions Siṁhavarmā, son of Jayavarmā, and father of Naravarmā. The Gaṅgdhār inscription of Mālava year 480=A.D. 423 mentions Viśva varmā as son of Naravarmā. The Mandasor inscription of Mālava year 493=A.D. 436 and 529=A.D. 472 refers to *Goptā* Viśvavarmā *Nṛipa*, and his son *Nṛipa* Bandhuvarmā, as feudatories at Daśapur under emperor Kumāra Gupta I. Thus these three inscriptions testify to the following line of Malwa kings: Siṁhavarmā—Naravarmā (A.D. 404)—Viśvavarmā (A.D. 423)—Bandhuvarmā (A.D. 426). The Siṁhavarmā of this list is counted by H. P. Sastri as identical with Siṁhavarmā, with his son Chandravarmā, as mentioned in the Susunia inscription, in which case Chandravarmā becomes a brother of Naravarmā.

H. P. Sastri sought support for his theory in the curious geographical fact that there is a place called Pokhraṇ in the Jodhpur State in Rajputana, with which he identified the Pishkaraṇā of which Chandravarmā was the king according to the Susunia inscription. Sastri advances his theory further by supposing that this Chandravarmā from distant Rajputana came on a conquering career as far as Bankura in Western Bengal and may be taken as identical with king Chandra of Meherauli inscription recording his conquests in Vaṅga and treating the Susunia inscription as another record of his conquest. The further history to which he is led is that this Chandravarmā was the same king who was expelled from Āryāvarta by Samudra Gupta after which he or his brother Nara varmā must have migrated to Malwa.

This theory is, however, now proved to be totally untenable. Pushkaraṇā is now identified with a place nearer home at Bankura and one need not go as far as Jodhpur to find its equivalent. Besides, the other inscriptions mentioned above do not at all refer Chandravarmā in their list of kings. His place in that list is only inferred from the name Siṁhavarmā in that list, who was quite a different person whose son is mentioned as Naravarmā and not Chandravarmā, as mentioned in the Susunia inscription. Thus Sastri's fallacy lay in fastening upon Siṁhavarmā as the connecting link between the Susunia and the Malwa inscriptions.

The difficulty now remains as to the identity of king Chandravarmā and of king Chandra of Meherauli inscription, who was defeated by Samudra Gupta. A plausible theory is to treat Chandra the conqueror of Bengal as a king of the Devarakshitas who ruled in Bengal about this time. After his death, king Chandravarmā of Pushkaraṇā emerged into prominence till he was disposed of by Samudra Gupta.

It is not also possible to equate king Chandra of Meherauli inscription with emperor Chandra Gupta I as has been done by some. King Chandra is given a long reign in the inscription (*suchirān*) with which Chandra Gupta I is not credited, while his dominion extended from Magadha along the course of the Ganges up to Prayāga and Sāketa without including any part of Vaṅga. It is Samudra Gupta whose dominion counted as its subjects the kingdoms of Samataṭa (lower and eastern Bengal) and Ḍavāka (probably northern Bengal or Tipperah district). But it is not clear how and by whom Bengal proper was annexed to the Gupta Empire. This question is discussed later [Some of these suggestions I owe to Dr. B. C. Sen's comprehensive treatise, *Some Historical Aspects of the Inscriptions of Bengal*, Calcutta University.]

CHAPTER II

ŚRĪ GUPTA (*c.* A.D 240-280) AND GHAṬOTKACHA (*c.* A.D. 280-319)

Origin: Śrī Gupta (*c.* A.D. 240-280). Like all things great, the Gupta Empire grew out of small beginnings which are shrouded in obscurity. The first evidence of Gupta connexion with Magadha cames from a foreign source. The Chinese traveller I-tsing, who came to India in A.D. 672 heard of 'Mahārāja Śrī-Gupta (*Che-li-ki-to*) who built a temple near Mṛigaśikhāvana for Chinese pilgrims and endowed it with 24 villages'. This was done '500 years before.' I-tsing stated this in A.D. 690 and so Śrī-Gupta must have ruled about A.D. 190. But the time of an event reported 500 years later cannot be strictly accurate. Some margin of error may be allowed. We find that the Gupta inscriptions mention 'Mahārāja Śrī-Gupta' as the founder of the dynasty who is also aptly called *Ādirāja* in the Poona plates of Prabhāvatiguptā Vākāṭaka [*EI.* XV, No. 4, p. 43] and he may be identified with the Gupta king mentioned by I-tsing who gives him the same name and title. We may further note that Mṛigaśikhāvana along with the villages granted to its monastery were all situated within Magadha and Gupta territory. I-tsing informs us that the aforesaid park was 'about 50 stages east of Nālandā down the Ganges', while Nālandā was '7 stages to the north-east of Mahābodhi'. This shows that I-tsing's 'stage' was about 5 or 6 miles. On the basis of this calculation, the territory of Gupta will have to be extended up to the Murshidabad district at a distance of 250 miles from Nālandā in Bihar Sharif. Now as to the probable date of Śrī-Gupta, considering the dates of his successors, we may take it to be A.D. 240-280, giving to his son Ghaṭotkacha the period A.D. 280-319 for his reign. Thus there is a difference of only about 50 years from I-tsing's computation which was given as a mere guess and not the result of any precise calculation.

We may further note that the name of this king is to be taken as 'Gupta' and the prefix '*Śrī*' as an honorific, as is shown in all the names of the Gupta emperors mentioned in their inscriptions. Where *Śrī* is a part of the name as in Śrīmatī in inscription No. 46 of Fleet, the prefix *Śrī* will still be added in the case of royalty, whence Śrī-Śrīmatī [*Ibid*]. Nor is the name *Gupta* by itself objectionable. We have analogous names like *Datta* or *Rakshita* in olden times, or such abbreviated names as Devaka for Devadattaka [Kātyāyana's *Vārttika* on Pāṇini, VII, 3, 45] or Harsha for Harsha-Vardhana.

Gupta figures in the inscription as a 'great king', *Mahārāja*. This points to earlier origins of his family but these are not traceable.

The Gupta kings were of the *gotra* known as *Dhāraṇa*, as is stated in the Poona Copper-plate inscription of Prabhāvatiguptā, the Vākāṭaka queen, who was a daughter of Chandra Gupta II and his wife Kuberanāgā born of the Nāga family [*EI*, XV, 41f].

Ghaṭotkacha (*c*. A.D. 280-319). The inscriptions name Mahārāja Ghaṭotkacha as the successor of Gupta. He should not be confused with Ghaṭotkachagupta named on some seals found at Vaiśālī which was not part of the Gupta kingdom in his time. Ghaṭotkachagupta issued those seals in his capacity as the chief officer of the province (*Bhukti*) whose headquarters were at Vaiśālī in the Empire of Chandra Gupta II. He might have been a scion of the royal family, as indicated in the prefix *Śrī* added to his name, but he is not called Mahārāja. He is called on the seals a Kumārāmātya, a Minister in attendance on the Prince who was 'Mahārāja Govinda Gupta', a son of emperor Chandra Gupta II by his queen 'Mahādevī Dhruvasvāminī', and serving as Viceroy at Vaiśālī but did not succeed his father on the Gupta imperial throne. It is possible that he may have been the same person mentioned as Governor of Eran in the Tumain inscription in Madhya Pradeśa of the year 116 (= A.D. 435) [M.B. Garde in *IA*, 1920, p. 114].

CHAPTER III

CHANDRA GUPTA I

(*c.* A.D. 319-335 ?)

His Conquests. While his two ancestors are each given the title of *Mahārāja*, Chandra Gupta I is described in the inscriptions as *Mahārājādhirāja*, 'King of Kings' or Emperor. He is thus taken to be the founder of the Gupta Empire. The title of 'King of Kings' must have been acquired by his conquests by which he was able to rule over an extensive territory. Unfortunately, there is not much known about his conquests and the exact extent of his territory. According to the *Purāṇas*, 'the kings born of the Gupta family will rule over the territories (*Janapadas*) situated along the Ganges (*anu-Gaṅgā*) such as Prayāga, Sāketa (Oudh), and Magadha.' This description of Gupta dominion applies to what it was before Samudra Gupta had achieved his extensive conquests which made him the paramount sovereign over a large part of India. Therefore, the passage from the *Purāṇas* may be taken to describe the extent of Gupta territory under Chandra Gupta I.

Prayāga. We have no details preserved as to his conquest of Prayāga or Sāketa. Certain inscriptions discovered at Bhiṭā bring to light three kings associated with Prayāga, viz., Mahārāja Gautamīputra Śrī-Śivamegha, Rājan Vāshishṭhīputra Bhīmasena whom Sir John Marshall assigns to the second or third century A.D., and Mahārāja Gautamīputra Vṛishadhvaja of the third or fourth century A.D.

Vaiśālī. As regards Magadha which may be taken to be South Bihar, it does not seem to include Vaiśālī as a part of the kingdom of Chandra Gupta I. But it may be noted that in the Allahabad Pillar inscription of Samudra Gupta, Nepal is mentioned as a State on the frontiers of his dominion, while what are known as 'Chandra Gupta Coins' associate the Lichchhavis with his sovereignty as the result of his marriage with their princess named 'Queen (Mahādevī) Kumāradevī in the inscriptions and 'Śrī Kumāradevī' on the aforesaid coins.

Magadha. Some light is thrown on Chandra Gupta's conquest of Magadha by literary texts but it is a doubtful light, because the texts are much later than the events.

Evidence of 'Kaumudī-Mahotsava'. According to the *Kaumudī-Mahotsava*, Magadha was then held by the dynasty (*Magadhakula*) of Sundaravarman (supposed to be a Maukhari) who died in the defence of Pāṭaliputra (Kusumapura) against the attack launched by his adopted son Chaṇḍasena helped by the Lichchhavis whose princess he had married. Chaṇḍasena as king of Magadha had to leave Pāṭaliputra to quell a revolt of his governors among the Śabaras and Pulindas on the frontiers of Magadha. Advantage was taken of his absence from the capital by a conspiracy which called back to the throne the last king's son Kalyāṇavarman whose power was strengthened by his marriage with a daughter of Kīrtisheṇa, the Yādava king of Mathurā. He celebrated his restoration to the throne of Magadha by the festival of *Kaumudī-Mahotsava*, the subject of the drama. The drama condemns the Lichchhavis as *Mlechchhas* and Chaṇḍasena as a Kāraskara. Perhaps the Guptas might have been Kāraskara Jāṭas and were settled somewhere on the borders of Magadha under Bhāraśiva suzerainty.

It has been suggested that Chaṇḍasena of the play may be identified with Chandra Gupta I whose marriage with the Lichchhavi princess had helped him to the throne of Magadha. The Lichchhavi alliance is the link of connexion between the drama and the inscriptions. Other stories of the drama, however, have no historical value. It condemns Chaṇḍasena as a usurper and of low caste whom the citizens of Magadha could not tolerate and drove him to die as an exile. Such a story does not support the identification of Chaṇḍasena with Chandra Gupta I.

Another suggestion in support of the historical value of the drama is that the *Koṭa-Kula* mentioned in the Allahabad Pillar inscription may be taken to be *Magadha-Kula* of the drama and that *Koṭa-Kulaja* of the inscription is no other than Kalyāṇavarman whose defeat by Samudra Gupta must have been recorded in certain missing syllables of line 13 of the inscription, while the inscription definitely tells that Samudra Gupta defeated Nāgasena, King of Mathurā, who was the brother-in-law of Kalyāṇavarman in the drama. Nāgasena is taken to be the son of King Kīrtisheṇa of Mathurā, the father-in-law of Kalyāṇavarman.

This agreement is somewhat far-fetched. The outstanding fact of the drama is against history and cannot be explained away. It is the extermination of the entire family of Chaṇḍasena (*Vaṁśānubandhaḥ nihitaḥ Chaṇḍasenaghātakaḥ*).

Evidence of Coins. We may take it for granted that in achieving his conquests and position as Emperor, Chandra Gupta I was materially helped by his Lichchhavi alliance of which even his illustrious progeny were so proud, and constantly making mention in their inscriptions. Samudra Gupta first proudly declares himself as a *Lichchhavidauhitra* in his inscription, and not a *Guptapautra*, although it is more usual to trace one's lineage on the father's side. The importance of the alliance thus affirmed in the inscriptions is also celebrated by the issue by Samudra Gupta of special coins commemorating the event. These coins (which were found in Burdwan, Gayā, and Ayodhyā) portray the marriage, some showing the husband offering with right hand a ring to his wife. They also bear the legends, *Chandra* or *Chandra Gupta* on obverse, and *Kumāradevī* or *Śrī Kumāradevī* on reverse, and on left; while on reverse, and on right, there is the significant legend, *Lichchhavayaḥ*, the Lichchhavis as a people to whom belonged the princess, and the Gupta Empire at its foundation owed so much. The conjecture may be hazarded that these coins were in circulation in Lichchhavi territory which now passed into the possession of Chandra Gupta I as one of the results of his Lichchhavi alliance.

The date of this matrimonial alliance may be roughly taken to be A.D. 308, if Chandra Gupta's son Samudra Gupta is taken to be his eldest son, and to have succeeded him on the throne in A.D. 335, when he should have been at least 25 years old for purposes of efficient kingship. Hindu legal texts point to the age of 25 years for kingship.

Gupta Era. According to Fleet, Chandra Gupta I marked his accession to the throne of Magadha by founding an era of which the first year was A.D. 319-320. Fleet also states that this era was also that of the Lichchhavis of Nepal from whom it was taken over by Chandra Gupta I who was so intimately connected with them. The time of Jayadeva I of Nepal approximates closely to A.D. 320. The Valabhī era is also identified with the Gupta era. The Valabhī kings, as feudatories of the Guptas, introduced the era of their overlords in their own dominion of Surāshṭra. We find that a son of the founder of the Valabhī dynasty uses the date 207 for one of his grants, showing that there was no independent era marking its foundation. The first year of the Gupta era as fixed by Fleet has been the subject of some controversy. But the controversy may be settled in the light of the following facts and considerations. The dates of the Śaka satraps of Ujjain support Fleet's conclusion, if it is taken for granted that they are in the Śaka era. It is an established fact that Śaka power was extinguished by Chandra Gupta II who issued his silver coins in imitation of those of the satraps. Now the last date of Chandra Gupta is 93, while that of the Śaka dynasty is 304[1]. It is only by taking the Gupta era to begin in A.D. 319 and Śaka era in A.D. 78 that these two phases of Gupta and Śaka history can be reconciled and brought together in time. The basis of fixing

1. The recently discovered hoards of coins of Svāmī Rudra Siṁha III at Uparkot and Sarvania show that his coinage ended in the Śaka year 274=A.D. 352, the time of Samudra Gupta who, accordingly, is supposed to have been the conqueror of Kshatrapa Kingdom (Jayachandra Vidyālaṅkār in *J. Gujarat R. S.*, No. 2, pp. 109-11).

the Gupta era is of course the statement of Alberuni that the Gupta era was separated from the Śaka era by an interval of 241 years. According to Sir R. G. Bhandarkar, 'the evidence in favour of Alberuni's initial date for the Gupta era appears to be simply overwhelming'. We may conclude by citing certain other pieces of epigraphic evidence on the subject: the Mandasor inscription of Kumāra Gupta and Bandhuvarman dated ME 493 and the Ganjam plates of Śaśāṇka dated GE 300. We may also add to this the evidence derived from a different locality and history. It is the rock inscription at Tezpur of Harjavarman, the Kāmarūpa king, of the year GE 510. Now Harjavarman is ninth in descent from Śālastambha whose date is ascertained from other sources to have been *c.* A.D. 650, whence the date of Harjavarman should be somewhere near the date A.D. 829 arrived at by taking the Gupta era to begin in A.D. 319.

CHAPTER IV

SAMUDRA GUPTA PARAKRĀMĀṄKA

(*c.* A.D. 335-380)

Date. His time is ascertained by his synchronism with king Meghavarṇa of Ceylon (A.D. 351-379) who sent him an embassy after his conquests were achieved, as indicated by the reference to Ceylon in his Allahabad Pillar inscription. If the Nālandā spurious plate inscription is to be believed, he came to the throne before GE 5 = A.D. 325, while the spurious Gayā copper plate record supposes him to reign in A.D. 328.

Name. The name *Samudra Gupta* is to be taken as a title which he had acquired by his conquests. The title means that he was 'protected by the sea' up to which his dominion was extended. The Mathurā inscription of Chandra Gupta II actually states that 'the fame of his conquests extended up to the four oceans' (*Chaturudadhisalilāsvāditayaśaḥ*). He must have had a personal name which is supposed to have been *Kācha* who issued coins describing himself as *Sarvarājochchhettā* (the exterminator of all kings), an epithet applicable fully only to Samudra Gupta among all Gupta kings. A personal name in addition to what may be called the official name was not unusual in those days, e.g. Virasena, Minister of Chandra Gupta II, who had a personal name Śāba (No. 6 of Fleet), or the personal name Vyāghra of Rudrasena (No. 15 of Fleet). That the name *Kācha* was also not unusual is shown in an Ajaṇṭā Cave inscription which refers to two chiefs named Kācha I and Kācha II. Vāmana in his *Kāvyālaṅkāra* (iii, 2, 2) refers to Chandraprakāśa as the son of Chandra Gupta and so it may be another name of Samudra Gupta. Even as regards the name which is usually taken as one word *Samudragupta*, it should be split up into two parts, viz., *Samudra* as a personal name, and *Gupta* as his surname. This assumption is suggested by the fact that the obverse of his earliest coins of standard type bears the legend *Samudra* on some specimens, while the reverse bears in common the legend *Parākramaḥ* as his title. Similarly, the name *Samudra* is also seen on some specimens of other types of coins, such as the *Archer* type and *Battle-Axe* type.

Succession. In the Allahabad Pillar inscription it is stated that Samudra Gupta was selected for the throne by his father who considered him to be fully worthy of it as an *ārya*, 'with an eye to truth, right, and justice' (*tattvekshiṇā chakshushā*), without being swayed by any other consideration, and declared his decision publicly before his Council (*Sabhā*) by telling the Prince: 'Protect ye this earth!' This decision was, however, not quite palatable to his kinsmen of equal birth (*tulyakulaja*) whose faces became pale (*mlāna*) with disappointment. His Council, however, were exultant (*uchchhvasita*) over the decision.

There is an assumption that the discontent of his brothers at this supersession led to a revolt headed by his eldest brother who is supposed to be no other than Kācha of the coins. It is pointed out that the inscription goes out of the way in referring to their resentment which is supposed to have led to a war of succession to which a reference is sought to be found in the gaps shown in its stanzas 5 and 6. The incomplete sentence 'conquered some by his arms in battle' is taken to refer to the battle among the brothers for the throne; and further below there occurs the expression 'pride had changed into repentance', which is also taken to refer to the discomfiture of his brothers. Those who support this theory suppose that some time must have elapsed between Chandra Gupta's selection of Samudra Gupta as his successor and his actual accession to the throne, and that this time was utilized by his jealous brothers to strike for the throne. It is further supposed that his eldest brother Kācha was able to seize the throne for a while during which he struck his coins. These coins show their gold to be of inferior quality indicative of political unrest. From this point of view, Kācha was a usurper and this explains why his name is not mentioned in the genealogical list of the inscriptions which also do not generally mention the name of a king who does not come in the direct line of succession.

It may be noted that the reference to Chandra Gupta's selection of Samudra Gupta as his successor in preference to his other brothers is also indicated in the Ṛiddhapura inscription in the expression *tatpāda-parigṛihīta*.

Allahabad Pillar Inscription. The main source of Samudra Gupta's history is this inscription which is engraved on one of the stone pillars set up at Kauśāmbī by Asoka who had used it for his own inscription; but, though appearing on the same pillar, the two inscriptions of the two kings are poles apart in the character of their contents. Samudra Gupta's inscription details his conquests achieved by force which Aśoka had abjured. But for this inscription Samudra Gupta would have remained unknown to history except for what could be gathered from his coins. Unfortunately, the inscription is not dated, and so it is taken by some to be posthumous. But this supposition has been disposed of by Bühler who pointed out that it must have been issued before Samudra Gupta had performed the *Aśvamedha*. Otherwise it would have mentioned such an important event. The posthumous character of the inscription is inferred from its line 31 where there is a reference to Samudra Gupta's fame (*kīrti*) which, resulting from his world-conquest (*Sarvapṛithivī-vijaya-janitodaya*), had spread over the whole universe (*Vyāpta-nikhilā-vanītalām*) and even went up to heaven (*Tridaśapatibhavanaga-manāvāpta*). But the fame of a man on earth may go up to heaven without the man himself going up to heaven. The inscription is not posthumous for another reason above stated—that it does not mention the *Aśvamedha* which was performed later by the king on completion of all his conquests and their consolidation. The inscription is valuable not only for Samudra Gupta's history but also for the political geography of India which it indicates, mentioning the different kings and peoples of India in the first half of the fourth century A.D.

Harisheṇa. The inscription states that it is the poetical composition (*Kāvya*) of Harisheṇa who combined in himself the important offices of the *Khādyaṭapākika*, (Officer controlling the Superintendents of the Royal Kitchen), the *Sāndhivigrahika*) (Minister for Peace and War), *Kumārāmātya* (Minister in attendance on the Prince) and *Mahādaṇḍanāyaka* (the Chief of the Police and Criminal Judge). It is also stated that one of his offices was hereditary, as his father Dhruvabhūti was also a *Mahādaṇḍanāyaka*.

The inscription is stated to have been executed (*anushṭhita*) by another *Mahādaṇḍanāyaka* named *Tilabhaṭṭaka*. As a responsible officer of the State, Harisheṇa was in a position to give an account of his master's exploits with which he was in direct touch as his Minister for War. Thus his inscription may be taken to be a faithful record of the events it narrates, and also of the order of their happenings. The order in which these are mentioned in the inscriptions is important for the history it records.

Campaigns and Conquests. These are detailed in the inscription which also classifies the conquests with reference to the different degrees in which they were achieved.

First Campaign in Āryāvarta. Some States were completely 'uprooted' (*unmūlya*). The kingdoms of Achyuta and Nāgasena suffered this fate.

Achyuta was the ruler of Ahichchhatra, the capital of ancient northern Pañchāla (modern Ramnagar in Bareilly district). Copper coins bearing the legend *Achyu* found in this locality may be attributed to him.

Nāgasena was one of the Nāga kings who, according to the *Purāṇas*, were ruling at the two centres, Champāvatī (same as Padmāvatī near Narwar), and Mathurā. Nāgasena was of Padmāvatī where Nāga coins have been found. Nāgasena has been mentioned by Bāṇa in his *Harshacharita* which states: 'At Padmāvati occurred (*āsit*) the doom of Nāgasena, born of the Nāga family (*nāgakulajanmanaḥ*), who was foolish enough to have the secrets of his policy discussed in the presence of the *Sārikā* bird which declared them aloud.'

At the same time, a king of the Koṭa dynasty (*Koṭa-kula*) was 'captured' by Samudra Gupta's army (*daṇḍagrāhayataiva*) while he was playing (*krīḍatā*) at the city of Pushpa (=Pushpapura= Pāṭaliputra). There are found some Koṭa coins which resemble the *Sruta* coins of a ruler of Śrāvastī and the Koṭa kings might have been ruling in that region.

Samudra Gupta thus began his reign by overthrowing his immediate neighbours. If the war of succession was a fact, then these three princes might have joined hands and tried to take advantage of Samudra Gupta's domestic troubles. Thus they became the first victims of his conquest by which Gupta dominion was extended far beyond Prayāga and Sāketa over regions round Mathurā and Padmāvatī. It is also ingeniously supposed that this battle against these treacherous princes was fought at Kauśāmbī where the Aśoka pillar was utilized as pillar of victory by Samudra Gupta.

Campaign in Dakshiṇapatha. If we may believe in the order of events recorded by Harisheṇa, Samudra Gupta, having consolidated his kingdom and the centre, opened the second phase of his activities by engaging on campaigns in the distant South. It is stated that he was able to inflict defeat upon all the kings of the South (*Sarva-Dakshiṇāpatharāja*).

His conquests in the South (*Dakshiṇāpatha*) are marked by three features: (1) *Grahaṇa* (capture of the enemy), (2) *Moksha* (liberating him), and (3) *Anugraha* (favouring him by reinstating him in his kingdom). This policy may be taken to be the only policy that the conqueror could pursue in the distant South where he was only anxious that his position as the paramount sovereign of India should be recognized.

Kosala. The route of his march to the South may be traced in the light of the order in which his campaigns are referred to in his inscription. Leaving the Jumna valley, Samudra Gupta must have marched through the modern Rewa State and Jubbulpore district and come up against his first object of attack, the kingdom of Kosala, which is Southern Kosala with its capital Śrīpura, modern Sirpur in M.P., and included the eastern and southern parts of M.P., the modern districts of Bilaspur, Raipur and Sambalpur and also parts of Ganjam district.

The king of this Kosala was Mahendra.

Mahākāntāra. Next, Samudra Gupta found himself in the

Vindhyan wilderness, the eastern Gonḍavana, aptly called Mahākāntāra, whose chief is more aptly called the 'tiger' of the forest, *Vyāghrarāja*, already mentioned as a feudatory of the Vākāṭakas. It may be noted that he had a son named Jayanātha of Uchchakalpa dynasty, whose date is 174 Kalachuri era, which shows that he was a contemporary of Chandra Gupta II, and so his father Vyāghra was a contemporary of Samudra Gupta.

Probably Sambalpur on the Mahānadī was its capital.

Kaurāla. As he emerged victorious from the forest-States, he came into the east coast and its first kingdom, that of Maṇṭarāja of Kaurāla. Kaurāla is severally identified with (1) Colair lake, (2) Sonpur district of M.P., of which the capital was known as Yayātinagarī on the Mahānadī, as stated in the *Pavanadūtam* of the poet Dhoyi who refers to *Keralīnām* city named above; (3) Korāḍa in South India.

B. V. Krishna Rao (*Early Dynasties of Āndhradeśa*, p. 366) proposes a new identification of Kaurāla. He thinks it should not be identified with the region of Kolleru lake, because it is very near Vengipura which Dandin also describes as Āndhranagarī on a lake. Samudra Gupta could not have advanced so far from the last stage of his campaign. Kaurāla may, therefore, be identified with the kingdom known as Kulūṭa (modern Chanda district of M.P.). It is mentioned in the Mahendragiri Pillar inscription of Velanauti Rājendra Chola I (*SII*, V. No. 135). Thus the last three places conquered by Samudra Gupta were all located in north-eastern Deccan.

Pishṭapura. The next objective of Samudra Gupta's campaigns was the Kingdom of Pishṭapura, modern Piṭhāpuram in Godāvarī district, then under its king, Mahendragiri.

Koṭṭūra. After Pishṭapura came the turn of Koṭṭūra under its king Svāmīdatta. Koṭṭūra is identified with modern Kothoor in Ganjam district or with a place called Koṭṭūra at the foot of the hills in the Vizagapatam district (District Gazetteer I, 137).

Erandapalla. The next king subdued was Damana of Eraṇḍapalla. This place is identified with (1) Erandol in Khandesh, (2) Eraṇḍapalli, which is a town near Chicacole in Vizagapatam district, (3) Yendipalli in Vizagapatam district, and (4) Endapilli in Ellore taluq.

Kāñchī. There is a long interval of space leading to the next conquest. It was that of Kāñchi or modern Conjeevaram under its king named Vishṇugopa.

Avamukta. The next conquest of Samudra Gupta was the kingdom of Avamukta under its king called Nīlarāja. It must have been a small kingdom in the neighbourhood of Kāñchī and Vengī. Nīlarāja may be connected with Nilapallin in Godāvarī district. He was also another member of the Pallava Confederation fought by Samudra Gupta. The kingdom of Kāñchī in those days embraced the whole territory from the mouth of the Kṛishṇa to the south of the river Palar and sometimes even Kāverī. To the east of this territory lay the kingdoms of Vengī, Palakka and Avamukta.

Vengī. The next conquest is that of Vengī under its king Hastivarman. It is to be noted that in proceeding against Kāñchī Samudra Gupta could not have left in his rear the king of Vengī. Very probably he had to give battle to a coalition of Pallava kings headed by Vishṇugopa and Hastivarman. Hastivarman is supposed to have belonged to Śālaṅkāyana dynasty (Peḍḍavegi plates of Nandivarman II).

Palakka. Samudra Gupta next proceeded against Ugrasena of Palakka. Palakka is supposed to be a place in Nellore district. There is a place called Palakkaḍa which was the seat of a Pallava Viceroyalty and so may be the same as Palakka.

Devarāshṭra. The next kingdom that came on his way was Devarāshṭra under its king Kubera. A copper-plate grant of the eastern Chālukya king, Bhīma I, mentions a village in Elamañchi Kaliṅgadeśa which was part of the province called Devarāshṭra. Elamañchi, capital of Kaliṅgadeśa, is identified with modern Yellamañchili in Vizagapatam district. Therefore, Devarāshṭra is to be located in this district. This location has been further confirmed by an inscription stating that Pishṭapura formed part of the kingdom of Devarāshṭra ruled in its time by king Guṇavarman (*EI.* XXIII, 57).

Kusthalapura. The last kingdom mentioned in the list of Samudra Gupta's conquest in the South is Kusthalapura under its king Dhanañjaya. This place may be located in the tract round about the river Kuśasthalī, in which case it must have been conquered by Samudra Gupta on his return march. The place ha also been identified with Kuttalur near Pollur in North Arcot district.

Route in the South. Some of the above identifications of the places mentioned in the inscription go against the theory held by Fleet and since strongly supported by several scholars, that Samudra Gupta, on his return march, conquered some of the kingdoms on the western coast. Kaurāla of the inscription was identified with Keralaputra (Madurā) or the Chera kingdom of Southern India. Similarly, Koṭṭūra was identified with a place called Koṭhurapollachi in the Coimbatore district, and Palakka with Pālaghāt on the Malabar coast. Eraṇḍapalla was identified with Erandol in the Khandesh district of Bombay as already stated, and Devarāshṭra was equated with Mahārāshṭra. Apart from the more satisfactory identifications which have been given above and which go against this theory, the theory is rendered untenable on another very decisive ground. If the inscription is to be taken as mentioning the conquests of Samudra Gupta in the order in which they had actually followed one another, Eraṇḍapalla and Devarāshṭra should have been mentioned after the southernmost kingdoms of Vengī and Kāñchī. It cannot be supposed that Samudra Gupta returned to the south after first conquering these kingdoms of Western India.

Second Campaign in Āryāvarta. Having now felt his power and measured his strength (*pratāpa*) by his campaigns in the South, he returned to his kingdom and found that it was surrounded by a belt of hostile States which were potential sources of danger to his sovereignty. He, therefore, resolved to make himself the king of these kings by a 'war of extermination' against them (*prasabhoddharaṇa*). It was a violent and bloody war waged against the remaining kings of Āryāvarta who were not conquered in the first campaign.

Rudradeva. The first of these kings was Rudradeva who is identified with Rudrasena I Vākāṭaka (A.D. 344-48) and who must have been deprived of the eastern part of his territory between Jumna and Vidiśā, i.e., Bundelkhand. Samudra Gupta did not carry his campaigns into the central and western parts of the Deccan which were left alone as a result of a possible alliance between him and Rudrasena's son Pṛithivīsheṇa I (A.D. 348-375) who must have acknowledged his suzerainty. Pṛithivīsheṇa's inscriptions show that his territory included the country from the south of the Jumna to the south-west of the Vindhyas. The Eran inscription of Samudra Gupta points to a part of Malwa being in his dominion, what is called *Airikiṇa-pradeśa* (now a village in Saugor district in M.P.), which he must have annexed by defeating Rudradeva=Rudrasena I Vākāṭaka.

Āṭavika (Forest) Kingdoms. The conquest of Āryāvarta was followed by the establishment of suitable relations with other States far and near. The inscription states that Samudra Gupta reduced to complete subjection (*parichārakīkṛita*, 'made servants of') the kings of 'all' the forest-States. Eighteen such States are mentioned in the copper-plate inscription of Parivrājaka king Basti and the Dabhāla kingdom (Jubbulpore) is one of them.

Frontier States. This succession of conquests made Samudra Gupta so powerful that the States on the frontiers of his empire, whether kingdoms (*Pratyantanṛipatibhiḥ*) or republics, were anxious to enter into friendly relations with him by rendering satisfaction (*paritosha*) of the demands of his imperial administration (*prachaṇḍaśāsana*) in the shape of payment of all taxes (*sarvakaradāna*), obeying his decrees (*ājñā-karaṇa*), and attending his imperial darbars to tender homage to him in person (*praṇāmāgamana*).

Among the frontier kingdoms are mentioned five of eastern India.

Samataṭa. The first is Samataṭa which the *Bṛihatsaṁhitā* places in the eastern division of India. Hiuen-Tsang placed it to the east of Tāmralipti country and bordering on the sea. Its capital was Karmmānta which is supposed to be modern Kamta in Comilla district by N. K. Bhattasali (*Iconography*, pp. 4f).

Davāka. According to Mr. N. K. Bhattasali, the chief city of Ḍavāka is to be identified with modern Dabok in the Nowgong district of Assam. Ḍavāka then corresponds to the valley of the Kapili-Yamunā-Kolong rivers of Assam.

Kāmarūpa. It may be taken to be the Gauhati District of Assam.

Nepal. The then king of Nepal was Jayadeva I, the new Lichchhavi king, who was a relation of Samudra Gupta on his mother's side. The submission of such a hilly kingdom to the suzerainty of Samudra Gupta is a great triumph for him and a proof of his invincible power.

Kartṛipura. This is another Himalayan State, the territory of Katuriya or Katyur kingdom of Kumaun, Garhwal, and Rohilkhand (*JRAS*, 1898, pp. 198-9).

The location of these frontier States shows that Bengal proper, excluding its part named Samataṭa, was already a part of the Gupta empire under Samudra Gupta, while in the time of his successor Chandra Gupta II, northern Bengal figures as a regular province of the empire under the name Puṇḍravardhana. It may, therefore, be assumed that the conquest of Bengal proper was the work of Samudra Gupta's father, Chandra Gupta I, and this assumption will support the view that Chandra Gupta I may be equated with *Chandra* of the Delhi Pillar inscription which refers to Chandra's victory over a coalition of Bengal chiefs (*śātrūn sametyāgatān vaṅgeshu*). With Bengal conquered and his rear thus secured, Chandra Gupta I was able to push his conquests farther along the course of the Ganges up to Prayāga and then beyond it up to Śāketa or Oudh, as stated in the *Purāṇic* passage whose meaning may be now correctly understood. There is, however, another view of the matter, which will be discussed later.

The Republican Peoples : Mālavas. These republican States were on the frontiers of Samudra Gupta's empire on its western and south-western side. Of these, the Mālavas have several centuries of history from the time of Pāṇini (*c.* 500 B.C.) and of Alexander's invasion (326 B.C.) which they had resisted. They are also known to the *Mahābhārata* (II. 32; 52). They came into conflict with Nahapāna's son-in-law Ushavadāta who subdued them with the help of

PLATE I

COINS OF SAMUDRA GUPTA

1. Standard Type

2. Kācha Type

3. Tiger Type

PLATE II

COINS OF SAMUDRA GUPTA

(Continued)

4. Chandra Gupta Type

5. Battle-axe Type

6. Asvamedha Type

[From Line-Drawing by Śrī Nanda Lal Bose]

his allies, the Uttama-bhadras, as already stated. The Mālava copper coins are found all over the wide area from the Sutlej to the Narmadā and have an equally wide range in time from 250 B.C. to A.D. 350, as shown by Cunningham. Their coins are not found after A.D. 350 when they ceased to be independent and submitted to Samudra Gupta. Their influence in the Mandasor region is proved by the fact that they were able to impose their tribal era beginning from 58 B.C. upon the Mandasor princes.

Ārjunāyanas. The *Bṛihatsaṁhitā* places them in the northern division of India. Ptolemy knows of a people in the Punjab whom he calls the Pandoonoi = Pāṇḍavas with whom the Ārjunāyanas (called after Arjuna) may be connected. Ārjunāyana coins are found in the Mathurā region and 'they may be assigned with probability to the region lying west of Agra and Mathurā, equivalent, roughly speaking, to the Bharatpur and Alwar States' (V. A. Smith's *Catalogue*, p. 160).

Yaudheyas. They are as old as Pāṇini who knows of them as a military clan (*āyudhajīvī saṁgha*) who lived by the profession of arms. They are also known to the *Mahābhārata* (II. 52; VII, 9). The Girnar inscription of Rudradāman (A.D. 150) mentions his victory over the Yaudheyas 'proud of their heroism'. The Bijayagaḍh inscription (No. 58 of Fleet) connects them with the Bharatpur State. In the Ludhiana district have been unearthed their votive tablets. Yaudheya coins have been found all over the area from Saharanpur to Multan. A rich find of their coin-moulds was recently brought to light by Dr. B. Sahni at Khokrakot near Rohtak where there seems to have existed a regular mint. In Samudra Gupta's time, they seem to have occupied northern Rajputana and south-east Punjab, and their territory extended up to the confines of the Bhawalpur State where their name survives in the name of the tract called Johiyāwār.

Madrakas. The Madradeśa is as old as the Upanishads which have immortalized its philosopher named Patañchala Kāpya to whom scholars from eastern India flocked for advanced knowledge. They are also known to Pāṇini (IV. 2, 121) and to the *Mahābhārata* (II, 52; VI, 61). They lived in the country between the Rāvi and the Chenab with their capital at Śākala (Sialkot). Their territory on the eve of Samudra Gupta's conquest seems to have been situated to the north of the Yaudheyas.

Ābhīras. They are known to the *Mahābhārata* which locates them near the Sarasvatī and Vinaśana in western Rajputana (IX. 37. 1.). The *Periplus* calls their country Abiria. They are also mentioned in the *Mahābhāshya* of Patañjali (1. 2, 3) in association with the Śūdras, the Sodrai of Alexander's time who lived in northern Sind. Ābhīra generals served in the armies of Saka satraps of western India in the second century A.D. as known from their inscriptions. An Ābhīra chief named Iśvaradatta attained to the position of a *Mahākshatrapa*. But the most famous Ābhīra was Iśvarasena (=Iśvaradatta?), son of Śiva Datta and Mādharī, who is believed to have defeated the Śātavāhanas and annexed their province of Mahārāshṭra in A.D. 248 from which also begins the era of the people known as the Traikūṭakas who were rulers of the Aparānta or Konkan and identified by some scholars with the dynasty of Ābhīra Īśvarasena. The Traikūṭaka kings known from their coins and inscriptions in the Gupta period are (1) Indradatta, (2) his son Dahrasena (A.D. 455), (3) his son Vyāghrasena (A.D.480). Dahrasena performed an *aśvamedha*. The dynasty seems to have succumbed to the Vākāṭaka King Harishena. Some Ābhīras settled in Central India where the tract named Ahirwār between Jhansi and Bhilsa may have been called after them.

Prārjunas. These are supposed by V. A. Smith to have belonged to the Narasiṁhapur district of M. P. Kauṭilya knows of a people called Prājjūnakas.

Sanakānikas. These are mentioned in one of the Udayagiri inscriptions of Chandra Gupta II (Fleet, No. 3). Their seat of power seems to have been near Bhilsa.

Kākas. They are mentioned in the *Mahābhārata* (VI. 9, 64). V. A. Smith connects them with Kākanāda (Sanchi). Hence they may have been neighbours of the Sanakānikas.

Kharaparikas. Dr. D. R. Bhandarkar takes them to be the Kharparas mentioned in the Batihāgaḍh inscription (*EI*, XII, 46) of the Damoh district of MP. (*IHQ*. I, p. 258).

Foreign States. Beyond the frontier States described above lay the foreign States towards the north-west, in Western India, and also in the distant south, Siṁhala and all other islands overseas, which were also ready to acknowledge the suzerainty of Samudra Gupta by rendering to him all kinds of service (*sevā*). These services are distinguished in thei nscriptions as comprising (1) *Ātmanivedanam* (offering their own persons for service to the emperor), (2) *Kanyopāyana* (gifts of maidens), (3) *Dāna* (presents) and (4), application (*yāchanā*) for charters bearing the imperial Gupta Garuḍa seal (*Garutmadaṅka*) by which they would be left undisturbed by the emperor in the enjoyment (*bhukti*) and administration (*śāsana*) of their respective territories (*svavishaya*). The foreign and overseas States thus entered into what may be regarded as Treaties of Alliance and Service so that they might be spared an invasion by the 'all-powerful emperor who brought the whole of India under his sway by the prowess of his arms' (*bāhuvīrva-*

prasaradharaṇībandhasya : svabhujabala parākramaikabandhoḥ parākramāṅkasya). These foreign States are enumerated below.

Daivaputra-Shāhī-Shāhānushāhī. These three titles were first used by the Great Kushān emperors. In the inscription of the year 8 found at Mathurā, Kanishka I uses the title *Shāhi*. In several other inscriptions, he uses the title *Devaputra* which has also been used by Huvishka and also by Vāsudeva I (*EI*. XVII, 11; I, 381; IX, 240; VIII, 182; IX, 242). The title *Devaputra* is of Chinese origin. The title *Shāhānushāhi* is derived from Iranian or Persian *Shāhānushāh*. It corresponds to the legend *Shaonono* appearing on the coins of Vāsudeva whom the legend calls *Bazodeo Koshano*. The later Kidāra Kushāns assumed for themselves the title *Shāhi*. The later Kushān king whom Samudra Gupta has in view may have been Grumbates who helped his Sassanian overlord Shāhpur II with a contingent of Indian elephants about A.D. 350. His Iranian title shows that he was not ruling in India proper. The later Kushān kings were ruling on Indian borderland and in the Kabul valley in the third and fourth centuries A.D., as already related, and were issuing coins modelled on those of the imperial Kushāns, Kanishka I, and Vāsudeva I (Smith's *Catalogue of Coins of Indian Museum*, p. 91.)

Śakas. The Śakas in India in the fourth century A.D. must be the Śakas of Western India with their capital at Ujjain and belonging to the satrapal family of Chaṣṭana and Rudradāman. In the time of Samudra Gupta, the Śaka ruler was Rudrasiṁha II whose successor, Rudrasiṁha, whose coins come up to A.D. 390 was killed by Chandra Gupta II. A Sāñchī inscription testifies to the existence of another Śaka principality under its chief named Mahādaṇḍanāyaka Śrīdhravarman, son of Nandī, who was ruling in about A.D. 319. His title seems to show that his position was that of a feudatory. That there were a number of such petty Śaka chiefs in the region of the Vindhyas is indicated by the discovery of what are called 'Puri Kushān' coins in this locality.

It may be noted that the Śaka homage to Samudra Gupta was not at all sincere and reliable since it was not tendered to his successor.

There is a view that the context of the inscriptions shows that these Śakas, instead of being the Western Kshatrapas, should be taken as the Śakas of the north whose coins were imitated by Samudra Gupta. These coins corresponded to Kushān types marked by *Ardochsho* reverse, and the title *Śaka* added to the initials of the individual rulers concerned, written in Brāmī script. These coins of the Śaka (Kushān) kings of the Punjab are distinct from the coins of the Kushān kings of Kabul, which are marked by the

Oesbo, reverse, and did not influence Samudra Gupta's coinage in any way.

Murundas. Muruṇḍa is a Śaka word for *Svāmī* or chief. The title *Svāmī* was used by the Kshatrapas of Surāshṭra and Ujjain. In the Girnar inscription of Rudradāman his grandfather is called *Svāmī* Chashṭana. But the people called here as the *Muruṇḍas* are to be distinguished from the Śakas and may be identified with the Kushāns, as Sten Konow suggests (*EI.* XIV, 292).

There is a view that the expression '*Daivaputra—Shāhi—Shāhānushāhi*' should be taken to indicate three different peoples. The Daivaputras were in possession of the Central Punjab, while the Shāhis and Shāhānushāhis were ruling beyond the Punjab and the frontiers in the region corresponding to modern Afghanistan. It is also to be noted that Samudra Gupta's coins copy Śaka and Kushān coins, proving his conquest of the Śaka and Kushān territories where these coins were in circulation. The parallel case is that of Gupta silver coinage which was inaugurated on the occasion of Gupta conquest of the kingdom of the Western satraps whose coinage had to be imitated by its new rulers.

Siṁhala. The epigraphic statement that Siṁhala and all other neighbouring islands brought presents to Samudra Gupta is supported by literary evidence. The Chinese author, Wang Hiuen-tse, relates that the king of Ceylon named Chi-mi-kia-po-mo (=Śrī Megha-Varman or -Varṇa, whose time is A.D. 350-380) sent to Samudra Gupta an embassy and gifts coupled with a request that he might be permitted to build at Bodh-Gayā a monastery for the use of Ceylonese pilgrims.

The inscription, however, does not confine the imperial Gupta influence to Ceylon. It mentions 'all other islands' to which it was extended, but does not name which islands these were. This influence laid the foundation of Greater India consisting of those islands which were presumably the islands of the Indian Archipelago like Java, to which the name Indonesia is applied.

Mattila. Mattila is supposed to be Mattila of a clay seal found in Bulandshahr but the seal appears to be that of a private person and not a prince in the absence of the honorific *Śrī* in the name.

Nāga Kings. Nāgadatta, Gaṇapati-Nāga, and Nāgasena, are presumbaly kings of the Nāga dynasty at its different centres already related. Gaṇapati-Nāga is stated to be *Dhārādhīśa*, Lord of Dhārā [K. P. Jayaswal in *Cat. of Mithilā MSS.* II. 105; also *Bhāvaśataka* I. 4. 800 (*Kāvyamālā* Text)]. Gaṇapati is further known from his coins found at Narwar and Besnagar. Nāgasena may be dubbed Nāgasena II or may have been of another branch of the wide-spread

Nāga family to distinguish him from the Nāgasena who was extirpated in the first campaign in Āryāvarta.

Chandravarman. He may be identified with Chandravarman mentioned in an inscription on Susunia hill near Bankura as son of Siṁhavarman and king of Pushkaraṇa, modern Pokharan, about 25 miles from Susunia hill. There is another view that Pushkaraṇa is modern Pokran or Pokurna in Marwar and that Chandravarman is to be taken as the son of Siṁhavarman mentioned in a second Mandasor inscription (*AI*, 1913, 217-19). This inscription mentions Naravarmā as son of Siṁhavarmā and brother of Chandravarmā and so both the Susunia and Mandasor inscriptions mention a common fact that Siṁhavarmā was the father of Chandravarmā.

Achyuta. Achyuta may be taken to be another king of Ahichchhatra to distinguish him from the first Achyuta already dispossessed of his kingdom. But repetition of these names of kings already defeated may be made for emphasis as a renewed declaration of his conquests.

Nandi. Nothing is known about Nandi, unless he is taken to be Śivanandi, a Nāga king (*ASR*, 1915). The *Purāṇas* mention Śiśu Nandi and Nandiyaśas as Nāga kings of Central India.

Balavarman. Balavarman is also an unknown name. He cannot be taken to be a king of Assam on the ground of the mere suffix -*Varman*, for Assam figures as a frontier State separate from Āryāvarta in the inscription.

A suggestion has been made by Rapson that these nine kings of Āryāvarta may be taken to be the nine Nāga kings referred to in the *Purāṇas*. In that case, Garuḍa is a very apt emblem of the Gupta dynasty which exterminated the Nāga dynasty, like Garuḍa eating up the *Nāgas* or serpents.

It is to be noted that this part of the inscription ends with the statement that besides these nine kings who were exterminated by Samudra Gupta, there were many other kings of Āryāvarta (*Anekāryāvartarājaprasabhoddharaṇa*) whose territories were annexed by him. Thus, as a result of his two campaigns, Samudra Gupta made a clean sweep of all the petty kingdoms of Āryāvarta the whole of which was now brought under his authority as its paramount sovereign. The political unification of Āryāvarta which was split up into so many small States was one of the great achievements of Samudra Gupta who thus built up the Gupta Empire. The geographical name Āryāvarta may be taken in the sense in which it is taken in the standard legal work *Manu-Smṛiti* where it denotes the land between the Himalayas and the Vindhyas and between the western and eastern seas (Manu, II, 22).

Aśvamedha. Samudra Gupta fittingly celebrated his *digvijaya* by celebrating the horse-sacrifice which had long fallen into desuetude. Therefore, his successors hail him as one who 'revived the horse-sacrifice after such a long time' (*Chirotsannāśvamedhāhartā*). The Allahabad *Praśasti* is silent about it, because the ceremony was performed after it was incised, and all the conquests were achieved. But his coins make up for this epigraphic deficiency. These may be dubbed as *Aśvamedha* coins, portraying, as they do, horse before *yūpa*, and on *Rev.* the queen (whose presence was required for the ceremony) and the definite legend *Aśvamedha-parākramaḥ*. The legend on the *Obv.* in its full form reads as follows: *Rājādhirājaḥ pṛithivīmavitvā divaṁ jayati aprativāryavīryaḥ*; "the king of kings, having conquered the earth, now conquers heaven with invincible valour." This legend makes it quite clear that the *Aśvamedha* had followed his conquests. Heaven can be conquered only by *dharma*, by the performance of a religious ceremony like *Aśvamedha*, by 'good deeds,' (*sucharitaiḥ*, as stated in the inscription or *Karmabhiḥ uttamaiḥ*, as stated on his coins).

A possible allusion to the horse-sacrifice may be found in the expression *Suvarṇadāne*, 'distribution of gold', occurring in the Eran stone inscription, or in the expression *aneka-go-hiraṇyakoṭi-pradasya*, 'the giver of many cows and crores of gold coins' occurring in Fleet's inscription No. 4. In the Poona plate of Prabhāvatiguptā, his grand-daughter, Samudra Gupta is described as 'one who performed many horse-sacrifices' (*anekāśvamedhayājī*) (*EI*, XV, 41).

Lastly, the ceremony may also be indicated in the inscription '*ddaguttassa deyadhamma*' occurring on the figure of a horse on view at the Lucknow Provincial Museum and also in a seal showing the figure of a horse with the legend *parākrama* (*JRAS*, 1901, 102).

Coins. Samudra Gupta issued coins of as many as eight different types, all of pure gold. It was his conquests which brought to him the gold utilized in his coinage and also the knowledge of its technique acquired from his acquaintance with Kushān (eastern Punjab) coins. His earliest coins began as imitations of these Kushān coins, and of their foreign features which were gradually replaced by Indian features in his later coins. Thus Samudra Gupta both inaugurated and Indianized Gupta coinage. The degree of Indianization of the Gupta coins is a key to their chronology. From this point of view, what are known as 'Chandra Gupta coins' already described cannot be attributed to Chandra Gupta I because, as will be shown below, they show a degree of independence of Kushān models which makes them later than several other types of coins issued even by his successor, Samudra Gupta. They cannot by any means be considered as the earliest Gupta coins from the point of view of technique.

The foreign Kushān name of *dīnāra* suggested by the Roman *denarius aureus* was also applied to Gupta coinage (Nos. 5-9, 62, 64 of Fleet's Inscriptions). In inscription No. 64, the foreign name is coupled with the Hindu name *Suvarṇa* of which the standard was 146.4 grains, to which only the later Gupta coins of the east correspond.

Standard Type. This is the commonest type of Samudra Gupta's coins, the closest copy of Kushān coins, and, therefore, the earliest type of Gupta coins.

Its *Obv.* shows 'King standing l. nimbate (i.e. with halo round head), wearing close-fitting cap, coat, and trousers, ear-rings and necklace, holding in l. hand *standard* bound with fillet, dropping incense on Altar, with his r. hand; on l., behind Altar, is a *Standard*, bound with fillet, surmounted by a *Garuḍa*. Some specimens show the king wearing shorts and full socks. The *Altar* may also be taken to be *Tulasīvṛindāvana*, a completely Indian feature'.

Beneath the king's l. arm is written vertically the name *Samudra* or in some varieties *Samudra Gupta*.

The *Obv.* also bears the legend which in complete form reads: '*Samaraśatavitatavijayo jitāripurājito divaṁ jayati*; the conqueror of unconquered fortresses of his enemies, whose victory was spread in hundreds of battles, conquers heaven.'

The *Rev.* depicts 'Goddess (Lakshmī) seated, facing, on throne, nimbate, wearing loose robe, necklace, and armlets, holding fillet in outstretched r. hand and cornucopia in l. arm; her feet rest on lotus; traces of back of throne on r. on most specimens; border of dots.' The *cornucopiae* (cornucopia) is the horn of plenty, the horn of the goat Amalthea by which Zeus was suckled. The horn is represented in art as overflowing with flowers, fruit, and corn. Thus, it is a pre-eminently foreign feature on these coins.

On r. is written the legend: *Parākramaḥ*.

A comparison of the features of the *Obv.* with those of the *Obv.* of later Kushān coins will show that they agree except in regard to the following: (1) the Gupta king wears a close fitting cap, instead of the peaked head-dress of the Kushān kings; (2) the *Garuḍa* standard in place of the Kushān trident; (3) the jewellery worn by the king is Indian. But the following Kushān features still remain: (1) the Gupta king is given Kushān dress; (2) his name is written vertically; (3) the standard is bound with a fillet, as on the Kushān coins; (4) the altar and sprinkling of incense are Kushān and found on Kanishka's coins; (5) the halo round the king's head is also Kushān, as well as the crescent to its l. According to Allan (*Gupta*

Coins, p. 1, XX), the crescent is reminiscent of the Greek 0.

The *Rev.* is a downright copy of the late Kushān Ardochsho *Rev.* Ardochsho is seen seated, facing, on a high-backed throne, holding cornucopia in l. arm and fillet in outstretched r. hand. This Ardochsho *Rev.* does not occur on early Kushān (Kanishka, Huvishka or Vāsudeva) coins. The back of the throne conveyed no meaning to the Kushān engravers or their Gupta copyists who, however, kept it up by giving only its r. side.

Another irrelevant Kushān feature slavishly copied on Gupta coins is the symbol or monogram appearing on the l. and probably treated as an ornament balancing the portion of the back of the throne on the r.

As has been already stated, the gradual elimination of these foreign features and elements which lost their meaning for the Indian public supplies the test by which Gupta numismatic chronology may be determined. It may also be noted that the *Standard* indicates the conquered territories where the flag of victory was planted. It is also appropriately associated with the legend *Parākramaḥ*.

Chandra Gupta Coins. Judged by the above criterion, the type of coins known as Chandra Gupta coinage cannot be attributed to Chandra Gupta I. If Chandra Gupta I had issued any coins, they should have been, as the earliest Gupta coins, of the Standard type as being the closest copy of the Kushān original. No such coins of Chandra Gupta I have been discovered. On the other hand, the Chandra Gupta type is more Indianized than the Standard type of Samudra Gupta, as shown (1) in the figure of the queen added on the *Obv.* and (2) in the lion taking the place of the throne, though its dependence on Kushān technique is seen in traces of the back of the meaningless throne being still kept up.

Further, the goddess seated on a lion first appears on the reverse of the Lion-slayer type of Chandra Gupta II coinage. Therefore, Chandra Gupta I type should be considered as the immediate predecessor of this type of coins of Chandra Gupta II.

It may be noted in this connexion that Gupta coins which bear most the traces of the Kushān throne are to be taken as both earlier and of the north where the Kushān prototype was more known. This applies to the Standard and Archer types. But the types like Chandra Gupta I and Battle-axe which show the throne the least must have been issued in the more southerly regions, in the original Gupta territory where Ardochsho did not penetrate. Some of the foreign elements such as the cornucopia of the throne *Rev.* also thus persist late in the north, even up to the time of Kumāra Gupta I Of these Chandra Gupta coins, the *Obv.* shows 'Chandra Gupta I

PLATE III

COINS OF SAMUDRA GUPTA

(Continued)

7. Lyrist Type
[From Line-Drawing by A. K. Haldar]

standing to l., wearing close-fitting coat, trousers, and head-dress, ear-rings and armlets, holding in l. hand a crescent-topped standard bound with fillet, and with r. hand offering an object, which on some coins is clearly a ring, to Kumāradevī who stands on l. to r., wearing loose robe, ear-rings, necklace and armlets, and tight-fitting head-dress; both nimbate'. 'On r. on either side of the standard, the legend *Chandra*, or *Chandragupta*; on l. the legend *Kumāradevī*, or *Śrī-Kumāradevī* or *Kumāradevī Śrīḥ*'.

The *Rev*. shows 'Goddess seated, facing, on lion couchant to r. or l., holding fillet in outstretched r. hand and cornucopia in l. arm; her feet rest on lotus; behind her on l. are the traces of the back of a throne on most specimens; border of dots; symbol on l. On r. the legend *Lichchhavayaḥ*'.

The significance of this legend may be understood in the light of the appellation assumed by Samudra Gupta in the inscriptions as a *Lichchhavi-dauhitra*, showing how he took pride in his pedigree on his mother's side and in the indebtedness of the Gupta Empire to the Lichchhavi connexion is thus declared on these coins.

The goddess on lion must be Durgā *Siṁhavāhanā* whose might and majesty (*māhātmya*) are described graphically in the sacred work called *Chaṇḍī* (a part of the *Mārkaṇḍeya-Purāṇa*) and who was worshipped according to popular tradition by Rāma on the eve of his encounter with Rāvaṇa. Thus Samudra Gupta became also a devotee of Durgā for the success of his military missions.

Archer Type. The *Obv*. shows 'King standing l., nimbate, dressed as in Standard type, holding bow in l. hand, while the r. holds arrow, the head of which rests on ground.; Garuḍa standard on l.; bearing legend *Samudra* beneath l. arm; also the legend "*Apratiratha vijitya kshitiṁ sucharitair* (or *avanipatir*) *divam jayati*" ("Unopposed by hostile chariots, conquering the earth, he conquers heaven by his good deeds.")'.

The *Rev*. shows 'Lakshmī seated as on Standard type; symbol on l.; and legend *Apratirathaḥ*'.

Battle-axe Type. The *Obv*. exhibits 'King standing l., nimbate, wearing close-fitting cap, coat and trousers, ear-rings and necklace, and sword, holding battle-axe (*paraśu*) in l. hand, while r. hand rests on r. hip; on l. boy or *dwarf* to r., behind whom is a crescent-topped standard; beneath l. arm, the legend (*a*) *Samudra* or (*b*) *Kṛi* or *Kṛitānta* or (*c*) *Samudragupta*; and "*Kṛitāntaparaśur jayatyajitarājajetājitaḥ*."' ["the holder of the battle-axe, the weapon of the invincible god of death (Yama), the unconquered conqueror of unconquered kings, achieves victory"].

The *Rev*. shows 'Goddess Lakshmī, nimbate, seated on throne with lotus footstool or lotus, facing, as on Standard type (but in some varieties, holding lotus in place of cornucopia); border of dots; symbol on l; on r. the legend *Kṛitāntaparaśuḥ.*'

On some varieties, the king on *Obv.* does *not* wear sword, while on *Rev.* the goddess is seated *not* on throne but on lotus (*padmāsanā*), a definitely Indian feature. The goddess is also unmistakably Lakshmī. On some coins, she is seated on throne *without* back (thus shedding a Kushān feature) and holds lotus.

The dwarf on some coins holds up an object, possibly an umbrella. The king's menial staff traditionally included personal attendants marked by physical deformities, such as the *Kubja* (hunchback), *Vāmana* (dwarf), *Kirāta* (*alpatanu*, 'of small body'), *Mūka* (dumb), *Badhira* (deaf), *Jaḍa* (idiot), and even *Andha* (blind) [see my *Chandragupta Maurya and His Times*, p. 106].

Both the Archer and the Battle-axe types mark an advance in their process of Indianization. The unmeaning standard copied from the later Kushān coins is replaced in these types by more understandable and appropriate objects like the bow, the battle-axe, or a crescent-topped standard, and the arrow takes the place of the altar. The bow and arrow recall Vishṇu *Śārṅgī*.

The Battle-axe type of coins was issued by Samudra Gupta to celebrate his conquests in different directions, proving the invincible might of his arm and justifying his title as *Kṛitāntaparaśu.* These should therefore belong to the later part of his reign.

Kācha Type. The *Obv.* shows 'King standing to l., dressed as in preceding types, holding standard surmounted by wheel (*Chakra*) in l. hand and sprinkling incense on altar with r. hand; legend *Kācha* beneath l. arm and "*Kācho gāṁ avajitya divaṁ karmabhir uttamair jayati*" ("Kacha, after conquering the earth, conquers heaven by means of good deeds")'.

The *Rev.* shows 'Goddess (Lakhshmī) standing to l., wearing loose robe, holding flower in r. hand and cornucopia in l. arm; border of dots; symbol on l.; or. the legend "*Sarvarājochchhettā*", ("the exterminator of all kings")'.

Some varieties show Lakshmī standing on lotus. Her husband, the god Vishṇu, is recalled by *Chakra* on *Obv.*

Tiger Type. The *Obv.* shows 'King standing l., wearing turban, waist-cloth, necklace, ear-rings and armlets, trampling on a tiger which falls backwards as he shoots it with bow in r. hand, l. hand drawing bow back behind ear; on l. behind tiger, crescent-topped standard as on Battle-axe type; legend "*Vyāghraparākramaḥ*".'

The *Rev.* shows Goddess (Gaṅgā) standing l. on *Makara*, nude to waist, wearing ear-rings, necklace, anklets and armlets, holding lotus in l. hand and r. hand outstretched empty; on l. crescent-topped standard bound with fillet; no symbol; legend "*Rājā Samudraguptaḥ.*"'.

This is a rare type, of which only four examples are so far known. The goddess Gaṅgā is introduced to indicate Samudra Gupta's conquests in the valley of the Ganges, with its swampy and forested regions which were the abode of the royal Bengal tiger, and gave scope to the king's big game hunting. Thus the goddess Gaṅgā and the tiger are aptly associated on these coins.

Lyrist Type. The *Obv.* shows 'King seated, nimbate, cross-legged to l., wearing waist-cloth, close-fitting cap, necklace, ear-rings and armlets on high-backed couch, playing on lyre or lute (*vīṇā*) which lies on his knees; beneath couch is a pedestal or foot-stool inscribed *Si;* legend "*Mahārājādhirāja-Śrī-Samudraguptaḥ*"'.

The Rev. shows 'Goddess nimbate, seated to l. on a wicker stool, wearing loose robe, close-fitting cap, and jewellery, holding fillet in outstretched r. hand and cornucopia in l. arm; border of dots; no symbol; on r. legend "*Samudraguptaḥ*"'. The *Vīṇā* or lyre on the *Obv.* suggests that the goddess on *Rev.* is to be taken as Sarasvatī associated with *vīṇā* as the Goddess of Music.

Both the Tiger and the Lyrist types are the most Indian of Samudra Gupta's coinage. The king's attitude and dress are perfectly Indian, free from all traces of Kushān influence. On some varieties of the Lyrist type, the king appears even bare-headed. The goddess on *Rev.* also sits on the Indian wicker-stool, marking an original deviation from the Ardochsho type. She may be taken more appropriately as Sarasvatī associated with Music and *vīṇā* (as *Vīṇāpāṇī*) than Lakshmī in the absence of lotus on the coin.

The inscription *Si* on footstool may be a part of the slogan *Siddhaṃ*.

Aśvamedha Type. The *Obv.* shows 'Horse standing l. before a sacrificial post (*yūpa*), from which pennons fly over its back; on some specimens a low pedestal below; beneath horse the letter *Si*; legend: "*Rājādhirājaḥ pṛithivīṁ avitvā divaṁ jayatyaprativāryavīryaḥ*" ("the king of kings, having gained the earth, conquers heaven, with his irresistible heroism")'. On one specimen the reading is '*Pṛithvīṁ vijitya*' and on another '*pṛithivīṁ vijitya divaṁ jayatyāhṛita-vājimedhaḥ*' (D. C. Sircar, *Select Inscriptions*, p. 268).

The *Rev.* presents 'the chief-queen (*Mahishī*) standing l. wearing loose robe and jewellery, holding *chowrie* over r. shoulder in r. hand, l. hanging by her side; on l. is a sacrificial spear bound with fillet; around her feet a chain (?) extending round spear and on some specimens gourd (?) at feet; no symbol; legend "*Aśvamedhaparākramaḥ*"'. The queen figured here must be Queen Dattā = Dattadevī, mother of Chandra Gupta II, as mentioned in his Eran Stone Pillar inscription (No. 4 of Fleet) and also other inscriptions such as (1) Bilsaḍ Stone Pillar inscription of Kumāra Gupta I of the year 96=A.D. 415; (2) Bhitarī Stone Pillar inscription of Skanda Gupta; (3) Bihar Stone Pillar inscription of Skanda Gupta; (4) Bhitarī Seal inscription of Kumāra Gupta III; and (5) Nālandā Seal inscription of Budha Gupta.

We may trace, in conclusion, the progressive Indianization of the coinage of Samudra Gupta by its relevant features and marks (technically called *lakshaṇas*) as given below:

1. The king's head-dress which from the start was a close-fitting cap in place of the Kushān peaked or conical head-dress. In the most Indian of the coins such as the Tiger type, the king wears the Indian turban and on some varieties is even bare-headed.

2. The jewellery worn by the king or queen or the goddess is Indian, such as ear-ring, necklace, armlet, or anklet (worn by goddess on Tiger type).

3. The king wears the Indian *dhoti* or waist-cloth on both Tiger- and Lyrist-types.

4. Introduction, in place of Ardochsho, of Indian goddess:

(i) Lakshmī marked by her favourite flower, lotus (a) which she holds in hand (as on Battle-Axe type) in place of the Greek and foreign object, the cornucopia; (b) which is used as a foot-stool (as on Battle-Axe type); (c) on which she is seated (as on some varieties of the Battle-Axe type). Lakshmī on some coins is seated on the Indian *moḍhā* or wicker stool (as on Lyrist type ?), or on throne without the Kushān back (as on some varieties of the Battle-Axe type).

(ii) Goddess on lion who is *Durgā-siṁhavāhanā* with her feet resting on lotus (as on Chandra Gupta I coins).

(iii) Goddess *Gaṅgā* on *Makara* (as on Tiger type).

(iv) Goddess *Sarasvatī* on the Lyrist type, seated on *Moḍhā* (as on some varieties of the Battle-Axe type).

5. Introduction of the queen on certain coins (the Chandra Gupta I and Aśvamedha coins).

6. *Garuḍa*, vehicle of Vishṇu surmounting the standard.

7. The Indian weapons of war and hunting such as Bow and Arrow (on Archer type), Sword and Battle-Axe (on Battle-Axe type) which take the place of the Kushān standard, the arrow taking the place of Kushān altar.

8. The *Dwarf* who had a traditional place in the Indian royal household (as seen on Battle-Axe type).

9. The *Aśvamedha* type inspired by a specifically Indian conception and institution.

It is interesting to note that there is a design behind this variety in types of Samudra Gupta's coinage. The figure of *Garuḍa* introduced for the first time on the *Obv.* of Standard type, being the vehicle of Vishṇu, suggests Lakshmī as the appropriate goddess on the *Rev.* The legend describing Samudra Gupta as the hero of hundreds of battles on the *Obv.* suggests the title of *Parākramaḥ* on the *Rev*, for it is to his *parākrama* or prowess that he owed his victories. Similarly, on Archer type, both Garuḍa and Lakshmī go together as associates of Vishṇu while the word of its legend *Apratirathaḥ* is picked up and carried forward to the *Rev.* as the royal title by itself. On the Chandra Gupta coins, as has been already noticed, the figure of *Kumāradevī* on the *Obv.* calls for the legend *Lichchhavayaḥ*, with whom she is connected, to appear on the *Rev.* Its meaning may be further understood in the light of the appellation applied to Samudra Gupta in some of the inscriptions, viz., *Lichchhavidauhitra*. The Gupta emperors took pride in their maternal pedigree to which they owed so much. On the Battle-Axe type, the term *Kṛitāntaparaśuḥ* of the *Obv.* legend is adopted as a new royal title on the *Rev.* On the Tiger type, as already pointed out, the tiger as the denizen of the forests of the Gangetic valley directly suggests the allied figure of *Gaṅgā Makaravāhanā* on the *Rev.* and the appropriate royal title, *Vyāghraparākramaḥ*. On the same principle, on Lyrist type, the *Vīṇā* on *Obv.* points to Goddess *Sarasvatī* on *Rev.* and not to *Lakshmī* as taken by Allan. There is, accordingly, no trace of lotus to point to Lakshmī on the *Rev.* Lastly, on the *Aśvamedha* type, the ceremony of horse-sacrifice depicted on *Obv.* inevitably requires its association with the Queen or *Mahishī* whose figure is, accordingly, brought up on the *Rev.* to complete the picture. The legend on the coin is inspired by the subject it depicts. Its key-word is *Aprativāryavīryaḥ* denoting the unopposed career of the conqueror who is appropriately designated as *Aśvamedhaparākramaḥ*.

A recent find of 21 Gupta gold coins in the Holkar State includes a coin of Samudra Gupta's Standard type bearing on *Rev.* the singular legend: *Śri ViKramaḥ* (*Journal of the Numismatic Society of India*, v. 136).

The Emperor. Glimpses of the many-sided genius and character of Samudra Gupta are given both by his inscriptions and coins.

Ruler. As a ruler, he was known for his vigorous and resolute government aptly described as *prachaṇḍa-śāsana* in the inscription.

Conqueror. As a conqueror, he was not moved by a lust for conquest or annexation for its own sake. He was at once a *Digvijayī* and a *Dharmavijayī* in accordance with circumstances. He could not tolerate the independence of his neighbouring States, the many petty kingdoms which threatened the unity and peace of the country, his first concern and consideration. He consecrated his military power to the supreme mission of unifying the country (*bāhuvīryaprasara-dharaṇībandhasya*). Therefore, the petty States of Āryāvarta were annexed by him, as we have already seen. But he had a different policy in respect of other States which were not such sources of trouble, the States on the frontiers of his dominion or situated at a distance. Some of these he conquered only to liberate on terms of peaceful neighbourliness and acknowledgement of his paramount sovereignty. He worked for an international system of brotherhood and peace replacing that of violence, war, and aggression. That is why his reputation spread abroad as one who vanquished kings whom he reinstated in their kingdoms in a new order of peaceful partnership. The expression used in the inscription is very appropriate and forceful: *Anekabhrashṭa-rājya-utsannarāja-vaṁśa-pratishṭhāpana*, 'restoring many a kingdom that was destroyed (*bhrashṭa*) and dynasty that was exterminated (*utsanna*)'; recalling the earlier expression *bhrashṭa-rājyapratishṭhāpaka* applied to Rudradāman I in the Girnar inscription of A.D. 150; corresponding to the poet Kālidāsa's description of the *Dharmavijayī*: '*Gṛihīta-pratimuktasya sa dharmavijayī nṛipaḥ*', suggesting the words of the inscription *grahaṇa-moksha-anugraha*. It is further stated that Samudra Gupta restored to many (*aneka*) vanquished (*vijita*) kings not merely their liberties but also their properties (*vibhava-pratyarpaṇa*) and kept his officers (*Yuktapurusha*) constantly employed (*nitya-vyāpṛita*) on this difficult work of restitution.

Warrior. All his conquests the king achieved by his personal prowess and fighting in the front-line as a soldier (*saṁgrāmeshu svabhuja-vijitāḥ*). He was a fearless fighter, possessed of 'the dash and drive of a tiger' (*vyāghra-parākramaḥ*), the hero of a hundred battles (*samaraśata*) which left on his body their scars (*vraṇa*) as marks of decoration (*śobhā*) and beauty (*kānti*), scars of various kinds caused by different weapons of war (*praharaṇa*), such as *paraśu* (battle-axe), *śara* (arrow), *śaṅku* (spear), *śakti* (spike), *prāsa* (barbed dart), *asi* (sword), *tomara* (iron club), *bhindīpāla* (javelin for throwing arrows of iron), *nārācha* (iron arrow) and *vaitastika* (scimitar) The king depended, indeed, on his personal heroism as his only ally (*svabhujabala-parākramaika-bandhoḥ*). Unable to stand his might (*vīryottaptāḥ*), Kings offered him submission (*śaraṇamupāgatāḥ*). His might knew no bounds (*udvelodita bāhuvīrya*). The Eran stone inscription describes him as 'possessed of prowess which was invincible' (*aprativāryavīryaḥ*). This epithet is repeated on his Aśvamedha coins, as noted above.

Philanthropist. Yet under his iron coat of mail was always beating a soft heart (*mṛiduhṛidaya*), full of compassion (*anukampā*) for those who deserved it by their humility (*avanati*), and regard for him (*bhakti*), for the lowly (*kripaṇa*), the poor (*dīna*), the destitute (*anātha*), and the afflicted (*ātura*), for the relief (*udharaṇa*) of whom he constantly worried himself (*mantradīkshādi-upagatamanasaḥ*). He is a shining (*samīddha*) image (*vigrahavān*) of philanthropy (*lokānugraha*) which showed itself in his vast charities, such as 'gifts of hundreds of thousands of cows'. These charities came out of his wealth which was lawfully acquired (*nyāyāgata* in No. 4 of Fleet) and not ill-gotten, the product of plunder.

Superman. His many actions were, indeed, those of a superman, and not of an ordinary mortal (*amanuja-sadṛiśa*), of a god among men who is beyond comprehension (*achintyapurusha*), one who is only a man (*mānusha*) by form in having to act according to the customs and conventions governing this life (*lokasamaya-kṛiyānuvidhānamātramānusha*). Otherwise, he is the equal of the gods : Kubera in wealth ; Varuṇa in justice ; Indra by power ; invincible like Antaka (Yama) ; a Bṛihaspati in sharp and penetrating intellect (*niśitavidagdhamatiḥ*) ; the hope (*udaya*) of the good (*sādhu*), and the destruction (*pralaya*) of the wicked (*asādhu*).

Poet. Harishena also extols the virtues of his chief as a man of letters, and as a poet. With a mind full of bliss (*sukhamanaḥ*), he was fit for the company of the sages (*prajñānushaṅgochita*) ; a master of the inner meaning (*tattvaḥ*) of the *Śāstras*. He gathered at his court the literary masters (*budhaguṇita*) by whose judgements (*guṇājñā*) he was able to check (*āhata*) those compositions which were against *viruddha*) the spirit (*śrī*) of true poetry (*satkāvya*). He himself composed a large volume of poetry (*bahukavitā*) which appealed to all for its clear (*sphuṭa*) meaning and brought him fame (*kīrti*). He ruled in the realm of letters (*viddvalloke*) as in that of politics, enjoying another kingdom of fame (*kīrtirājya*). He revived the extinct title of *Kavirāja*, 'the prince of poets', by his many poetical works (*anekakāvyakriyābhiḥ*) which might serve even as sources of livelihood to learned men by virtue of their quality and popularity (*vidvaj-janopajīvya*).

He was also the refuge of religion (*dharmaprāchīrabandhaḥ*) into the deepest truths of which his learning penetrated (*vaidushvaṁ tattvabhedi*).

The *Mañju-Śrī-Mūlakalpa* characterizes Samudra Gupta as 'a superman, ever vigilant, unmindful about himself, unmindful about the hereafter'.

Lastly, we may note that Samudra Gupta's achievements and character, his work and worth, are very well summed up in the Bilsad Stone Pillar inscription of his son's successor, Kumāra Gupta I, as follows : *Sarvva-rājochchhettuḥ Prithivyāmapratirathasya chaturuda-*

dhisalilāsvāditayaśaso-Dhanada Varuṇendrāntaka samasya Kṛitāntaparaśoḥ nyāyāgatānekagohiraṇyakoṭipradasya chirotsannāśvamedhāharttuḥ. This characterization of Samudra Gupta was standardized and is also repeated in several later inscriptions such as Bhitarī and Bihar Stone Pillar inscriptions of Skanda Gupta and partly in the Bhitarī Seal inscription of Kumāra Gupta III.

In conclusion, we may bring together the many epithets applied to him in inscriptions on coins which aptly point to the many sides of his complex character and personality. Some of these have been already noticed. The epigraphic epithets are: *Ārya*, *Amanuja*, *Achintya-purusha*, *Sukhamanaḥ*, *Sucharita*, *Kavirāja*, *Pṛithivyāṁ apratirathaḥ* and *Parākramāṅka*. The numismatic appellations suggested by the legends are: *Apratiratha*, *Kṛitāntaparaśu*, *Sarva-rājochchhettā*, *Vyāghraparākrama*, *Aśvamedhaparākrama*, *Aprati-vārya-vīrya*, *Parākramāṅka*, *Samaraśatavitatavijaya*, *Jitāripura*, *Ajita*, *Ajitarājajetājitaḥ* '('the unconquered conqueror of unconquered kings'), *Rāja*, *Rājādhirāja* and *Mahārājādhirāja-Śrī*.

A NOTE ON VĀKĀṬAKA HISTORY

Vākāṭaka history has been recently placed on a satisfactory footing by Principal V. V. Mirashi in *Hyderabad Archaeological Memoir* No. 14 on the basis of a re-reading of the Vākāṭaka inscription in Cave XVI at Ajaṇṭā in the light of the new data furnished in the newly-discovered Bāsim copper-plate grant which was issued by the Vākāṭaka king Vindhyaśakti II (= Vindhyasena) at his capital called Vatsagulma (= modern Bāsim, the headquarters of a *taluq* in Akolā district).

These inscriptions contain many names of Vākāṭaka kings whose relationships in their genealogical lists have been the source of much confusion and controversy. Principal Mirashi has sought to solve the difficulties by suggesting that Vākāṭaka history had split up into two branches with separate histories, the mixing up of which has created confusion. The separation seems to have taken place after Pravarasena I, the son and successor of the founder of the dynasty, Vindhyaśakti I.

As the *Purāṇas* tell us, Pravarasena I had four sons who, after his death, divided his vast kingdom among themselves. The eldest son Gautamīputra predeceased his father because in none of the copper-plate charters mentioning his name is the usual epithet *Vākāṭakānāṁ Mahārājā* applied to him. His son, Rudrasena I, therefore, succeeded Pravarasena I, and founded the northern branch of the dynasty ruling over northern Berar and the western districts of M.P. where are found their inscriptions. For instance, an inscription of Rudrasena I has been found at Deoṭek in the Chāndā district of M.P., while copper-plates of his great-grandson, Pravarasena II, record gifts of land in the districts of Amraoti, Wardha, Nagpur, Betul, Bhaṇḍārā and Bālāghāṭ. At first, the capital of this branch was Nandivardhana as mentioned in the Poona plates of Prabhāvatiguptā (*EI.* XV. 39 f.) and the Belorā (*EI.* XXIV, 260 f.) and Kothūraka (*EI*) grants of her son Pravarasena II. Pravarasena II changed the capital to the city founded by him and called Pravarapura.

The genealogy of this northern branch of the Vākāṭaka dynasty may be thus presented :

Vindhyaśakti I
|
Son Pravarasena I
|
(Son Gautamīputra)
|
Son Rudrasena I
|
Son Pṛithivīsheṇa I
|
Son Rudrasena II (married to Prabhāvatiguptā, daughter of emperor Chandra Gupta II)
|
Son Pravarasheṇa II
|
Son Narendrasena
|
Son Pṛithivisheṇa II

The genealogy of the other branch of the dynasty which may be called the Vatsagulma branch will be as follows :

Vindhyaśakti I
|
Son Pravarasena I
|
Son Sarvasena
|
Son Vindhyasena (=Vindhyaśakti II)
|
Son Pravarasena II
|
Son (whose name is lost)
|
Son Devasena
|
Son Harisheṇa

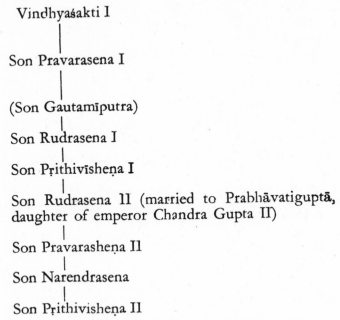

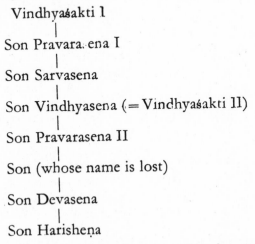

It is to be noted that the name Sarvasena has been taken from the Bāsim plate which mentions him as a son and successor of Pravarasena I. The name cannot be traced in the Ajaṇṭā record but has been restored by Principal Mirashi on the ground that it is suggested by the phrases *Jita-Sarvasenaḥ* in accordance with the epigraphist's use of *yamakas*.

So far, only five inscriptions of this family have been known: (1) Bāsim plates of Vindhyaśakti II; (2) a fragmentary copper-plate inscription of Devasena; (3) inscription in Ajaṇṭā Cave XVI of his minister Varāhadeva; and (5) inscription of Varāhadeva in Ghaṭotkacha Cave near Ajaṇṭā.

The date of Rudrasena II as the son-in-law of Chandra Gupta II gives a clue to the Vākāṭaka chronology. Vindhyaśakti II and Pravarasena II may be taken to be contemporaries of Pṛithivīsheṇa I and Rudrasena II of the other branch. Thus the reign of Vindhyaśakti II may be taken to have closed by A.D. 400. His predecessors are given abnormally long reigns by the *Purāṇās*, while the Bāsim plates mention the 37th year of the reign of Vindhyaśakti II. Thus we may assume a period of 150 years at the least for the reigns of the four kings from Vindhyaśakti I to Vindhyaśakti II and the date A.D. 250 for the foundation of Vākāṭaka I dynasty by Vindhyaśakti I. Granting 100 years for the four successors of Vindhyaśakti II, the last of the dynasty, Harisheṇa, may be taken to have ruled between A.D. 475 and 500. It may be noted that, on architectural grounds, Cave XVI of Ajaṇṭā is also assigned to A.D. 500 by Fergusson and Burgess.

The inscription of this Cave mentions among the conquests of Harisheṇa the following countries: Kuntala, between the Bhīmā and Vedavatī, comprising the Kanarese districts of Bombay and Madras Presidencies and of Mysore state, and also perhaps a part of Mahārāshṭra with Vidarbha, with its capital at Pratishṭhāna (Paithan in Nizam's Dominion) on the Godāvarī (page 9, footnotes, of Principal Mirashi's *Memoir*); Avanti, western Malwa, with its capital Ujjain; Kaliṅga, between the Mahānadī and Godāvarī on the east coast; Kośala or Dakshiṇa Kośala, corresponding to modern Chhatisgarh and adjoining parts of the Eastern State Agency; Trikūṭa, located in Aparānta or North Koṅkan and comprising the country to the west of Nāsik (ibid, p. 10); Lāṭa, between the Māhī and Tāpti, comprising central and southern Gujerat; and Āndhra to the south, of the Godāvarī.

CHAPTER V

CHANDRA GUPTA II VIKRĀMADITYA

(*c.* A.D 375-414)

Date. His dates may be deduced from a number of dated inscriptions discovered for his reign. The first of these is the Mathurā Pillar inscription of G.E. 61=A.D. 380 (*EI.* XXI). The inscription has some significant words read by Dr. D. C. Sircar (*Select Inscriptions*, I. 270) as '*Mahārājā-Rājādhirāja—Śrī—Chandraguptasya vijaya-rājya-saṁvatsare-pañchame*', showing that his inscription dated G.E. 61 (*saṁvatsare ekashashṭhe*) was issued in the fifth year of the reign of Chandra Gupta II. His reign, therefore, commenced in G.E. 61—5=G.E. 56=A.D. 375. This inscription is important as mentioning the earliest date of the Gupta era which may be taken to be as defined by Alberuni in his statement that 'the epoch of the Guptas falls 241 years later than *Śaka-kāla*', i.e., in A.D. 78 + 241 = 319 (Sachau, *Alberuni*, *India*, *II.* 7).

The second dated inscription of his reign is the Udayagiri Cave inscription of Gupta year 82 = A.D. 401, which was issued by his feudatory belonging to the Sanakānika family.

The third is the Sāñchī Stone inscription of Gupta year 93 = A.D. 412 issued by Āmrakārdava who seems to have been a Minister of Chandra Gupta II 'to whose favour (*prasāda*) he owes the fulfilment of the object of his life (*āpyāyita-jīvita-sādhanaḥ*), and who was the hero of many a battle'. (Fleet No. 6).

The fourth inscription is the Gadhwa Stone inscription of Gupta year 88=A.D. 407. Parts of the inscription are lost including Chandra Gupta's name, but that it belonged to his reign may be taken for granted both from the date and his titles, *Paramabhāgavata* and *Mahārājādhirāja* still preserved.

The date of Chandra Gupta II may also be inferred from that of his silver coins which he had issued after his conquests of Surāshṭra and modelled on the coins of its previous rulers, the Kshatrapas. It will appear that the latest coins of the western Kshatrapas, those of Rudra Siṁha III, are of the Śaka year 310 = A.D. 388. The earliest date of the Kshatrapa coins as restruck by Chandra Gupta II is 90 + X (Gupta Era) = A.D. 409 (410).

Name. Chandra Gupta II appears to have several names. The name *Devarāja* is given to him in Sāñchī inscription (Fleet, No. 5). A Vākāṭaka inscription mentions Prabhāvatiguptā as the daughter of Devagupta and Kuberanāgā and describes Devagupta as *Mahārājādhirāja*, while the Riddhapura grants of Queen Prabhāvatiguptā

PLATE IV
COINS OF CHANDRA GUPTA II

1. Couch Type

2. Archer Type

3. King as Bowman
(a variety of Archer Type)
[From Line-Drawing by P. Neogy of Scindia
Public School, Gwalior]

PLATE V

COINS OF CHANDRA GUPTA II

(*Continued*)

4. Chhatra Type

5. Lion-Slayer Type

mention her father's name as Chandra Gupta II. This shows that Devagupta is another name of Chandra Gupta. The grant of Vākāṭaka king Pravarasena II also mentions his maternal grandfather as Chandra Gupta II and Devagupta. It also appears that Chandra Gupta had a third name, Deva-Śrī, as used on his Archer- and Couch-type of coins.

Nomination. The Eran Stone inscription of Samudra Gupta (Fleet, No. 2) refers to the 'many sons and grandsons' of Samudra Gupta, while the Mathurā Stone inscription of Chandra Gupta II (Fleet, No. 4) states that he was chosen for the throne out of all his sons (*tat-parigṛihītena*) by Samudra Gupta. The same fact is repeated in the Bihar and Bhitarī Stone Pillar inscriptions of Skanda Gupta (Fleet, Nos. 12 and 13), where the phrase *tat-parigṛihīta* is used in respect of Chandra Gupta II. Chandra Gupta II has also been described as the *sat-putra* of his father in the Mathurā Pillar inscription of year 61. The repetition of this fact of Chandra Gupta II being deliberately preferred for the throne to all his sons by Samudra Gupta shows that it was an outstanding fact in Gupta history, and should, therefore, dispose of the theory based on certain later texts and traditions that the immediate successor of Samudra Gupta was another son of his, known as Rāma Gupta. The inscriptions shut out the supposition that there was another Gupta king between Samudra Gupta and Chandra Gupta II. Samudra Gupta in fact pays to his son the same compliment as was paid to him by his father who acclaimed him before all his kinsmen (*tulyakulaja*) as the fittest to succeed him on the throne. These references rule out room for any other king lacking his predecessor's nomination for the throne.

Family. His mother, the wife of Samudra Gupta, is called *Dattā* in the Eran inscription and *Dattadevī* in the Mathurā Stone inscription, as also Bilsad Stone Pillar inscription of Kumāra Gupta I, Bihar and Bhitarī Stone Pillar inscriptions of Skanda Gupta, with the title *Mahādevī*.

Chandra Gupta had at least two wives, named Dhruvadevī and Kuberanāgā. Dhruvadevī is mentioned in three Gupta inscriptions (Nos. 10, 12 and 13 of Fleet) in which she is described as Mahādevī and as the mother of Prince Kumāra Gupta I. One of the seals found at Vaiśālī describes it to be of 'Mahādevī Dhruvasvāminī, queen of Mahārājādhirāja Chandra Gupta II, and mother of Mahārāja Govinda Gupta'. Dhruvasvāminī of this seal is no other than Dhruvadevī of other inscriptions. As already stated, Queen kuberanāgā is known as the mother of Chandra Gupta's daughter, Prabhāvatiguptā, and as born of Nāga family (*Nāgā-Kulasaṁbhūtā*) in the Poona Copper-plate inscription of Prabhāvatiguptā (*EI*, XV, p. 41 f).

This Vākāṭaka matrimonial alliance brought to the Gupta

family several offshoots and extended political influence. This will be clear from Vākāṭaka history.

Samudra Gupta, as already stated, had defeated the Vākāṭaka king Rudradeva, i.e., Rudrasena I (A.D. 344-48) who had to cede to him the eastern part of Vākāṭaka territory (Bundelkhand), leaving room for its expansion towards the west. Vākāṭaka power was very much extended by the next king Pṛithivīsheṇa I by his conquests in Central India and the Deccan including Kuntala. This increase of Vākāṭaka power led Chandra Gupta to seek its alliance by marrying his daughter Prabhāvatiguptā to Rudrasena II, son of Pṛithivīsheṇa. I. The result was that Vākāṭaka politics came under the influence of the Gupta empire. The change is indicated in certain literary texts and inscriptions. Pṛithivīsheṇa I had a long reign (up to *c.* A.D. 375). But Pṛithivīsheṇa's son, Rudrasena II, the son-in-law of Chandra Gupta, had a short one followed by the regency of his daughter and its control by himself. As stated by the commentator of the Prākṛita Kāvya, *Setubandha*, Chandra Gupta's grandson, Pravarasena II, was in his court, and composed a work which underwent revision at the hands of Kālidāsa at the instance of Vikramāditya. This tradition makes Chandra Gupta II Vikramāditya, Kālidāsa, and Pravarasena II Vākāṭaka, contemporaries. Again, Bhoja, in his *Śṛiṅgāraprakāśa*, has a verse which is ascribed to Kālidāsa who is said to have made a report to the Gupta emperor on the luxurious life at the court of the Lord of Kuntala who must have been his grandson Pravarasena II. The embassy of Kālidāsa to the Kuntala court is also referred to as *Kuntaleśvara-dautya* in Kshemendra's *Auchitya-Vichāra*. The Pattan plates of Pravarasena II also mention a Kālidāsa as the writer of that record. These references do not, however, settle the point whether the Kālidāsa they mention was the great poet, but they establish Gupta contact with Kuntala, which was brought on by the regency administration of Queen Prabhāvatiguptā seeking her father's intervention which was further increased under the inefficient rule of her son given to a life of luxury and poetical pre-occupation.

Gupta contact with Kuntala is further attested by the Tālgunda Pillar inscription which states that a Kadamba king of Vaijayanti in Kuntala (Kanarese country) gave his daughters in marriage to Gupta and other kings. It seems that the Kadamba king Kākusthavarman married his daughter to Kumāra Gupta (or to his son). Some mediaeval chiefs of Kuntala trace their lineage to Chandra Gupta. Several grants of the Western Gaṅgas indicate that Kākusthavarman is to be assigned to A.D. 435-475 (Dandekar, *History of the Guptas*, pp. 87-91 ; Raychaudhuri, *Political History*, p. 475, notes).

Events. The most important event of his reign is his conquest of Western Malwa and Saurāshṭra (Kathiawad) which were under the rule of Śaka satraps. It would appear from the Eran stone inscription of Samudra Gupta that Eastern Malwa had already passed under the rule of the Guptas. Airikiṇa (Eran) was the city situated in a sub-division of modern Saugor district of M.P. and is described in the inscription as the city of Samudra Gupta's own enjoyment (*svabhoganagara*). Eastern Malwa must have been the base of Chandra Gupta's operations against the Śaka Kingdom in Western India. The Udayagiri Cave inscription of Chandra Gupta II which is not dated like the other inscriptions in the same cave describes how the king came to that place in Eastern Malwa in person in pursuit of his programme of 'world conquest (*kṛitsna-pṛithivījayārthena*) and with him came his Minister (*sachiva*) named Vīrasena Śāba hailing from the city of Pāṭaliputra. It is also stated that Chandra Gupta II who is described as the royal sage (*rājarshi*) appointed Vīrasena as his Minister for Peace and War. The other Udayagiri Cave inscription (Fleet, No. 3) of Gupta year 82=A.D. 401 indicates how the chief of Sanakānika tribe (near Bhilsa) was acknowledging Chandra Gupta II as his liege-lord (*Chandragupta-pādānudhyāta*). The Sāñchī inscription (Fleet, No. 5) of Gupta year 93=A.D. 412 also shows how Chandra Gupta's authority was very well established in that region, administered by his officer called Āmrakārddava known for his 'victories in many battles'. These inscriptions show the successive steps in the advance of Gupta power towards the west. This advance was materially aided by Chandra Gupta's alliance with the Vākāṭaka king whose geographical position could affect movements to its north against the Śaka Satrapies of Gujarat and Surāshṭra.

The actual conquest of these Śaka territories is proved by his coins. As has been already stated, the latest coins of the western Kshatrapas are not later than A.D. 388, while the earliest coins of Chandra Gupta II in this region are not earlier than A.D. 409. It was thus by a protracted war of about twenty years that Gupta power was extended up to the western sea. Although Chandra Gupta II modelled his coinage, which was in silver, on that of the Kshatrapas, he was careful to impress upon it marks of his conquest. The *Obv.* of the coins does not show any change. It still shows the king's head with traces of Greek inscription appearing as before with date behind, but on the *Rev.* the place of the Chaitya is taken by the specific Gupta emblem of Garuḍa along with the Gupta legend, *Paramabhāgavata*.

There is also a piece of literary evidence pointing to the victory of Chandra Gupta II against the Śaka king in Bāṇa's *Harshacharita*, where it is stated how Chandra Gupta 'in the disguise of a woman coveted by the lustful Śaka king, had killed him on the spot at his own capital'.

Ministers. Chandra Gupta had a number of able Ministers who are thus mentioned in his inscriptions :

(1) A chief (*Mahārāja*) of the Sanakānika family who served (*pādānudhyāta*) Chandra Gupta as his overlord (*Mahārājādhirāja*) as stated in the Udayagiri Vaishṇava Cave inscription of year 82. He must have been one of the Governors in charge of parts of eastern Malwa conquered by Samudra Gupta, and visited by Chandra Gupta as the place of preparation for his expedition towards the west.

(2) Āmrakārddava, hailing from Sukuli-deśa and associated with the Mahāvihāra of Kākanāda-boṭa (old name of Sāñchī) to which he gave an endowment out of his abundance which he owed to the patronage (*prasāda*) of the king whom he loyally served by fighting and winning his many battles, as stated in the Sāñchī Stone inscription of year 93.

(3) Śāba Virasena, hailing from Pāṭaliputra, who was Chandra Gupta's Minister for Peace and War (*sandhi-vigraha*) by hereditary right (*anvayaprāpta-sāchivya*), and thus accompanied the king on his far-reaching military expeditions, as stated in a second Udayagiri Śaiva Cave inscription.

(4) Śikharasvāmī who is described as a Councillor (*Mantrī*) of Mahārājādhirāja Chandra Gupta II, with the title of *Kumārāmātya*, in an inscription on a stone *liṅga* found at Karmadāṇḍa in the Fyzabad district, of the Gupta year 117=A.D. 436 and belonging to the reign of Kumāra Gupta I (*EI.* X, 71-72).

(5) Mahārāja Śrī Govinda Gupta, a son of emperor Chandra Gupta II, who appears to have been the Governor of the province called Tīra-*bhukti* with its headquarters at Vaiśālī, from the seal issued by him and discovered by Bloch at Basāṛh (*ASR*, 1903-4, pp. 101-20). It appears that Govinda Gupta is also mentioned in the newly discovered Mandasor inscription of the Mālava-Vikrama year 524 (*ASI*, Annual Report, 1922-23, p 187; *EI.* XIX, App. No. 7).

Administrative Offices. The excavations carried out at Basāṛh (ancient Vaiśālī) by Bloch brought to light numerous clay seals which were issued by Prince Govinda Gupta, the various officials of his administration, and the prominent citizens and communities of his Province. They mention the following offices or officials :

(1) *Kumārāmātyādhikaraṇa*, office of the Prince's Ministers. The officer *Kumārāmātya* is given the curious title of *Yuvarāja*, a title that is repeated on another seal and coupled with another significant title, *Bhaṭṭāraka*, as the chief of the Prince's Ministers ;

(2) *Balādhikaraṇa*, office of the Head of the Army, who also bears the title of *Yuvarāja* and *Bhaṭṭāraka* ;

(3) *Raṇabhāṇḍādhikaraṇa;* the Military Exchequer;
(4) *Daṇḍapāśādhikaraṇa*, office of the Chief of the Police;
(5) *Vinayaśūra*, Chief Censor;
(6) *Mahāpratihāra*, Chief Chamberlain;
(7) *Talavara*, (uncertain);
(8) *Mahādaṇḍanayāka*, Chief Juctice;
(9) *Vinayasthiti-Sthāpaka*, Minister for Law and Order;
(10) *Bhaṭāśvapati*, Head of the Infantry and Cavalry;
(11) *Uparika*, Governor of the Province, as in *Tīrabhukti-uparika-adhikaraṇa*.

It may be noted that the terms *Śrī-paramabhaṭṭāraka-pādīya* and *Yuvarāja-pādīya* as used on these seals for the officer called *Kumārāmātya* indicate the Chief Minister in waiting on the King and the Crown Prince respectively.

The office of the District Officer of Vaiśālī is called *Vaiśālī-adhishṭhāna-adhikaraṇa*. The City of Udānākūpa was governed by the Committee or Municipality called *Parishad*. The monastery (*Vihāra*) of Kākanādaboṭa was governed by the *Ārya-Saṁgha* and also an Assembly of Five called *Pañcha-Maṇḍalī* (Fleet, No. 5).

Guilds. A large number of these seals was issued by the *Nigamas* or guilds of different classes of economic interest. These were of Bankers (*Śreshṭhīs*, modern *Seṭhs*), Traders (*Śārthavāhas*) and Craftsmen (*Kulikas*). These Guilds functioned like Chambers of Commerce of modern times. Many seals were issued jointly by these three classes of guilds as shown in their legend *Śreshṭhī-Sārthavāha-Kulika-Nigama*, or by two, as in the legend *Śreshṭhī-Kulika-Nigama*. The Artisans' guilds bear an appropriate symbol, a money-chest [See my *Local Government in Ancient India* (Oxford) pp. 111-3].

Some of these Corporations operated as Banks of those days. The *Ārya-Saṁgha* in charge of the *Śrī-Mahāvihāra* of Kākanādaboṭa receives a donation in cash of 25 *dīnāras* to be kept in permanent deposit with the *Saṁgha* with the stipulation that the money will be held by it as a trust-fund, out of the interest of which provision will be made for feeding daily five *bhikshus* and for burning a lamp in the *Ratnagṛiha* (probably the *Stūpa* as the abode of the three *Ratnas* or jewels, viz., the *Buddha*, the *Dharma* and the *Saṁgha*) in the great *Vihārā*, 'as long as the moon and the sun exist' (Fleet, No. 5). The *Saṁgha* is here thus functioning as a bank of deposit and also as a trustee, holding in safe custody, and in perpetuity, a fund in aid of the beneficiaries fixed by the donor, while keeping the corpus of the donation intact. A similar transaction is indicated in the Gadhwa Stone inscription of Gupta year 88 (Fleet, No. 7).

Administrative Divisions. The empire was divided into convenient administrative units. The largest unit was the Province called *Deśa*; e.g. *Śukuli-Deśa* (Fleet No. 5)., The Province was also called a *Bhukti*, e.g. *Tīra-Bhukti* in a Basāṛh Seal inscription. A Province again was made up of divisions which were called *Pradeśas* or *Vishayas*, e.g., *Airikiṇa-Pradeśa* (Fleet, No. 2).

Religion. The Gupta empire treated all religions equally. The principal religions of the times were Vaishṇavism, Śaivism and Buddhism. Permanent benefactions in support of each of these religions were encouraged by the State. The Gupta emperors themselves were orthodox Hindus. Chandra Gupta II takes the title of *Paramabhāgavata* which is a Vaishṇava title (Fleet, No. 4). No. 5 of Fleet refers to the grant by a prominent Minister of Chandra Gupta II of a village, or an allotment of land, called Īśvaravāsaka, and a sum of money to the Community of Buddhist Monks called *Ārya-Saṁgha* belonging to the great *Vihāra* at Kākanādaboṭā (Sāñchī). As the donor was a Buddhist, he does not apply to Chandra Gupta his usual epithet of '*Paramabhāgavata*', 'the sincerest devotee of Vishṇu'. One of the Udayagiri Caves bears an inscription of another Minister of Chandra Gupta II who was a devoted Śaiva. It records that the cave was excavated as a temple of the god Śambhu or Śiva (Fleet No. 6). It also naturally omits as irrelevant the mention of the king as a *Paramabhāgavata*. The other Udayagiri Cave which bears the dated inscription of Gupta year 82 appears to be a Vaishṇava Cave (Fleet, p. 23) from its sculptures representing the figures of (1) the four-armed Vishṇu with his two wives and (2) a twelve-armed goddess who might be Lakshmī. The Gadhwa Stone inscription of Gupta year 88 repeats the title of *Paramabhāgavata* for Chandra Gupta II, because it is a Brahminical inscription. The inscription is very much mutilated, but the fragments that remain record two gifts of 10 *dīnāras* each as contributions in aid of a Brahminical institution, a perpetual alms-house or a charitable hall (*Sadā-sattra*) for its Brahmin residents. This gift shows that the religious sense of the people encouraged endowments of social srevice as a form of worshipping God through service of man.

The Mathurā Pillar inscription of A.D. 380 testifies to an offshoot of Śaivism, the Sect of Māheśvaras, flourishing at Mathurā under the teacher named Uditāchārya. In the inscription ,he mentions as his preceding teachers Kapila-vimala, Upamita-vimala, and Parāśara from whom he is thus fourth in descent (*Bhagavat-Parāśarāt chaturthena*). He also describes himself as being tenth in descent from Bhagavat-Kuśika, who was thus the founder of this particular Śaiva sect, that of the Māheśvaras. It will appear that this Kuśika is mentioned in the *Vāyu-* and *Linga-Purāṇas* as the first disciple of the great Lakulī described as the last incarnation of Śiva Maheśvara.

Lakulī had four disciples each of whom was the founder of a Pāśupata sect.

The inscription further states that Āchārya Udita, for the sake of addition to his own religious merit (*sva-puṇya-āpyāyananimittam*), and also for the glory (*kīrti*) of his teachers (*Gurus*), set up in the 'Shrine of Teachers' (*Guru-āyatane*) what are called *Upamiteśvara* and *Kapileśvara*. The term *Īśvara* as used here is taken to indicate that what were installed (*pratishṭhāpita*) were *Liṅgas*, together with the images or statues of the teachers. A *Liṅga* was set up in the name of each teacher and the fact that it was set up in the *Guru-āyatana* shows that the *Liṅgas* were accompanied by the statues. Bhāsa's drama called *Pratimā-Nāṭaka* mentions a royal gallery of portrait-statues called *Deva-kula*, and this *Guru-āyatana* was perhaps also planned as a *pratimā-griha*, a house of teachers' statues. The inscription reads: '*Upamiteśvara-Kapileśvarau Gurvvāyatane guru*......' The missing words after *guru*, showing space for at least five letters, may be taken to be (*guru*) *pratimāyutau*, as suggested by by Dr. D. R. Bhandarkar (*EI.*, XXI, p. 5). Āchārya Udita repeats that this monument is not meant for his own fame (*naitat-khyātyartham*) but for the attention (*vijñapti*) of the Māheśvaras, and the admonition of the *āchāryas* that they should consider it as their own property (*āchāryāṇāṁ parigraham*) and, without any reservation (*viśaṅkam*), worship it with offerings (*pūjā-puraskāraṁ*) and maintain it with gifts (*parigriha-pāripālyam*). It may be noted that the expression '*Deva-kula-sabhā-vihāra*) occurs in the Mandasor Stone inscription of Kumāra Gupta and Bandhuvarman (No. 18 of Fleet).

Apart from the inscriptions, the coins of Chandra Gupta II indicate his personal religion of Vaishṇavism. It is indicated by the legend *Paramabhāgavata* appearing on his gold coins of the Horseman type. The same title also appears on his silver coins which were meant for circulation in his newly conquered territory which was under the rule of the Western Kshatrapas, and were modelled on their coins. As conqueror, he had to observe as far as possible the manners and customs of the conquered country, and especially the characteristics of the currency to which it was used. Thus, on the *Obv.* of his new-struck coins, he kept up the conventional head which had done duty for centuries as a portrait of the reigning satrap, but their *Rev.* he utilized to indicate his conquest and the change in its sovereignty. Even on the *Obv.* Gupta conquest is indicated by replacing the Śaka era by the Gupta era. The *Rev.*, however, introduces a specific feature of Gupta coinage. Garuḍa, the bird of Vishṇu, the deity of Chandra Gupta II, takes the place of the Kshatrapa *Chaitya*.

The copper coins of Chandra Gupta II declare his religion of Vaishṇavism in the figure of Garuḍa on the *Rev.*

Centres. The capital of the empire was Pāṭaliputra called Pushpa in the Allahabad Pillar inscription. His campaigns and conquests show that Chandra Gupta II was also associated with the city of eastern Malwa, Vidiśā, while, as we have seen, some of the chiefs of the Kanarese country claiming connexion with him describe him as 'the Lord of Ujjayinī, the foremost of cities' (*Ujjayinī-puravarādhīśvara*) as well as of Pāṭaliputra. His association with Ujjayinī also follows from his supposed identification with the Śakāri Vikramāditya of tradition. We have already seen how Vaiśālī was also an important city of the empire.

Coins. Like his father, Chandra Gupta II issued various types of coins in accordance with the needs of a large empire. They were (1) Archer, (2) Couch, (3) Chhatra, (4) Lion-Slayer, and (5) Horseman. All these types also show varieties in features.

Archer Type. This type is the commonest of his coins and shows great variety. The first variety is that of the *Rev.* showing either throne or lotus as the seat of the goddess, while within each class there are minor varieties depending on the position of bow and of the name *Chandra* on the *Obv.*

Throne Reverse : This variety shows on Obv. 'King standing l., nimbate, as on Archer type of Samudra Gupta, holding bow in l. hand and arrow in r.; Garuḍa standard bound with fillet on l.; *Chandra* under l. arm; around the legend *Deva-Śrī-Mahārājādhirāja-Śrī Chandraguptaḥ*'.

It shows on *Rev.* 'Lakshmi seated facing, nimbate, on throne with high back, as on similar coins of Samudra Gupta, holding cornucopia in l. hand and fillet in r.; her feet rest on lotus; border of dots; on r. *Śrī-Vikramaḥ*'. There is a variety showing goddess seated on the throne *without back* and holding lotus in l. hand, instead of cornucopia, and is thus more Indianized.

Lotus Reverse : This variety shows on Obv. 'the king drawing an arrow from a quiver standing at his feet on l.' and on *Rev.* 'Goddess, nimbate, seated facing on lotus, holding lotus and fillet in outstretched l. and r. hands respectively'.

Other varieties of this class show (1) 'King l. holding arrow in r. hand', as in Throne *Rev.* class; Crescent above standard on *Obv.*; (3) Wheel (Vishṇu's *chakra*) above standard on *Obv.*, (4) 'King standing r. wearing waist-cloth and ornaments only, holding bow in l. hand and arrow in r. hand; (5) 'King standing to l. with bow in r. hand but leaning his l. arm on his hip without holding an arrow', a very rare variety.

It is to be noted that varieties (2) and (3) are marked by heavy weight and debased metal, while variety (4) drops the conventional Kushān dress in favour of Indian waist-cloth with sash.

Very probably the Throne class, by its features, was more in vogue in the northern, and the Lotus class in the central and eastern provinces, where foreign features were not suitable.

The design determining the variety of types may be noted. Garuḍa on *Obv.* prepares the way for goddess Lakshmī to appear on *Rev.*, for both are linked together with Vishṇu. The wheel on the *Obv.* of some specimens similarly recalls Vishṇu and Lakshmī, like Garuḍa.

Couch Type. The Obv. shows 'King wearing waist-cloth and jewellery, seated, head to l. on high-backed couch, holding flower in uplifted r. hand, and resting l. hand on edge of couch; legend *Deva-Śrī-Mahārājādhirāja-Śrī-Chandraguptasya*'. The *Rev.* shows 'Goddess (Lakshmī) seated facing on throne without back, holding lotus in uplifted l. hand, resting feet on lotus' as on some specimens of Archer type; 'on r. the legend *Śrī-Vikramaḥ*'. On the specimen at the Indian Museum, the legend on the *Obv.* contains the additional word *Vikramādityasya* and, beneath couch, the word *Rūpākṛiti*. The expression evidently refers to his physical and cultural qualifications. It may be noted that the Couch type depicts on *Obv.* the king in the enjoyment of his success and prosperity which he owes to goddess Lakshmī appropriately represented on the *Rev.* This type is rarely found and was issued early in the king's reign, as indicated by the throne *Rev.*

Chhatra Type. There are two main varieties of this type marked by a variety in the *Obv.* legend. The first shows on *Obv.* 'King standing l., nimbate, casting incense on altar on l. with r. hand, while l. hand rests on sword-hilt; behind him a dwarf attendant holds *chhatra* (parasol) over him; legend *Mahārājādhirāja-Śrī-Chandraguptaḥ*' as against the legend *Kshitim̐ avajitya sucharitair divam̐ jayati Vikramādityaḥ* occurring on the *Obv.* of the other variety. The *Rev.* shows 'Goddess (Lakshmī) nimbate, standing l. on lotus, holding fillet in r. and lotus in l. hand, and legend *Vikramādityaḥ*. In the other variety, the goddess appears to rise from lotus (as *padmasambhavā*). It also shows specimens containing representations of the goddess in different positions or postures.

The meaning of the *Obv.* legend is that 'Vikramāditya, having conquered the earth, conquers heaven by his good deeds'.

The design of this type may be noted. The *Obv.* shows the umbrella of royal authority won by the favour of the Goddess of Fortune appropriately depicted on the *Rev.* Equally appropriate is the figure of the dwarf as the bearer of the umbrella on *Obv.* as well as the royal title *Vikramāditya* on *Rev.*

Lion-Slayer Type. This type is represented in a large variety of specimens showing on *Obv.* 'the king hunting down lion in different positions and on *Rev.* the appropriate goddess *Durgā Siṁhavāhanā* seated on lion in different positions.'

Class I shows on *Obv.* 'King standing r. or l., wearing waist-cloth with sash which floats behind him, turban or ornamental head-dress, and jewellery, shooting with bow at lion which falls backwards and trampling on lion with one foot.'

The *Rev.* shows 'Goddess seated, nimbate, facing, on lion couchant to l. or r., holding fillet in outstretched r. hand and cornucopia in l. on certain varieties; lotus on other varieties, border of dots; symbol on l.'

The hunting scene on *Obv.* is portrayed on coins in the following different ways:

1. King to l. shooting lion as described above but *not* trampling on it.
2. King shooting lion which falls back from its spring.
3. King with l. foot on back of lion which retreats with head turned back, shooting at it with bow in l. hand.
4. Lion on l. retreating.
5. King standing r. with l. foot on lion which retreats with head turned, snapping at the king as he strikes at it with sword in uplifted r. hand.

Vincent Smith described these varieties as Lion-trampler, Combatant Lion and Retreating Lion types.

The *Rev.* portrayal of the goddess also shows some differences among coins, e.g. (1) Goddess seated facing on lion which is *walking* to r.; (2) Goddess seated to l. astride of lion, with her l. hand resting on lion's haunch; (3) Goddess seated facing on lion couchant l., with head turned back.

Now as to legends, that on class I on *Obv.* reads in its full form as follows:

Narendrachandraḥ prathitaśriyā divaṁ |
jayatyajeyo bhuvi Siṁhavikramaḥ ||

"The moon among kings, with established fame, invincible on earth, conquers heaven, with the valour of a lion.'

On class II, the *Obv.* has a different legend which may be constructed as follows: *Narendrasiṁha-Chandraguptaḥ pṛithivīṁ jitvā divaṁ jayati*: 'Chandra Gupta, the lion among kings, having conquered the earth, conquers heaven.'

On the *Rev.* the legend is generally *Śrī-Siṁhavikramaḥ*. On one variety it is *Siṁha-chandraḥ*.

We thus see that the sport of lion-hunting captured the king's imagination which suggested a variety of designs in its treatment by the craftsmen who were set to reproduce all possible positions in which the royal hunter and his big game found themselves on different occasions of hunting. It is to be noted that, while Samudra Gupta was thinking of the tiger as his game, his son was more obsessed by the lion. There seems to be a deep reason for this difference between the father and son as to big game hunting by each. As has been already stated, the Tiger type of coins celebrates Samudra Gupta's conquests of the Gangetic valley abounding to this day in forests breeding the royal Bengal tiger. The Lion-type of coins issued by Chandra Gupta II has a similar regional significance and celebrates his conquest of regions which are the habitat of the lion. It celebrates his conquest of the region of western Malwa and Surāshṭra or modern Kathiawad which is still the abode of lions to this day in India. Further, like the tiger and goddess Gaṅgā linked together, the lion on the *Obv.* has very naturally suggested for the *Rev.* the goddess Durgā with whom it is associated as her sacred seat, and *vāhana* or vehicle. She rides on the lion as the picture of Śakti, Invincible Might, invoked by Chandra Gupta II in his arduous adventure for the conquest of the Śaka satrapy of Surāshṭra. There is thus an underlying design and purpose shaping Gupta coinage, giving to it a profound historical and territorial significance.

The Obv. shows 'King riding on fully caparisoned horse to r. or l.; his dress includes waist-cloth with long sashes which fly behind him, and jewellery (ear-rings, armlets, necklaces, etc.): on some specimens he has a bow in l. hand, on others he has sword at l. side.'

The *Rev.* portrays 'Goddess seated to l. on wicker stool, holding fillet in outstretched r. hand and lotus with leaves and roots behind her in l.; border of dots.' This design marks its purely Indian character and its complete divergence from the Ardochsho coinage.

The legend on the *Obv.* is *Paramabhāgavata-mahārājādhirāja-Śrī-Chandraguptaḥ* or *Bhāgavata* and on the *Rev.* *Ajitavikramaḥ*

The use of the new title *Bhāgavata* shows that the king is no longer the worshipper of Śakti, for he has already accomplished his programme of conquests. He can now devote himself to the tasks of peace and leave the sword for the flute as worshipper of Vishṇu and his consort, Lakshmī, appropriately figured on *Rev.* as the goddess of peace and plenty, consecrating himself as a *Bhāgavata* to the cult of non-violence.

Silver Coins. While the above types of coins were in gold, Chandra Gupta II, after his conquest of the western Kshatrapa kingdom, had to keep up its silver coinage, stamping on it some Gupta features. The *Obv.* of these restruck silver coins shows the king's bust to r., as on Kshatrapa coins, with traces of Greek letters, and on l., the word *va* (*rshe*) and date, in Brāhmī numerals, in the

Gupta in place of the Śaka era. The *Rev*. shows a completely Gupta design, the figure of Vishṇu's bird Garuḍa, standing, facing with outspread wings, and the corresponding legend describing the king as a devotee of Vishṇu: *Parama-bhāgavata-Mahārājādhirāja-Śrī Chandragupta - Vikramāditya - Vikramāṅkasya*. Another variety shows the legend: *Śrī-Gupta-kulasya Mahārājadhirāja-Śrī-Chandragupta-Vikramāṅkasya*.

Copper Coins. Chandra Gupta II was also the first to issue copper coins of which the general type shows king on *Obv*. and Garuḍa on *Rev*. with variations in the figuring of both. There is a bust, three quarters, or half-length of the king, with flower in r. hand? while Garuḍa is seen nimbate, standing facing with outspread wings, or with or without human arms, or standing on an altar, or holding a snake in his mouth, or merely holding it. There is also a *Chhatra* type of these copper coins, showing king at altar, with dwarf attendant holding *chhatra* over him. There are also types omitting the king but keeping up the Garuḍa, with the *Obv*. legend *Śrī-chandra* completed by the legend *Guptaḥ* on the *Rev*., or simply the name of *Chandra* by itself, without the suffix *Gupta*, on some examples. On some specimens there is a variety replacing Garuḍa by a flower-vase, with flowers hanging down its sides.

Thus Chandra Gupta's numismatic innovations comprise the figures of Couch, *Chhatra*, Lion, Horse, and Garuḍa and of goddess Lakshmī on lotus in place of the throned goddess (Ardochsho), and also silver and copper coinage.

Titles. His coins give Chandra Gupta II the following titles: *Rūpākṛiti*, *Vikramāditya*, *Vikramāṅka*, *Siṁhavikrama*, *Narendrachandra*, and *Paramabhāgavata* (which is also mentioned in his inscriptions). The Bilsad Pillar inscription of his son applies to Chandra Gupta II the epithet—*svayamapratiratha*.

Condition of the Country as seen by Fa-Hien. It would appear that Chandra Gupta ruled over an empire which extended from the peninsula of Kāthiawad in the west to eastern Bengal, and from the Himalayas to the Narmadā. The efficiency of Gupta administration was demonstrated by the material and moral progress of the people, of which glimpses are given in the record of the travel undertaken in the country by the Chinese pilgrim Fa-Hien, between the years A.D. 399 and 414, i.e. in the time of Chandra Gupta II, whose name, however, is not mentioned by him.

Fa-Hien, however, was not the sole and solitary instance of this cultural intercourse between India and China. India for long had been looked up to by China as the seat of saving knowledge and the highest wisdom which were eagerly and devoutly sought after by her best minds. These were found in Buddhism of which India was the cradle. Buddhism became known in China as early as the third century B.C. Since then it created a stir in Chinese religious circles and a movement to wards India for drinking in her wisdom at its very sources.

Fa-Hien very keenly felt that the Buddhist 'Disciplines' were very imperfectly known in China. In A.D. 399 he organized a joint mission with several Chinese scholars, Hui-Ching, Tao-Cheng, Hui-Ying and Hui-Wei, to travel together to India to get at these 'Rules', in the face of the risks to which such overland journey to India was exposed in those days. On the way, this band of missionaries met others who had preceded them on the same errand. They were Chih-Yen, Hui-Chien, Song-Shao, Pao-Yun, Seng-Ching, and others.

The first country where they saw Buddhism being followed was *Shan-Shan*. Here were 'some 4000 and more priests, all belonging to the lesser vehicle (Hīnayāna)'. 'The common people of these countries, as well as the *Shamans*, practise the religion of India', states Fa-Hien.

Next, the party passed through several *Tartar countries* where also they found 'all those who have "left the family" (priests and novices), study Indian books and the Indian spoken language.'

In the country of *Kara-shahr*, the Buddhist Hīnayāna monks numbered 'over 4000'.

After undergoing 'hardships beyond all comparison' on their journey through uninhabited tracts, and across difficult rivers, the party came to the hospitable country of *Khotan* where the monks were mostly Mahāyāna and numbered 'several tens of thousands'. They were accommodated in a Monastery known by the Indian name of *Gomatī*, where, 'at the sound of a gong, 3000 monks assembled to eat.' There were 14 such large monasteries in *Khotan*.

There was in the neighbourhood another Monastery which was '250 feet high', overlaid with gold and silver, 'and took 80 years to build and the reigns of three kings.'

The next seat of Buddhism was *Kashgar* where the pilgrims found the king 'holding the *pāñcha-parishad*' for purposes of making offerings including 'all kinds of jewels, such as *Shamans* require.' There were here 1000 Hīnayāna monks, along with some sacred relics, the Buddha's spittoon and tooth.

From *Kashgar*, after crossing snowy ranges, the travellers came to northern India and to a place called Darel where there were many Hīnayāna monks.

Next, they had to negotiate 'a difficult, precipitous and dangerous road', with the Indus flowing along the deepest gorge. Coming down 700 rock-steps, they crossed the Indus by 'a suspension bridge of ropes' and met monks who anxiously asked Fa-Hien 'if he knew when Buddhism first went eastward,' to which Fa-Hien answered: '*Shamans* from India began to bring the *Sūtras* and Disciplines across this river from the date of setting up the image of Maitreya Bodhisattva 300 years after *Nirvāṇa*.'

After crossing the Indus, the pilgrims came to the country called *Udyāna* where Buddhism was 'extremely flourishing' and the language used was that of 'Central India or Middle Kingdom'.

The next stage reached was *Gāndhāra* followed by *Takshaśilā* and Peshawar where king Kanishka 'built a pagoda over 400 feet high with which no other could compare in grandeur and dignity'.

This whole region was studded with monuments enshrining the relics of the Buddha or incidents of his life: his foot-prints, the stone on which he dried his clothes, his alms-bowl; the spot where he cut off his flesh to ransom a dove, or his eyes, or his head, for a fellow-creature, or gave his body to feed a hungry tiger.

From here Fa-Hien was left with only two companions, Hui-ching and Tao-cheng; the rest all went back to China.

Fa-Hien next reached the country of Nagarahāra, with a shrine containing Buddha's skull-bone to which kings of neighbouring countries 'regularly send envoys to make offerings.' At the capital of Nagarahāra was a Buddha-tooth pagoda, as also a shrine holding Buddha's pewter-topped staff, and another shrine containing one of Buddha's robes; there was also the cave of Buddha's shadow, and yet another pagoda 80 feet high at the spot where the Buddha shaved his head and his nails.

Fa-Hien and his two companions now crossed the little snowy Mountain (Sufed Koh) where Hui-Ching died of cold, saying to Fa-Hien: 'I cannot recover; you had better go on while you can; do not let us all pass away here.' Gently stroking the corpse, Fa-Hien cried out in lamentation: 'It is destiny: what is there to be done?'

Crossing the range, the pilgrims arrived at the country of Afghanistan and found there about 3000 monks of both Hīnayāna and Mahāyāna Schools.

A similar number of monks they also found at Falona or Bannu whence, travelling eastwards, they again crossed the Indus and came to a country called *Bhida* in the Punjab where Buddhism was very flourishing.

Passing through the Punjab with its 'many monasteries containing in all nearly 10,000 monks', the pilgrims came to Mandor or Muttra and found about '20 monasteries with some 3000 monks' along the banks of the Jumna.

To the south of Muttra is 'the country called the *Middle Kingdom* (of the Brāhmaṇas), where the people are prosperous and happy, without registration or official restrictions. Only those who till the king's land have to pay so much on the profit they make. Those who want to go away, may go; those who want to stop, may stop. The king in his administration uses no corporal punishments; criminals are merely fined according to the gravity of their offences. Even for a second attempt at rebellion, the punishment is only the loss of the right hand. The men of the king's body-guard have all fixed salaries. Throughout the whole country no one kills any living thing, nor drinks wine, nor eats onions or garlic; but *Chaṇḍālas* are segregated. *Chaṇḍāla* is their name for foul men (lepers).'

'In this country they do not keep pigs or fowls, there are no dealings in cattle, no butcher's shops or distilleris in their market-places. As a medium of exchange, they use cowries. Only the *Chaṇḍālas* go hunting and deal in fish.'

Since the time of the Buddha, 'the kings, elders, and gentry, built shrines and gave land, houses, gardens, with men and bullocks for cultivation. Binding title-deeds were written out, which subsequent kings did not dare disregard.'

'Rooms, with beds and matresses, food, and clothes, are provided for resident and travelling monks without fail; and this is the same in all places.'

'Pagodas are built in honour of Sāriputta, Mugalan, and Ānanda, and also in honour of the *Abhidhamma*, the *Vinaya* and the *Sūtras*.'

'Pious families organize subscriptions to make offerings to monks, various articles of clothing and things they need, after the annual Retreat.'

It may be noted that the *Middle Kingdom* was the stronghold of Brāhmanism and heart of the Gupta Empire, where India's Civilization was seen at its best. The observations of Fa-Hien show how the people were allowed by government considerable individual freedom not subject to vexatious interference from its Officers in the shape of registration, or other restrictions; economic liberty with unfettered mobility of labour, so that agriculturists were not tied to holdings like serfs; and humane criminal law. The moral progress and public spirit of the people are shown in their liberal endowments of religious and educational institutions. These endowments took the form of permanent grants of lands, with full apparatus necessary for their cultivation by men and bullocks. This shows that these cultural institutions had to maintain efficient agricultural departments to make out of their landed properties, cultivated fields as well as gardens or orchards, enough income to meet their expenditure. Monetary grants in aid of schools and colleges were unknown in those days. The ways of life were based on the cult of non-violence, with vegetarian diet, ruling out heating spices like onion or garlic, also distilleries, piggeries and butcheries.

Fa-Hien now visited the sacred places of Buddhism: *Sankisa* (Kapitha) where Aśoka built a shrine and a pillar 60 feet high with a lion-capital; with about 1000 monks, and another six or seven hundred in a neighbouring monastery; *Śrāvastī* with its many monuments of Buddhism.

Here Fa-Hien arrived with his only companion Tao-Cheng. The monks asked Fa-Hien: 'From what country do you come?' And when he replied, 'From China', the monks sighed and said, 'Good indeed! Is it possible that foreigners can come so far as this in search of the Faith? Ever since the Faith has been transmitted by us monks from generation to generation, no Chinese adherents of our Doctrine have been known to arrive here.'

Fa-Hien saw at Śrāvastī the famous Jetavana Vihāra which he calls the Shrine of the Garden of Gold built by 'Sudatta who spread out gold money to buy the ground.'

He saw 'all those spots where men of later ages have set up marks of remembrance.'

'In this country there are 96 Schools of Heretics (non-Buddhists), each with its own disciples, who also beg their food but do not carry alms-bowls.

'They further seek salvation by building alongside of out-of-the-way roads, Homes of Charity where shelter, with bed and food and drink, is offered to travellers and to wandering monks passing to and fro; but the time allowed for remaining is different in each case.'

This is remarkable testimony to public philanthropy inspired by the spirit of social service, the religion which inculcated worship of God as embodied in humanity, *Nara-Nārāyaṇa*, and expressed itself in the establishment of *Dharmaśālās* open to all without distinction of caste or creed, to Hindus of all sects as well as to Buddhists, though the people were predominantly followers of Brāhmanical religions. It is also interesting to note that these ancient *Dharmaśālās* anticipate the rules of residence obtaining in their modern substitutes limiting residence to short periods.

Fa-Hien still found places associated with Devadatta, and previous Buddhas such as Kāśyapa, Krakuchchhanda, or Kanakamuni.

He found Kapilavastu a wilderness, with its many Buddhist monuments 'still in existence'. 'On the roads wild elephants and lions are to be feared.' He also visited Lumbinī and Rāmgrāma, and Vaiśāli, and crossing the Ganges, came to Pāṭaliputra in Magadha.

At Pāṭaliputra, 'formerly ruled by King Aśoka', 'the king's palace, with its various halls, all built by spirits who piled up stones, constructed walls and gates, carved designs, engraved and inlaid, after no human fashion, is still in existence.'

These remarks rather suggest that Pāṭaliputra did not occupy the same position of importance in the Gupta empire that it had in the Maurya empire.

Up to Pāṭaliputra, Fa-Hien was accompanied by his companion, Tao-Cheng, but now he too was to part from him. Tao-Cheng was so much impressed by the spirituality of the *Shamans* of Central India that he prayed that 'from this time forth until I become a Buddha, may I never live again in an outer land.' 'He, therefore, remained and did not go back; but Fa-Hien's object being to diffuse a knowledge of the Discipline throughout the land of China, he ultimately went back alone.'

F-Hien found at Pāṭaliputra one Mahāyāna and another Hīnayāna monastery. The former had a Brāhmaṇa Buddhist teacher named Raivata, 'a strikingly enlightened man of much wisdom, there being nothing which he did not understand. All the country looked up to him and relied upon this one man to diffuse widely the Faith in Buddha.' It also had as its resident another famous Brāhmaṇa teacher named Mañjuśrī who was 'very much looked up to by the leading *Shamans* and religious mendicants throughout the kingdom.'

Fa-Hien has some interesting observations on the country of Magadha and its civilization. 'Of all the countries of Central India, this has the largest cities and towns. Its people are rich and thriving and emulate one another in practising charity of heart and duty to one's neighbour.'

At their festivals such as procession of images 'in four-wheeled cars of five storeys', 'the Brahmans come to invite the Buddhas', and were thus quite catholic in their religious outlook.

As regards public philanthropy endowing social service, Fa-Hien says: 'The elders and gentry of the countries have instituted in their capitals *free hospitals*, and hither come all poor or helpless patients, orphans, widowers, and cripples. They are well taken care of, a doctor attends them, food and medicine being supplied according to their needs. They are all made quite comfortable, and when they are cured, they go away.'

Fa-Hien found an Asoka pillar bearing an inscription near his pagoda (*stūpa*) at Pāṭaliputra and another in its neighbourhood with a lion-capital and inscription.

He next passed through Nālandā 'where Sāriputra was born' and where was a pagoda of old still existing, and Rājagṛiha where he visited the numerous sacred spots of Buddhism including the

Vulture Mountain where Fa-Hien's 'feelings overcame him,' but he restrained his tears and said, 'Buddha formerly lived here and delivered the Sūrāgama Sūtra. I, Fa-Hien, born at a time too late to meet the Buddha, can only gaze upon his traces and his dwelling-place.'

He next proceeded to Gayā and Bodh-Gayā, seeing all the Buddhist sacred places and monuments, and then retraced his steps towards Pāṭaliputra and arrived at Benares and its deer-forest where he found two monasteries with resident monks.

Now, he commenced his return journey home, coming back to Pāṭaliputra and 'following the course of the Ganges down stream' came to Champā, whence, proceeding farther, he arrived at the country of Tamluk, 'where there is a sea-port.' He saw here 24 monasteries and stayed for 2 years, 'copying out Sūtras, drawing pictures of images,' and then 'set sail on a large merchant-vessel,' reaching Ceylon after 14 days. He remained in Ceylon for 2 years and obtained copies of some sacred works in Sanskrit, copies of Discipline, Āgamas, and selections from the Canon. Then he 'took passage on board a large merchant-vessel on which there were over 200 souls, and astern of which there was a smaller vessel in tow, in case of accident at sea and destruction of the big vessel.' Such an accident did happen. After two days, they encountered a heavy gale which blew on for 13 days and nights, and the vessel sprank a leak which was stopped up when they arrived alongside of an island. The passengers had to throw their bulky goods into the sea and Fa-Hien fervently prayed that the books and images he was carrying to China might be spared and the labour of his life not lost.

They 'went on for more than 90 days until they reached a country named *Jāvā* where heresies and Brāhmanism were flourishing, while the faith of the Buddha was in a very unsatisfactory condition.'

Fa-Hien remained in Jāvā 'for 5 months or so and again shipped on board another large merchant-vessel which also carried over 200 persons. They took with them provisions for 50 days.'

They again encountered a heavy gale. The Brāhman passengers complained: 'Having this *Shaman* on board has been our undoing. We should leave him on an island. It is not right to endanger all our lives for one man.' The bold attitude taken by another passenger in support of Fa-Hien silenced them. In the meanwhile, the captain of the vessel lost his reckoning. 'So they went on for 70 days until the provisions and water were nearly exhausted, and they had to use sea-water for cooking, dividing the fresh water so that each man got about 2 pints.' Then changing direction, they reached land after 12 days' sailing. The Prefect of the place, who was a Buddhist, on hearing that 'a *Shaman* had arrived who had brought Sacred Books and Images with him in a ship immediately proceeded with his retinue to the seashore to receive him.'

Thus was completed Fa-Hien's journey on which he thus commented : 'Looking back upon what I went through, my heart throbs, involuntarily, and sweat pours down. That in the dangers I encountered I did not spare my body was because I kept my object steadily in view.'

It may be recalled that Fa-Hien practically walked all the way from Central China across the desert of Gobi, over the Hindu Kush, and through India down to the mouth of the Hooghly, where he took ship and returned to China by sea, after so many hair-breadth escapes, passing through nearly 30 different countries, spending 6 years on mere travelling, and another 6 years on stay and study in India.

The main object of his mission which was to get copies of sacred works and images was hard to fulfil under the system of education in India where study and teaching were carried on by the oral method and not on the basis of written literature which could be copied and carried in MSS. The subjects of study were not reduced to writing and instruction had to be received directly from the lips of the teacher uttering the words that had to be 'heard, pondered over, and contemplated' as *Śruti*. All lessons and literature had to be heard. Thus Fa-Hien states that 'in the various countries of North India, the sacred works were handed down orally from one Patriarch to another, there being no written volume which he could copy.' It was only at one place that he found a copy of the Discipline, 'a further transcript of same running to 7,000 stanzas as used by the Sarvāstivāda School, which also have been handed down orally from Patriarch to Patriarch without being committed to writing, extracts from the Abhidharma in about 6,000 stanzas, and a complete copy of a Sūtra in 2,500 stanzas, as well as a roll of the Vaipulya Parinirvāṇa Sūtra in 5,000 stanzas. Therefore, Fa-Hien stopped here for 3 years, learning to write and speak Sanskrit (and Pali ?) and copying out the Disciplines.'

A NOTE ON RAMA GUPTA

A Supposed Successor of Samudra Gupta

According to contemporary epigraphic evidence set forth above, the immediate successor of Samudra Gupta was his worthy son (*Satputra* in Mathurā Pillar inscription of Chandra Gupta II) Chandra Gupta II. But of late, much has been made of evidence derived from later literary works to prove that there was an elder brother of Chandra Gupta II, Rāma (Śarma ?) Gupta by name, who succeeded his father before him. This literary evidence may be set forth here.

The earliest evidence invoked on the subject is a passage of Bāna's *Harshacharita* (*c.* A.D. 620) stating merely that 'Chandra Gupta, in the guise of a female, killed the Śaka king possessed of lust for another's wife at the very city of the enemy (*aripure*).'

Next, a work of dramaturgy named *Nāṭyadarpaṇa* written by Rāmachandra and Guṇachandra makes citations from a dramatic work named *Devīchandraguptam* based on the following story: 'Rāmā Gupta, an impotent (*klība*) king, for the sake of his subjects, was bent upon surrendering his queen, Dhruvadevī, to the Śaka chief invading his kingdom. Then, his younger brother, Prince Chandra Gupta, resolved to save the situation, went to the camp of the Śaka chief disguised as the queen, and killed him, as he came up to him. Chandra Gupta then killed his cowardly brother, and married his widow, Dhruvadevī.' The author of the play is Viśākhadatta who may be identified with the author of the drama *Mudrārākshasa* of about 6th or 7th century A.D. As Sylvian Levi points out, these later historical dramas cannot be considered as trustworthy sources of the history they make for purposes of the drama. *Mudrārākshasa* is not considered as a reliable source of Maurya history.

There are, however, late epigraphic records supposed to refer to the story of *Devīchandraguptam* somewhat vaguely. In the Sanjan plates of the Rāshṭrakūṭa king Amoghavarsha I of A.D. 781, it is stated: 'That donor, in the Kaliyuga, who was of Gupta lineage, having killed his brother, we are told, seized his kingdom and wife.' This passage omits the main point of the story of *Devīchandraguptam* concerning the assassination of the Śaka king by Chandra Gupta and also the name of the fratricide whom Bhandarkar even identifies with Skanda Gupta.

Again, a similar story is referred to in the Cambay (A.D. 930) and Sangli (A.D. 933) plates of Rāshṭrakuṭa king Govinda IV. These mention the murder of his elder brother by a king named Sāhasāṅka, and his marrying his brother's widow. It is supposed that Sāhasāṅka may be taken to be Chandra Gupta II who assumes on his coins the title Vikramāṅka. Besides, Rājaśekhara in his *Kāvyamīmāṁsā* (IX 47) (of *c.* A.D. 900) also mentions a Sāhasāṅka as a patron of learning, and in that respect he is sought to be identified with Chandra Gupta II.

It is thus clear that the original story mentioned by Bāṇa received additions and embellishments later texts, literary and epigraphic.

A good deal is also made of the story of Rawwal and Barkamaris as related in an Arabic work translated into Persian by Abul Hasan Ali (A.D. 1026) (Elliot and Dawson, *History of India*, I, 110-111.). In the story, the two are brothers, and princes. The elder brother Rawwal, the king, proposed to escape from an invader of his kingdom by offering to surrender his queen to him. His brother, Barkamaris, then saved the situation by approaching the enemy in the dress of the queen and killing him. Later, he killed his cowardly brother and married the widowed queen. Rawwal here is taken to be Rāma and Barkamaris, Chandra Gupta, while Safar named as the Prime Minister of Rawwal is taken to be Śikharaswāmī, the Minister of Chandra Gupta II mentioned in the Karamadāṇḍā inscription of A.D. 436.

A NOTE ON KING CHANDRA OF MEHARAULI PILLAR INSCRIPTION

It is to be noted at the outset that this iron pillar was not originally located at its present site, the village called Mihirapurī, about 9 miles south of Delhi. It was brought to this place from its original location on a hill near the Beas by a ruler of Delhi who seems to have been fired by the same enthusiasm which led Feruz Shah Taghlak to remove to Delhi the two pillars of Aśoka.

The question of the identification of king Chandra of this inscription is one of the puzzling problems of Gupta history. It is best approached by the inductive method, and objective analysis of the contents of this inscription.

The inscription credits king Chandra with the following achievements: (1) Conquest of the Vaṅga countries (*Vaṅgeshu*) by his battling alone against a confederacy or enemies united against him (*Śatrūn-sametyāgatān*); (2) Conquest of the Vāhlikas in a running fight across the seven mouths of the river Sindhu; (3) Spread of his fame as a conqueror up to the southern seas; (4) Achievement of sole supreme sovereignty in the world (*aikādhirājyam*) by the prowess of his arms.

The inscription then relates how the king celebrated his conquests by setting up his pillar in honour of Lord Vishṇu on the hill known as *Vishṇupada*.

It will thus appear from this description of king Chandra's conquests that they covered a wide range of territory, of which the inscription indicates only the extreme limits. The northern limit was the Vāhlika country, the southern limit was the ocean (*dakshiṇa-jalanidhi*), the western limit was the mouths of the Indus, and the eastern limit was Vaṅga.

With all this remarkable achievement to his credit, king Chandra remains an isolated figure in Indian history in which it is difficult to assign his proper place. Accordingly, there have been many guesses and theories as to his identification. These have to be considered on their merits so as to pave the way to a conclusion if possible, for it may be a conclusion in which nothing may be concluded.

Firstly, he is sought to be identified with king Chandravarman who is mentioned in an inscription on Susunia Hill near Bankura in Bengal as son of Siṁhavarman and king of Pushkaraṇa, modern Pokharan, about 25 miles from Susunia Hill. This inscription makes out the king to be a Vaishṇava, as it refers to a pillar set up by him in honour of god Chakrasvāmī. This fact is supposed to connect Chandravarman with king Chandra who is also a Vaishṇava.

There is another view that Pushkaraṇa is modern Pokran or Pokurna in Marwar and that Chandravarman is to be taken as the son of Siṁhavarman mentioned in a second Mandasor inscription (*IA.*, 1913, 217-19). This inscription mentions Naravarmā as son of Siṁhavarmā and brother of Chandravarmā and so both the Susunia and Mandasor inscriptions mention a common fact that Siṁhavarmā was the father of Chandravarmā.

The weak point of this theory is that these two inscriptions say nothing about any conquest achieved by Chandravarmā. On the contrary, the Mandasor inscription makes him out to be a mere local chief to whom the panegyric of the Iron Pillar inscription cannot even remotely apply.

The next theory is that king Chandra may be taken to be the Gupta emperor, Chandra Gupta I. This theory is tenable if it can be shown that Chandra Gupta I was able to conquer Bengal, as stated in the Iron Pillar inscription. It is, however, difficult to settle this point. The record of Samudra Gupta's conquests gives him credit for conquering certain remote parts of Bengal, which are named Samataṭa which was probably to the east of Tāmralipti and bordered on the sea, as stated by Hiuen Tsang; and Davāka which is located in Assam, as already explained. The other conquest of Samudra Gupta in eastern India is stated to be Kāmarūpā or Assam. It may thus be inferred that the conquest of Bengal proper, of its central parts, was the work of his father, while his own work was the completion of his father's work by conquering the outlying parts of Bengal. In this view, as has been stated above, 'with the conquest of Bengal, and his rear thus secured, Chandra Gupta I was able to push his conquests farther up to Prayāga and then beyond it up to Sāketa or Oudh, as stated in the passage from the *Purāṇa* with reference to Chandra Gupta's dominion, which may be correctly understood in the light of this theory.' One has to admit the fact that Bengal formed a part of the Gupta empire under Chandra Gupta II, because under his son, Kumāra Gupta I, its northern part figured as a province of the Gupta empire and was known as Puṇḍravardhana-*Bhukti*. One has also to find out which Gupta emperor was the conqueror of Bengal. The difficulty of this view is that by no stretch of imagination can Chandra Gupta I figure as a conqueror of territories in the Punjab and North-West which Samudra Gupta was the first of the Gupta kings to deal with. As regards annexation of Bengal to the Gupta empire, it may have been the work of either Chandra Gupta I or Chandra Gupta II in the absence of any definite evidence on the subject.

There is the last theory that the conqueror of Bengal was

Chandra Gupta II himself, who may be thus indentified with king Chandra, the record of whose conquests applies very well to him.

On paleographical grounds, the pillar inscription presents a script which is similar to that of the Allahabad Pillar inscription, Brāhmī of the northern class of the fifth century A.D.

The grounds of identification of Chandra Gupta II with king Chandra appear to be deeper historical grounds. The recently discovered Mathurā inscription of Chandra Gupta II as the first Gupta emperor whose inscription has been discovered in that city shows that the last outpost and stronghold of Śaka-Kushān power at Mathurā succumbed to the onrush of Gupta expansion. The full details of the struggle between the Gupta empire and the Śaka power have not been fully and critically studied. The Gupta conquest of the Śaka Kshatrapa kingdom of Surāshṭra and Kathiawad in western India does not admit of any doubt on acount of the unimpeachable evidence furnished by the coins of his Śaka predecessors, as has already been stated. But it appears that this conquest was the culmination of his previous conquest of Śaka territory in other parts of northern India. He undertook an expedition against the Vāhlikas by getting across the seven mouths of the Sindhu. He thus followed in the wake of his father's conquests of the territories of the Devaputras, Shāhis and Shāhānushāhis, who represented the remnants of the retreating Kushān power in the north-west up to Balkh but perhaps his conquest remained to be completed by his son.

There seems to have been a recrudescence of Śaka power under Rudrasena II whose coins date from A.D. 348 to 378 and give him the title of *Mahākshtrapa* which was for a long time in abeyance (from A.D. 305 to 348). As shown by Rapson, in the first part of this period there were two Kshtrapas and in the latter part there was no issue of their coins at all. It was probably due to the unrest created by invasions launched by Pravarasena I Vākāṭaka, and followed by Samudra Gupta. Under the next Vākāṭaka king, Pṛithivīsena, I, there was further expansion of Vākāṭaka power resulting in a corresponding decline of Kshtrapa power, so much so that some coins of the Kshtrapa Rudrasena are, according to Scott, 'in mint condition, and, therefore, unworn,' probably showing that these coins were 'secreted and hidden away,' owing to political unrest. After Prithivīsena II, i.e. after A.D. 375 there seems to have been a recovery of Kshatrapa power under Rudrasena II and Rudrasena III and also his successor Mahākshtrapa Svāmī Siṁhasena who was his sister's son. This expansion of Kshatrapa power became thus a menace to the Gupta empire and had to be dealt with by Chandra Gupta II. The Śaka king who was killed by Chandra Gupta II according to Bāṇa must have been this Siṁhasena.

As has been already stated, the destruction of Śaka power in western India was a long process, a war of about twenty years, from A.D. 388.

This view of Chandra Gupta's conquests in northern India by which Gupta power was consolidated and attained its acme seems to be supported by the history which may be gathered from Meharauli Pillar inscription regarding the exploits of king Chandra who was in that case no other than Chandra Gupta II. It is also to be noted that of the nine types of copper coins attributed to Chandra Gupta II, type VIII has on its *Obv.* the legend *Śrī Chandra* followed by the suffix *Guptaḥ* on the *Rev.*, but on type IX occurs on the *Obv.* simply the name *Chandra.* This point removes an objection to the identification of the name *Chandra* with Chandra Gupta II. We may also note in this connexion that some varieties of Lion-Slayer type of coins bear the king's title Narendra-*Chandra* or Siṁha-*Chandra* which may be taken to indicate that the king's personal name was *Chandra*, while *Gupta* was added to it as his surname.

CHAPTER VI

KUMĀRA GUPTA I MAHENDRĀDITYA

(c. A.D. 414-455)

Date. His earliest date is Gupta year 96=A.D. 415 as stated in the Bilsad inscription (No. 10 of Fleet) found in Eta district. It refers to the reign of 'ever-extending victory' (*abhivarddhamāna-vijaya-rājya*) of the new king, 'the son of Mahādevī Dharmadevī.' An inscription on *liṅgam* found at Karamdāṇḍā in the Fyzabad district and now kept at Lucknow Museum mentions the date 117 of Gupta era=A.D. 436, 'the fame of Kumāra Gupta being tasted by the waters of the four oceans' (*Chaturudadhi-salilāsvādita-yaśo*), and a minister of Kumāra Gupta I whose father was also a minister of the king's father. The long Mandasor Stone inscription of Kumāra Gupta I and Bandhuvarman refers to the Mālava year 493=A.D. 436 and the time when Kumāra Gupta 'was regning over the whole earth' (*Kumāragupte pṛithivīm praśāsati*). The earth or Mother India under Kumāra Gupta I was an extensive empire. Mother India is described as having 'her swinging *mekhalā* formed by the rolling four oceans' and 'breasts by the mountains Sumeru and Kailāsa. This means that Sumeru and Kailāsa formed the nothern boundaries of the empire, the Vindhyan forests (*Vanānta*) its southern boundaries, and the seas those on the other two sides. Thus Kumāra Gupta I was at the zenith of his power and Gupta empire had its largest extent in A.D. 436.

The inscription bears another date, Mālava year 529 (*Vatsara-śateshu pañchsu viṁśatyadhikeshu navasu chābdeshu*)=A.D. 472 which falls within the reign of the later King Pūru Gupta.

The main facts recorded by the inscription are: (1) A temple of the Sun (*dīpta-raśmi*) was constructed by silk-cloth weavers (*paṭṭavāyaiḥ*) organised as a guild (*śreṇībhutaiḥ*) at the city called Daśapura (modern Mandasor, the chief town of the Mandasor district of Gwalior State in the western Malwa division of Central India) to which they emigrated from the Lāṭa *Vishaya* (west of west Mālwa, with Navasārikā or Nausāri as one of its chief cities), in spite of the discomforts (*asukhāni*) of the journey, being attracted by the virtues of the kings of the country (*deśa-pārthiva-guṇāpahṛitāḥ*). These local kings are mentioned as (i) Viśvavarmmā, *Nṛipa* and *Goptā*, and (ii) his son Bhandhuvarmmā *Nṛīpa* who was then the governor (*pālayati*) of Daśapura. The construction of the Sun-temple is stated to have taken place in the year 493 of *Mālava-Gaṇa-Sthiti*. The Mālava year 493=A.D. 436. The Mālava era is also known as *Kṛita* era but it was known as Viktama era and connected with Vikarmāditya about 8th century A.D. It is curious that the year 103 mentioned in the inscription of Gondopharnes on Takti-i-Bāhī Stone appears to be a year in the *Kṛita* (or *Krita=Krīta*) era from the king's known date in the first century A.D. The inscription rightly records that in A.D. 436 it was Kumāra Gupta I who was ruling over the Gupta empire.

(2) In the course (*samatītenā*) of a long time (*bahunā kālena*), under other local kings of this region (*anyaiścha pārtthivaiḥ*) part of this temple fell into disrepair. And now (*adhunā*), the whole of this noble (*udāram*) temple of the Sun (*Bhānu-mato gṛihaṁ*) was once again (*bhūyaḥ*) reconstructed (*saṁiskāritam*) by the same philanthropic (*udāra*) guild (*Śreṇī*). And so once again the whole of this noble city (*puraṁ akhilaṃ udāraṁ*) was decorated (*alaṁkṛitam*) with this best of buildings (*bhavana-vareṇa*), as the cloudless sky (*nabho vimalaṁ*) is decorated with the Moon or god Śārṅgi's breast with *Kaustubha* jewel. As stated above, the reconstruction of the temple took place after a long interval from the time of its first construction in A.D. 436. The reconstruction took place in the Mālava year 529=A.D. 472 in the time of 'other kings' who are called *pārtthivas* or local kings of this region. Thus, while the first date refers itself to the time of Kumāra Gupta I, and of his feudatories, the second date is later and belongs to other kings.

Another inscription, the Gangdhar inscription of Viśvavarman (No. 17 of Fleet) bears an earlier date, Mālava year 480=A.D. 423. The inscription states that in the time of Viśvavarmmā, son of Naravarmmā, 'that bravest of kings ruling the earth' (*Tasmin praśāsati mahīm nṛipati-pravīre*), his minister (*Sachiva*), who was 'the third eye of the king' (*Rājñas-tṛitīyaṁ-iva chakshuḥ*), caused to be built (I) a temple of Vishṇu (*Vishṇoḥ Sthānam*) by his worthy sons (*Śrī-Vallabhaiḥ*), Vishṇubhaṭa, and Haribhaṭa (2) a temple of the Divine Mothers full of female ghouls (*dākinī-saṁprakīrṇṇam*) and (3) a large well of drinking water.

Another date of Kumāra Gupta is the year 129=A.D. 488 given in the Mankuwar (Allahabad district) Stone Image inscription which curiously calls Kumāra Gupta not *Mahārājādhirāja* but only *Mahārāja-Śrī*. It may be explained as the error of the scribe, or as indicating deterioration in the status of Kumāra Gupta during the later years of his reign troubled by the invasions of enemies, as alluded in the Bhitarī inscription of Skanda Gupta (Fleet No. 13). But the latter supposition is unlikely against the evidence of three inscriptions of the same time, viz., two Damodarpur Copper-plate inscriptions of the year 124=A.D. 443, 128=A.D. 447, and the Baigram plate inscription of the same year 128. All these inscriptions show that the authority of Kumāra Gupta I as paramount sovereign was fully recognized in eastern India which was administered under the Gupta emperor by his Governors ruling over its different provinces like Puṇḍravardhana-*bhukti*. At least for 4 years, G.E. 124-128, the Governor of North Bengal under Kumāra Gupta I continued to be *Uparika* Chirātadatta, while *Kumārāmātya* Vetravarman ruled over Koṭivarsha as its *Vishyapati* or District Magistrate. Another inscription dated 120=A.D. 439 has been recently discovered at Kalaikuri in Bogra district of north Bengal.

The latest known date of Kumāra Gupta I occurs on an inscription on one of his silver coins and is read as G.E. 136=A.D. 445 (*JASB*, 1894, P. 175).

Family. The only queen of Kumāra Gupta I mentioned in the extant inscriptions is Anantadevī. The Bhitarī Seal inscrption of Kumāra Gupta III mentions Anantadevī as Mahādevī, or Chief Queen, who is also described as the mother of Mahārājādhirāja Pura Gupta. Kumāra Gupta I had another son who immediately succeeded him, viz. Skanda Gupta, as is stated in the Bihar and Bhitarī Stone Pillar inscriptions (Fleet, Nos. 12 and 13). But the name of the mother of Skanda Gupta is not mentioned in the inscriptions unless it is taken to be Devakī mentioned in the Bhitarī Pillar inscription. The inscription mentions Devakī as the mother of Kṛishṇa but mentions Skanda Gupta's mother as a weeping widow to whom Skanda Gupta brings the glad tidings of the victory won by him against his enemies, just as Kṛishṇa rushed to his mother Devakī after his enemies were slain. As Kṛishṇa's mother was not a widow, there is no point in bringing together in this reference the two Devakīs except on the basis that Skanda Gupta's mother happened to have the same name as Kṛishṇa's mother.

According to Dr. R. N. Dandekar (*History of the Guptas*, p. 102), Queen Anantadevī, mother of Pura Gupta, was a Kadamba princess. The Talgunda Pillar inscription of Kadamba king Kākusthavarman refers to his matrimonial connexion with the Guptas. Kākusthavarman and Kumāra Gupta I were contemporaries. This is shown by some Western Gaṅga records according to which Kṛishṇavarman, the second son of Kākusthavarman, whose sister was married to the Gaṅga king Mādhava III, belonged to the period A.D. 475-500 and therefore his father must have lived earlier, *c*. A.D. 435-475. The Bihar Stone Pillar inscription of Skanda Gupta is supposed to mention another wife of Kumāra Gupta, the sister of some, minister of his.

Budha Gupta is taken to be another son of Kumāra Gupta I. This is suggested by Yuan Chwang calling Budha Gupta a son of Śakrāditya, Śakra may be equated with Mahendra and Śakrāditya

PLATE VI
COINS OF KUMĀRA GUPTA

1. Horseman Type

2. Swordsman Type

3. Peacock Type
[From Line-Drawing by Nanda Lal Bose]

PLATE VII

COINS OF KUMĀRA GUPTA I

(Continued)

4. Elephant-Rider Type

CAPITALS OF GUPTA PILLARS

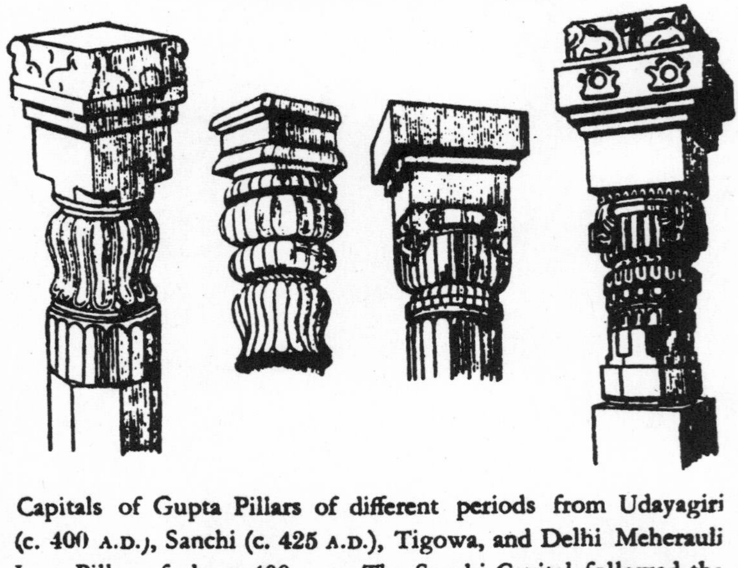

Capitals of Gupta Pillars of different periods from Udayagiri (c. 400 A.D.), Sanchi (c. 425 A.D.), Tigowa, and Delhi Meherauli Iron Pillar of about 400 A.D. The Sanchi Capital followed the design of Aśoka's; the Tigowa shows a new design of *Pūrṇa-Kalasa* or 'the Bowl of Plenty'.

with Mahendrāditya, the title assumed by Kumāra Gupta I on his coins.

Another son of Kumāra Gupta I may be taken to be Ghaṭotkacha Gupta mentioned as Śrī Ghaṭotkacha Gupta in an inscription on a Vaiśālī seal. It may be noted that another Vaiśālī seal mentions Mahārāja Śrī Govinda Gupta as a son of Chandra Gupta II who was his Viceroy at that place. Perhaps Ghaṭotkacha Gupta who was a Prince (as indicated by the prefix *Śrī* added to his name), was a Viceroy under Kumāra Gupta I. A Ghaṭotkacha Gupta is also mentioned in the Tumain fragmentary inscription of Gupta year 116=A.D. 435 found at the place it calls Tumbavana, a village in the Esagarh district of Gwalior State near Eran. This inscription throws new light on Gupta history in its locality. Its line I refers to Samudra Gupta and eulogizes Chandra Gupta II who conquered the earth as far as the ocean. Line 2 mentions his son Kumāra Gupta I as protecting the earth as a chaste and devoted wife, showing that there was no diminution in the extent of the empire under him nor in his authority which was strengthened by his popularity. Line 3 contains the significant reference to Ghaṭotkacha Gupta as having won by his arms the great fame achieved by his ancestors. Line 4 gives the date of the inscription and also states that Kumāra Gupta was then ruling over the earth. Thus this Ghaṭotkacha Gupta of the inscription may be identified with Śrī Ghaṭotkacha Gupta of the seal, but the difficulty is that it is a far cry from Vaiśālī to Airikiṇa of which apparently Ghaṭotkacha Gupta was the provincial Governor under his father Kumāra Gupta I. Only the dates of the seal and the inscription tally. There is another piece of evidence regarding Ghaṭotkacha Gupta on a coin noticed by Allan (*Gupta Coins*, pp. liv and 149.) The coin has on *Obv.* the legend *Ghaṭo* below (*gu*) *pta* (*h*). If these three Ghaṭotkacha Guptas are one and the same person, it is to be assumed that his original status at Vaiśālī where he served under the Crown Prince Mahārāja Govinda Gupta as its Governor was now improved by his transfer under Kumāra Gupta I as his Governor in East Malwa (M.B. Garde in *IA*, 1920, pp. 114, 115; *EI*, XXVI, p. 117). It appears from the Mandasor record of the Mālava year 524=A.D. 467 issued by Dattabhaṭa, son of Govinda Gupta's general Vāyurakshita, that he was also the Viceroy in Malwa under his brother Kumāra Gupta I (Bhandarkar's List, No. 7).

Events. We have already seen that the Gupta empire did not suffer any diminution of its extent and authority under Kumāra Gupta up to the date of the Damodarpur Copper-plate and Baigram plate inscriptions of A.D. 443 and 448. The vastness of his dominion is also reflected not merely in the wide distribution of his incriptions but also of his coinage. For instance, the find-spots of his silver coinage with the figure of Garuḍa stamped on the *Rev.* indicate that he was able to retain intact his father's conquests in western India. The other class of silver coins with the Peacock *Rev.* points by its provenance to his hold on the central parts of the empire, the valley of the Ganges.

Allan considers that some of the coins of western India which show some variations from Kshatrapa coins were in circulation in districts outside Kshatrapa dominion. Similarly, there is another class of silver coins which are more allied to the coins of Traikūṭaka dynasty and were probably in circulation in southern Gujarat. And, again, there is a numerous series of silver-plated coins with a copper core found only around the site of ancient Valabhī, where, accordingly, they were in circulation. It may also be noted that the other find-spots of the coins of Kumāra Gupta I in western India are Ahmedabad, Satara, the States of Bhawnagar and Nawanagar, and Ellichpur. These western issues were carried far and wide by merchants, as they have been most commonly found at places like Benaras, Ayodhya, Mathura, Kanouj, Hamirpur, Saharanpur, Buriya on the Jumna, etc. (Allan, p. cxxx).

It may be thus surmised on the basis of all this epigraphic and numismatic evidence that Kumāra Gupta I may be credited not merely with the negative and static work of maintaining in toto his imperial inheritance but also with some positive and bold exploits in adding to the extent of that inheritance by some new conquests and records. The fact of these conquests achieved by him is indicated by his issue of the significant Aśvamedha type of gold coinage bearing on *Obv.* the legend *Jayati divaṁ Kumāraḥ* (Kumāra conquers heaven) and, on *Rev.* *Śrī Aśvamedhamahendraḥ*. The celebration of horse-sacrifice is a sure proof of some considerable conquests achieved by the king.

If the legends on coins are any indications of history, the power and glory of the Gupta empire seem to be at their height under Kumāra Gupta I. We may instance the following legends: (1) *Vijitāvanir avanipatiḥ*, 'the Lord of the earth who has conquered the earth', (2) *Mahītalaṁ jayati*, 'who conquers the whole earth'; (3) *Kṣhitipatirajito Vijayī Mahendrasiṁho divaṁ jayati*, 'the Lord of the earth, the unconquered conqueror, Mahendrasiṁha, conquers heaven', (4) *Sākshādiva Narasiṁho Siṁha-Mahendro*, 'like another Narasiṁha *avatāra* or incarnation of Vishṇu is Siṁha-Mahendra'; (5) *Yudhi Siṁha-Vikramaḥ*, 'with the valour of a lion in war'; (6) *Vyāghrabala-parākrama*, 'possessed of the strength and prowess of the tiger'; (7) *Guptakula-Vyomaśaśī*, 'the Moon in the firmament of the Gupta dynasty'; and (8) *Gupta-Kulāmalachandro*, 'the Moon without spots in the Gupta dynasty'. Some of these legends which endow Kumāra Gupta I with some singular epithets describing him as the glory of the Gupta family upon which he shed lustre like the Moon, attributing to him the invincible valour of both the lion and the tiger, and comparing him to that embodiment of supreme power, Vishṇu as Narasiṁha, must have been inspired by an adequate record of military achievements.

But this Moon among the Guptas seems to have suffered an eclipse in later years. There was a set-back in Gupta imperial history, as is indicated in an inscription belonging to the reign of his son and successor, Skanda Gupta, the Bhitarī Stone Pillar inscription. The inscription refers to 'enemies prepared for conquests' (*svabhimata-vijigīshā-pradyotānāṁ Pareshām*); the fortune of the family (*kula-Lakshmī*) rendered unsteady (*vichalitā*); to the efforts of the Crown Prince Skanda Gupta towards making it firm and steady (*stambhanāya udyatena*); to Skanda Gupta being reduced to such straits in making these efforts for the restoration of the fallen fortunes of the family that he had to spend a whole night sleeping on bare earth in the battle-field. The task of this restoration was not an easy one for him. The enemies of the empire for a time succeeded in overwhelming its fortunes (*viplutāṁ vaṁśa-Lakshmīm*). These enemies are specified as *Pushyamitras* who had their resources of man-power and wealth fully mobilized (*samudita-bala-koshān*) to try conclusions with the Gupta empire whose yoke they were preparing to throw off as its feudatories. Skanda Gupta, as Crown Prince, was given the necessary training (*saṁvidhānopadeśa*) to be applied for subduing these enemies (*pareshāṁ praṇihite*). These *Pushyamitras* may be identified with those who are associated in the *Vishṇu Purāṇa* with the allied peoples called Patumitras, Durmitras, and others of the region known as Mekala of the Narmadā valley.

It may be noted that Mekala supplies a point of contact between Gupta and Vākāṭaka history. In the Balghat copper-plates of the Vākāṭaka king Pṛithivīsheṇa II, the sovereignty of his father Narendrasena (A.D. 435-470) is started to have embraced Kośala, Mekala, and Malwa. Narendrasena appears as the paramount sovereign of the entire Vindhyan region including the Berar-Maratha Country, Konkan, Kuntala, Western Malwa, Gujarat, Kośala, Mekala, and Andhra, as also Kuntala of the Kadamba kingdom in the south. Thus he was contesting Gupta overlordship in parts of western India and was coming into conflict with Skanda Gupta whose defeat of the peoples of Mekala gave a set-back to his aggression. That is why Narendrasena's son Pṛithivīsheṇa II found his family to be 'sunken' and had to undertake the task of 'raising and restoring it', as stated in the inscription. Thus the enemies whom Skanda Gupta had to deal with included the Vākāṭakas, along with the Pushyamitras and other peoples of Mekala. After Skanda Gupta, the Vākāṭakas recovered their lost ground and glory by the conquests of Pṛithivīsheṇa II who was able to assume the title : '*Kośala-Mekalā—Mālavādhipatyabhyarchitaśāsana,*' 'Lord of Kośala, Mekala, and Mālava'. The time of Pṛithivīsheṇa II is *c.* A.D. 470-485.

The defeat of the Pushyamitras by Skanda Gupta was complete. The panegurist says that he was able to 'place his left foot on their king as his footstool' (*kshitipa-charaṇa-pīṭhe*).

'The unsullied fame (*amalakīrti*) of this exploit, the purity of his character (*śubhraṁ charitaṁ*), are sung with great gratification (*paritushṭi*) in all quarters (*diśi diśi*) by all down to children (*ākumāraṃ manushyaiḥ*)'.

But the full programme of subjugation of the enemies of the empire was not accomplished by Skanda Gupta in his father's lifetime. It was after his father's death (*pitari divamupete*) that he was able 'to subdue all his enemies by the prowess of his arms' and 'to rehabilitate once again (*pratishṭhāpya bhūyaḥ*) the submerged (*vipluta*) fortune of his family'. He brought the glad tidings of his complete victory (*jitamiti*), in the absence of his deceased father, to the widowed Queen, his mother, and 'filled her eyes with tears of joy'. He firmly established (*pratishṭhāpya*) the power of his family and empire which was shaken by its enemies and tottering to its fall (*parichalitaṃ vaṁśam*).

Religious and Charitable Endowments. These endowments represent the principal religions of the country. The Bilsaḍ inscription refers to a temple of god Svāmi-*Mahāsena* (*Kārtikeya*). The Mankuwar Buddha Image inscription refers to the construction of an image (*pratimā*) of Buddha Bhagavān, the perfectly enlightened One (*Samyak Saṁbuddha*) and unrefuted doctrine (*Svamatāviruddha*) by Bhikshu Buddhamitra in Gupta year 129=A.D. 448 who may be identified from this date with Buddhamitra, the teacher of Vasubandhu (*IA*, 1912, p. 244). The Sāñchī Stone inscription of 131=A.D. 450 records the gift of (1) 12 *dīnāras* for feeding daily out of the interest of the amount one new recruit of a Bhikshu (*Saṁgha-madhya-pravishṭaka*), (2) 3 *dīnarās* and (3) 1 *dīnāra* for provision, out of the interest of the fund, for permanent lighting of lamps before the images of the Buddha. These gifts were made by *Upāsikā* Harisvāminī, wife of Sanasiddha, for the sake of her parents (probably out of her *Strī-dhana*) to the *Ārya Saṁgha* of Kākanādaboṭa-Śrī-Mahāvihāra who were to hold them as permanent trust-fund (*akshaya-nīvī*), keeping its corpus intact and spending only the income of the endowments in aid of its beneficiaries (Fleet, No. 62).

The Karamadaṇḍā Stone Linga inscription of the year 117=A.D. 436 invokes Mahādeva and records the gift made by a Minister of Kumāra Gupta I, Pṛithivīsheṇa by name, for the worship, with proper and righteous offerings, of Pṛithivīśvara (Mahādeva), probably the *liṅga* on which the inscription is incised. The genealogy of Pṛithivīsheṇa is interesting from the social point of view. He belonged to a Brāhmaṇa family, the son of Chandra Gupta's *Kumārāmātya* Śikharasvāmin, who was the son of Vishṇupālitabhaṭṭa, son of Kuramāravyabhaṭṭa, of the Chhándogas, whose *gotras* were Aśva and Vājin. The donees also are stated to have been Brāhmaṇas from Ayothyā, who were living in the vicinity of Mahādeva Śaileśvara, belonged to various *gotras* and *charaṇas*, and were proficient in *tapa* and *svādhyāya*, ascetic practices and Vedic study, in *Mantra*, *Sūtra*, *Bhāshya*, and *Pravachana*. There is also a reference to the festival called *Devadroṇī*, a procession of images (of Śiva) or idols.

The construction of a temple for worship of the Sun is the subject of the Mandasor inscription already noticed.

The Udayagiri Cave inscription of the year 106=A.D. 425 'in the prosperous reign of the best of Gupta kings' refers to the construction of an image (*ākṛiti*) of Jina vara Pārśava at the mouth of a cave (*guhā mukha*) by Śaṅkara who hailed from a region of the north like Uttarakuru (Fleet, No. 61).

Another inscription records the installation of a Jaina image at Mathurā in the year 113=A.D. 432 (*EI*, II. 210).

Among charitable endowments may be mentioned that of a *Sattra* (alms-house) with 10 *dīnāras* and another with 3 *dīnāras* at Gadhwa (No. 8 of Fleet).

Another Gadhwa inscription (Fleet, No. 9) refers to a gift of 12 *dīnāras* for the perpetual maintenance of a charitable hall or alms-house (*sadā-sattra*).

We have already seen how the Gaṅgdhar inscription refers to the construction of temples of Vishṇu, Śakti (the Divine Mother), and also the construction of a large well of drinking water. This inscription shows how in the same family worship was offered equally to the two seemingly opposed cults of Vaishṇavism and Tāntrikism and how father and son could be votaries of different cults.

The Dhānāidaha Copper-plate inscription records a gift of land made by a government servant (*āyuktaka*) to a Sāmavedin Brāhmaṇa (*EI*, XVII, op. 345). The Damodarpur Copper-plate grant of A.D. 443 records the sale of land by government to a Brāhmaṇa to help him in the performance of his *agnihotra* rites. The second Damodarpur grant of A.D. 447 records another sale by government of land to a Brāhamaṇa for the maintenance of his five daily sacrifices (*pañcha-*

mahāyajñas). The Baigram Copper-plate grant of the same date records gift of land to the temple of Govinda-Svāmī.

The Kalaikuri Copper-plate inscription of *c.* 120=A.D. 439 records the gift of land made by a group of traders, writers, and record-keepers to three learned Brahmins to finance their daily performance of Pañcha-Mahāyajñas.

Thus the religious endowments of the times represented the different religions then prevailing in the country such as Buddhism and Jainism and those centering round the Brahminical dieties, Vishṇu, Śiva, Kārtikeya, Śakti, and Sūrya. These religions also inspired social service as a form of worship of God embodied in huminity, of *Nara-Nārāyaṇa*.

Architecture. Some examples of architecture are mentioned in the inscriptions. The Gaṅgdhar Stone inscription mentions Viśvavarman equipping his city, built on the bank of the Gargarā, with wells for irrigation, (*vāpī*), tanks (*taḍāga*), temples and halls of gods (*surasadmasabhā*), drinking-wells (*udupāna*), parks (*upavana*) of various kinds, causeways (*saṅkrama*) and reservoirs of water (*dīrghikā*).

The Mandasor Stone inscription refers to the district of Lāṭa adorned with temples (*Deva-kula*) and Assembly-halls of the gods (*Deva-sabhā*), and *Vihāras.* It also describes the city of Daśapura 'embraced by two charming rivers', 'decorated with rows of storeyed mansions (*prāsāda-mālā*) like rows of aerial chariots (*vimāna-mālā*), and with paintings (*chitra-karmmāṇi*). The houses were very high (*adhikonnata*), 'resembling the peaks of white clouds lit up with forked lighting' or the lofty peaks of Mount Kailasa. In the city was built a temple of the Sun with broad and lofty spires (*vistīrṇṇa-tuṅga-śikharam*) resembling a mountain. The temple had later to be thoroughly repaired and then it became 'one of the beauties of this beautiful city, like the Moon shining in cloudless sky or the Kaustubha blazing on the breast of Śārṅgin'.

The Bilsaḍ inscription refers to the construction of a gateway with a flight of steps (*pratoli*) at the temple of god Svāmī-Mahāsena.

Administration. The empire is called Pṛithivī (Mandasor inscription). The emperor is given the titles of *Parama-daivata*, *Parama- bhaṭṭāraka*, and *Mahārājādhirāja* (as in Damodarpur Copper-plates). Below the emperor was the feudatory or the local king called severally *Nṛipa*, *Nṛipati*, *Pārthiva* or *Goptā* (Mandasor inscription). The local kingdom was called a *Deśa*, e.g., *Deśapārthiva* (*ibid.*).

The empire was divided for administrative purposes into Provinces. A Province was called a *Bhukti*. A Province was sub-divided into Districts called *Vishayas*. Under Kumāra Gupta I, Puṇḍravardhana-*bhukti* looms large in several inscriptions. These show that for 4 years, G.E. 124-128=A.D. 443-447, the *Bhukti* was ruled by Governor Chirātadatta. The title of provincial Governor was *Uparika-Māhāraja*. Under him was *Vishayapati* or the District Magistrate. Thus Vetravarmā was the *Vishayapati* of Koṭivarsha. The term *Adhishṭhāna* was applied to the headquarters of the District. The Distrct Office was called *Vishayādhikarṇa* (Damodarpur Copper-plates, 1 and 2). The Dhānāidaha (Rajshahi district grant of year 128 mentions another District or *Vishaya* called Khādā (ṭā) pāra which might have been also a *Vishaya* of Puṇḍravardhana-*bhukti*, but the name of the *Bhukti* cannot be clearly traced. The Baigram (Charter of year 128=A.D. 447 was issued from a District Office, *Vishayādhikaraṇa*, located at the town called Pañchanagarī. The District Officer is also named. He was Kulavṛiddhi, and had the title *Kumārāmātya*. The Mandasor inscription gives a glowing account of the prosperity of a District of Western India, viz., Lāṭa-*Vishaya*. A District had its Sub-Division called *Vīthī*. The officer in charge of the Sub-division is called *Āyuktaka* in the Kalayakuri inscription.

We have already seen that some of the Princes served as provincial Governors. Prince Govinda Gupta was the Governor of Tīrabhukti under Chandra Gupta II, while Prince Ghaṭotkacha Gupta was Govenor of Airikiṇa-*pradeśa* (another term for Province). Earlier, he perhaps served under Prince Govinda Gupta in a high and responsible office so as to issue seals in his name. Both his seals and those of Govinda Gupta were found together at Vaiśālī (Basarh), as already stated.

The Baigram Charter indicates an interesting administrative practice. *The Vishayapati* Kulavṛiddhi is mentioned as directly paying his homage to the emperor, as indicated by the expression *Bhaṭṭāraka-pādānudhyāta*, and not tendering that homage to his immediate superior, the provincial chief. It was because the appointment of the *Vishayapatis* or District Magistrates was made by the emperor himself who entered into direct relations with such responsible officers. The Damodarpur Plates, on the other hand, definitely state that the *Vishayapati* was appointed by the *Uparika* or Governor of the Province (*tanniyuktaka*). The two statements may be reconciled by the consideration that the appointment of the District Officer by the Governor was subject to formal sanction by the king to whom the homage of both was due.

Besides these Provincial Governors and District Officers, there were Ministers in attendance on the emperor at the headquarters of government. One such Minister is named Pṛithivīsheṇa who came to his exalted office by heredity. At first he started as a *Mantri* with the title *Kumārāmātya* but was later promoted to the higher office of *Mahābalādhikṛita* as the executive head of both civil and military administration (Karamdāṇḍā inscription). The term for a Minister was *Sachiva* (Mandasor inscription).

The Damodarpur Copper-plates give some interesting details of local administration. The district headquarters were called *Adhishṭhānas* where were located the District Offices and Courts called *Adhikaraṇas*. The District Magistrate was associated in his administration (*puroge saṁvyavaharati*) with an Advisory Council of non-officials representing the different interests of the locality, viz., (1) *Nagara-Śreshṭhi*, President of the Town Corporation (Mayor), (2) *Sārthavāha*, representative of the Guild of Merchants, (3) *Prathama-kulika*, Chief of the Guild of Artisans, and (4) *Prathama-kāyastha*, Chief of the Union of Writers or Scribes, Chief Secretary.

The Kalaikuri inscription gives some details of administration of the Sub-division of a District called *Vīthī*, as stated above. It mentions the Śṛiṅgavera *Vīthī*, and the office (*adhikaraṇa*) of the Sub-division located at its headquarters or civil station, the town named Pūrṇakāśilā. The Sub-divisional Officer, like the District Officer, was associated in his administration with a Council of non-official members called *Vīthī-Mahattaras* or the Elders of the locality, and *Kuṭumbins* or representative householders. The staff of the Sub-divisional Office included the Keepers of Records called *Pusta-pālas*, clerks or scribes called *Kāyasthas*, and *Kulikas* or representative craftsmen to deal with the interests of local handicrafts.

Transactions relating to land formed an important part of the functions of the District Magistrate, *Vishayapati*. Government gave facilities to private donors intending to make gifts of land for a religious or a charitable purpose. Such gifts were facilitated by a prescribed procedure. Ordinarily, land could not be transferred or alienated without the permission of government. Its tenure was regulated by what is called *Nīvī-dharma* or *Apradākshaya-Nīvī*. *Pradā* means gift and so *Apradā* means land that is not settled away or transferable. The *Nīvī-dharma* meant that the *nīvī* or principal or *mūladhana* was to be kept intact as *akshaya-nīvī*, while its interest alone could be spent on the purposes of the endowment. When the State sanctioned the grant of land, it was on the basis of *Nīvī-dharma*, i.e., the condition that the public purpose, charitable or religious, for which the grant was sanctioned was to be permanently promoted out of the income from the land granted, so that the land could not be transferred or alienated in any way for profit and should not change hands as private property. Thus sale or transfer of land was subject to sanction of government. That sanction was given on the report of its officers called *Pustapālas*, the Record-Keepers, to whom the petition for purchase of land had to be submitted in the first instance (*etat vijñāpyaṁ upalabhya*). The Record-Keepers, who generally formed a body of three, placed the matter before (1) the elders of the village concerned, who were called *Mahattaras*; (2) the officers of the village called *Ashṭakulādhikaraṇas*, i.e., officers in charge of groups of eight households; (3) officers called *Grāmikas* or village chiefs; and (4) representative householders (*Kutumbinaḥ*). These, in their turn, notified the petition (*vijñāpayati*) to the leading Brāhmaṇas, the prominent citizens, and householders of the village. The land in question was then inspected (*pratyavekshya*) by the said *Mahattaras* and other officers (*Mahattarādyadhikaraṇa*) and householders, and finally referred to the *Pustapāla* for report. Sale was sanctioned if the *Pustapāla* reported to the following effect: (1) 'Land may thus be given' (*evaṁ dīyatām*); or (2) 'The application is a proper one (*yuktam*). This is a case which conforms to the customary rule of sale (*vikrayamaryādā-prasaṅgaḥ*)'. The petitioner had to state in his petition the conditions on which the land is transferred, viz., (1) that it was according to *Nīvī-dharma* by which it was assured that the land thus transferred was to be a permanent gift for the purposes stated, such as 'facilities for performing *agnihotra* rites' (*agnihotropayogāya*), or 'for instituting the *pañchamahāyajñas* (2) that the land was '*khila*, as yet unploughed, and not already given to anyone' (*apradā-prahata-khila-kshetra*) and free of revenue (*samudayabāhyāprada-khila-kshetra*); (3) that the price to be paid was according to the rate prevailing in the village (*grāmānukrama-vikraya-maryyādā*). Lastly, the transfer was effected by suspending the condition as to non-transferability (*anuvṛitta-apradākshaya-nīvī*). At the concluding stage of the transaction, the *Mahattaras* and others were empowered to take measurement of the land by 8 × 9 reeds and then separate it from other plots (*apaviñchhya*). The sale price of land is also indicated. It was at the rate of 3 *dīnāras* for 1 *kulyavāpa*. The word *kulya* may be connected with *kula* which, according to Kullūka (on Manu VII, 119), means that amount of land which can be ploughed by two ploughs. *Vāpa* means the area which is sown. According to Sanskrit lexicons, 1 *kulya*=8 *droṇas*. In Damodarpur Copper-plate No. 2, the land bought was 5 *droṇas*=2/3 *Kulyavāpa*, 1 *kulyavāpa* being=8 *droṇavāpas*. [Dhānāidaha Copper-plate inscription of the year 113 (*EI*, XVII, p. 345); Damodarpur Copper-plate inscriptions, No. 1 of year 124; No. 2 of year 129; and some data cited for comparison from No. 3 undated (*EI*, XV. pp. 113 f)].

An inscription on a Copper-plate of Gupta year 120=A.D. 439 and thus belonging to the reign of Kumāra Gupta I has been recently discovered at a village called Kalaikuri in Bogra District of north

Bengal which has contributed so much to Gupta History by its other inscriptions found in the Bogra, Rajshahi, and Dinajpur Districts such as the five Damodarpur inscriptions and those of Baigram, Paharpur, or Dhānāidaha. The inscription has been edited and published by Dr. D. C. Sircar (I.H.Q., XIX). It is noteworthy for some of its concrete touches and details and new data of local administration. It mentions the city of Puṇḍravardhana (identified with modern Mahāsthān) as the capital of the *Bhukti* or Province of that name. Śṛiṅgavera is identified with modern Singra Police station in the Natore Sub-division of Rajshahi district. The Record also mentions the individual names of all the officers and parties concerned in its transaction, names of *Kulikas*, *Kāyasthas*, *Pustapālas*, the *Vīthī-Mahattaras*, and also of the *Kuṭumbins* who are quite numerous. The three Brahmin beneficiaries are also named and described as being proficient in the four Vedas and belonging to the Vājasaneya-Charaṇa.

The inscription mentions the usual conditions for the validity of an application for land, viz. (1) that the land applied for must be fallow and not settled so that its transfer was not subject to compensation payable to the dispossessed proprietor (*apratikara*); (2) that it should be given in perpetuity and remain as *Akshayanīvī*; (3) that it should be given for a public or religious purpose (such as performance of the five daily sacrifices in the present case); and (4) that it be paid for at the customary rate of the locality (*maryādā*). The application is then referred, as usual, to the *Pustapālas* for report. In the present case, they reported that it was in order, in accordance with (*anuvṛitta*) the customs of the *Vīthī*, and did not militate in any way against the interests of the State (*Nāsti virodhaḥ kaśchit*).

The inscription also shows that it was not always possible to find the required land situated in one area. In the present case, the application was for 9 *kulyavāpas* of land, out of which eight had to be found out of 3 villages and the remaining one in a fourth village. Even of the strips of land situated in the same village, their revenues (*prāveśya*) were payable to different owners or landlords. These facts indicate that there was considerable progress achieved in these parts of rural Bengal in intensive cultivation and farming coupled with the creation of small holdings under the laws of inheritance leading to their fragmentation.

Another interesting inscription to be noted in this connexion is the Baigram (Bogra district) Copper-plate inscription dated Gupta year 128 = A.D. 447-8 and thus belonging to the time of Kumāra Gupta I. The emperor is not named but is referred to in the expression *Bhaṭṭārakapāda*.

The inscription gives some interesting administrative data, some of which are repeated in the Damodarpur inscriptions discussed above. The repetition is useful as pointing to established administrative traditions, practices and institutions.

Two householders of the locality (*vāstavya-kuṭumbī*) named Bhoyila and Bhāskara, brothers, wanted to make a gift of land to the temple (*Devakula*) of Govindasavāmī which was founded by their father but was poorly endowed (*alpa-vṛittika*). They wanted to create provision for repair (*pratisaṃskāra*) of the breaches (*khaṇḍa*) and cracks (*phuṭṭa=sphoṭa*) of the temple and also for supply of requisites of worship such as scents (*gandha*), incense (*dhūpa*), light (*dīpa*) and flowers. They apply for land to the district officer named Kulavṛiddhi and described as *Kumārāmātya*, as already noticed. The district office is called *Vishayādhikaraṇa* and is located at Pañchanagarī which was apparently the headquarters of the district.

The application was made for purchase of 3 *kulyavāpas* of *khila* (fallow) land which was (1) not paying any rent or revenue to the State (*samudayabāhya*), (2) devoid of vegetation (*astamba*) and hence uncultivated waste, and (3) not liable for paying compensation to any dispossessed proprietor (*akiñchitpratikara=apratikara*). In addition, Bhoyila applied for 1 *droṇavāpa* of *sthala-vāstu* or homestead land which he required for the construction of *talavāṭaka*, trenches, and garden. Bhāskara also applied for the same. Thus these lands were unsettled government lands.

As shown in the Damodarpur inscriptions, the first stage in the transaction is the report, on the application, of the government Record-Keepers (*Pustapālas*) who were two in this case. They recommended the sale of government lands to private persons on the following grounds:

(1) that the lands are *astamba* (devoid of vegetation) and *khila* (fallow);

(2) that they are incapable of yielding revenue to the king (*samudaya-bāhya*);

(3) that there can be no objection to such sale on the ground of any financial loss to the king (*na kaschidrājārthavirodha*) from sale of lands which did not yield any revenue (*apratikara*);

(4) that there is, on the contrary, some material gain (*upachaya*) to accrue to the king from its sale, as well as spiritual gain in the shape of *Dharma*;

(5) that they are located in areas which will not affect the cultivation of the settled land (*svakarshaṇāvirodhisthāne*).

Thus the sale is approved and effected on the basis of the prevailing price being paid. The price paid was 6 *dīnāras* for 3 *kulyavāpas* of *khila* land and 8 silver coins (*rūpakas*) for

2 *droṇavāpas* of *vāstu* land. These prices show that, while the rate of fallow land was 2 *dīnāras* for 1 *kulyavāpa*, that for a dwelling site was 4 silver coins for 1 *droṇavāpa*. Taking the area of 1 *kulyavāpa*= 8 *droṇavāpas*, 1 *droṇavāpa* of *vāstu* land= $\frac{1}{8}$ of *kulyavāpa*= 4 *rūpakas* in value. If we assume the same rate of *khila* and *vāstu* land, 1 *dīnāra*=16 *rūpakas* on the basis that 1 *kulyavāpa* of *khila* land is valued at 2 *dīnāras*. But the assumption that the price of both the *khila* and *vāstu* land is the same is not tenable. While *khila* land is sold in larger quantities on the basis of *kulyavāpa* as a unit, building sites are sold on the basis of a smaller unit of land viz., *droṇavāpa*, because a building site is more valuable and costly than fallow land and is required in smaller quantity. It is fortunate that a proof of this difference in the rates of fallow and building land is given in one of the Damodarpur Copper-plate inscriptions of the time of Budha Gupta stating that 1 *kulyavāpa* of *vastu* land=3 *dīnāras* as against 2 *dīnāras* for a *kulyavāpa* of *khila* land, as stated in this inscription.

Coins. As has been already stated, Kumāra Gupta I is noted for the large number of his coins and the variety of their types, pointing to the vast extent of the territories within which the various types of coins were in circulation.

Kumāra Gupta issued the following types of coins: (1) Archer, (2) Swordsman, (3) Aśvamedha, (4) Horseman, (5) Lion-slayer, (6) Tiger-slayer, (7) Peacock, (8) Pratāpa, (9) Elephant-rider.

Archer type. It has varieties which are varieties of legends. The following legends appear on their *Obv.* (1) *Vijitāvaniravanīpatiḥ. Kumaragupto divaṁ jayati;* (2) *Jayati mahitalam* on r. and ending with (*Kumāragu*) *ptaḥ* on l.; (3) *Jayati mahītalaṁ* on r. with (*Ku*) *māragupta* on l.; (4) *Parama-rājādhirāja-Śrī-Kumāraguptaḥ;* (5) *Kumāra* and *Mahārājādhirāja Śrī-Kumāraguptaḥ;* (6) *Guṇeśo mahītalaṁ jayati Kumāraḥ.*

The *Rev.* bears the single legend *Śrī-Mahendraḥ.*

Swordsman type. This type is an innovation of Kumāra Gupta. The *Obv.* shows 'king standing l., nimbate, wearing waist-cloth and jewellery, casting incense with r. hand on altar on l., while l. hand rests on hilt of sword at his side; Garuḍa standard on l.' The king's dress does not show the Kushān features noticeable on the Archer type.

The *Rev.* shows 'Goddess (Lakshmī), nimbate, seated facing on lotus, holding fillet in outstretched r. hand and lotus in l., which rests on hip'. The Garuḍa, as usual, is linked with Lakshmī on *Rev.*

The legend on *Obv.* is *Gāṃ avajitya sucharitaiḥ Kumāragupto divaṃ jayati* and that on *Rev.* is *Śrī-Kumāraguptaḥ.*

Aśvamedha type. Its Obv. shows 'Horse standing r., wearing breast band and saddle, before sacrificial pole (*yūpa*) on altar, the pennons from which fly over its back.' On Samudra Gupta's type, the horse is not saddled. The *Rev.* represents 'Queen (Mahishī Anantadevī) standing l., mimbate, holding *chowrie* over r. shoulder and uncertain object in l. hand, wearing ear-rings, necklace, armlets, and anklets. On l. is a sacrificial spear bound with fillets.'

The *Obv.* bears the legend *Jayati divaṁ Kumāraḥ* and between legs of horse, *śvamedha*. On one specimen the legend reads: *Jayatadava Kumāra=Jayati divaṁ Kumāraguptoyaṁ*. On the *Rev.* is the legend *Śrī Aśvanedhamahendraḥ*.

The figure of Queen on *Rev.* appears as a religious necessity. The legend *Jayati divaṃ Kumāraḥ* indicates that by his conquest of heaven the king achieves the status of god Indra or Mahendra and assumes the appropriate new title, *Śrī-Aśvamedha-Mahendraḥ*.

Horseman type. This type shows six varieties in their legends. The *Obv.* shows the standard figure of 'King riding to r. on fully caparisoned horse,' and the *Rev.* 'Goddess (Lakshmī) seated to l. on wicker stool, holding lotus with long stalk and leaves in outstretched r. hand, while l. rests by her side.' There is a variety showing the king 'wearing long sash, the ends of which fly behind' and Goddess 'offering fruit to peacock'. Another variety shows very distinctly Goddess 'with r. hand feeding peacock from bunch of fruit.' The Goddess is to be identified as *Durgā*, the Goddess of War, feeding Her vāhana Mayūra, on the basis of a passage in *Śrī-Chaṇḍī* [Uttara-Charitra, VIII. 17] which is a part of *Mārkaṇḍeya Purāna*. The passage describes Goddess Kaumarī Ambikā as *Mayūra-Vara-Vāhanā* and *Guharūpiṇī* (resembling Kārtikeya in appearance) like the Brahmānī on *Haṁsa* and Māheśvarī on *Vṛisha*. Another passage [XI. 15] describes the Goddess as surrounded by peacocks and calls Her *Nārāyaṇī*.

The type is marked by the following variety of legends on *Obv.*: (1) *Pṛithivītalaṁ divaṁ jayatyajitaḥ*, (2) *Kshitipatirajito vijayī Mahendrasiṁho divaṁ jayati*, (3) *Kshitipatirajito vijayī Kumāragupto divaṁ jayati*, (4) *Guptakulavyomaśaśī jayatyajeyājita Mahendraḥ*, (5) *Guptakulāmala-chandro Mahendrakarmājito jayati*. The legend on *Rev.* is uniformly *Ajitamahendraḥ*.

Lion-slayer type. Its *Obv.* shows 'King standing r., wearing waist-cloth with sash floating behind and jewellery, shooting lion, which falls backward on r. from leap, with bow in l. hand, r. drawn behind head.' The *Rev.* shows 'Goddess nimbate, seated facing on lion couchant r., holding fillet in outstretched r. hand and lotus in l. hand or lotus only.' The goddess, as usual, is *Durgā Siṃhavāhanā*.

Varieties of this type are mainly those of legends which are: (1) *Sākshād iva (Narasiṁho) Siṃha-Mahendro jayatyaniśam*, 'Like God Narasiṃha in flesh and blood, King Siṁha-Mahendra is ever-victorious:' (2) *Kshitipatirajitamahendraḥ-Kumāragupto divaṃ jayati:* (3) *Kumāragupto vijayī Siṁha-Mahendro divaṃ jayati:* (4) *Kumāragupto yudhi Siṁha-vikkramaḥ.*

The legend on the *Rev.* is *Śrī-Mahendrasiṃhaḥ* or *Siṁha-mahendraḥ.*

Tiger-slayer type. Its *Obv.* shows 'King to l., wearing waist-cloth, jewellery, and head-dress, shooting tiger which falls backwards on l., with bow held in r. hand, l. hand drawing string of bow; his r. foot tramples on tiger; crescent-topped standard bound with fillet on l.' On *Rev.* is shown 'Goddess standing l. in lotus plant (?), holding lotus with long stalk behind her in l. hand and feeding peacock with fruit in r. hand.'

The legend on *Obv.* is *Śrīmān Vyāghrabalaparākramaḥ* and on *Rev. Kumāraguptodhirāja.*

The goddess feeding peacock is to be taken as goddess Durgā, as explained above. The peacock introduced on coinage for the first time directly suggests the regular Peacock type of coinage.

Peacock type. The *Obv.* shows 'King, nimbate, standing l. wearing waist-cloth with long sashes and jewellery, feeding peacock from bunch of fruit held in r. hand, l. hand behind him.' The *Rev.* show 'Kārtikeya, nimbate, three-quarters to l., riding on his peacock Paravāṇī, holding spear in l. hand over shoulder (*Śakti-dhara*), with r. hand sprinkling incense on altar on r. (?); the peacock on a kind of platform.'

The legend on *Obv.* is *Jayati svabhūmau guṇarāśi*, followed by five more characters on r., and ends *Mahendra-Kumāraḥ* on l. The legend on *Rev.* is *Mahendra-Kumāraḥ.*

Pratāpa type. The *Obv.* shows 'Male figure, wearing long loose robe, with arms on breast in (*jñānamudrā* attitude) standing facing; on his l. female figure to r., wearing long loose robe and helmet, with shield on l. arm, and holding out r. hand (closely resembling Minerva); on his r. a female figure wearing long loose robe, standing l., holding out r. hand and resting l. on hip; the two latter appear to be addressing the central figure; Garuḍa standard behind central figure.' The *Rev.* shows 'Goddess seated facing on lotus, holding lotus in uplifted r. hand and resting l. on knee.'

The legend on *Obv.* is *Kumāraguptaḥ* on either side of the central figure. There is a long inscription on the margin, of which only the lower parts of the letters remain on the plan. On the *Rev.* is the legend *Śrī-Pratāpaḥ* after which the type is named. This title may be taken to indicate restoration of his *pratāpa* or power by the victories of his Crown-Prince, Skanda Gupta, over the Hūṇas and the Mlechchha peoples.

The *Obv.* type is unique. 'It seems to be restruck on another, perhaps non-Indian coin. The central figure is Indian in style, while the two others are quite foreign.' These probably came from the conquered foreign peoples. Kings by tradition had female-attendants in their menial service.

Elephant-rider type. The *Obv.* shows 'King holding goad in r. hand, seated on elephant which advances l.; behind him is seated an attendant holding *chhatra* over him.' The *Rev.* shows 'Lakshmī standing facing on lotus flower, grasping stalk of lotus growing beside her in her r. hand and holding lotus flower in l. arm.' There is no clue to connect this coinage with Kumāra Gupta. The elephant is associated with Lakshmī on whose head it pours water according to tradition.

Silver Coins. It is to be recalled that the first Gupta silver coinage was inaugurated by Chandra Gupta II as the result of his conquests of the western Kshatrapa territories in which he had to keep in circulation the old familiar coins of the displaced rulers, with some modifications indicative of the new regime. But this conquest took place in the later period of his reign and so his silver issues are not known for their number or variety. His son, Kumāra Gupta I, however, had a longer control of these territories and more opportunities for issuing his silver coins in greater abundance and variety.

They fall broadly under four classes with some varieties in each.

Class I most closely resembles the coins of Chandra Gupta II and may be regarded as their immediate successors whose features they continue such as the Kshatrapa bust on the obverse, traces of *varshe* and corrupt Greek letters and well-executed Garuḍa on *Rev.* with 7 stars above it, and also the same legend: *Paramabhāgavata Mahārājādhirāja-Śrī-Kumāragupta-Mahendrādityaḥ.*

It is to be noted that even Skanda Gupta also struck coins of this type, proving that they belonged to a particular locality in western India, perhaps Surāshṭra, where Chandra Gupta II first had to strike these coins.

Class II does not copy so closely the features of the Kshatrapa coins. It omits the Greek letters on *Obv.* on which the bust also is nominally kept up, as well as the figure of Garuḍa on *Rev.* which drops the seven fillets. Thus these coins belonged to a locality in western India where Kshatrapa coins were not so known.

Class III, however, returns to Kshatrapa features, carefully executed bust and Greek letters on obverse, but rudely treated Garuḍa, which is all body and no neck but with prominent wings, on *Rev.* Their small thick fabric points to their similarity to the coins of the Traikūṭaka dynasty meant for southern Gujarat.

The legend on Class II is *Paramabhāgavata-Rājādhirāja-Śrī-Kumāragupta-Mahendrādityaḥ*, but on some specimens the first word is *Bhāgavata* and not *Paramabhāgavata*.

The legend on Class III is *Paramabhāgavata-Mahārājādhirāja-Śrī-Kumāragupta-Mahendrādityaḥ*.

The first three classes of silver coins were meant for circulation in the western Provinces.

Class IV comprises silver coinage which was introduced by Kumāra Gupta I for the first time to the central parts of the Gupta empire, in the Ganges valley. As it is far removed from western India, it also eliminates most of the Kshatrapa features. For instance, the bust on *Obv.* shows more of portraiture. Greek letters are replaced by a date in Brāhmī. On *Rev.* again, the degraded Garuḍa is discarded in favour of a peacock standing facing with outspread wings and tail. The peacock here appears as the vehicle (*Paravāṇi*) of god Kārtikeya who is also called Kumāra, of whom Kumāra Gupta was a devotee, as his father was a devotee of Vishṇu.

These coins also discard the *Vaishṇava* legends and bear a legend inspired by the military spirit: *vijitāvanīravanipatiḥ Kumāragupto divaṃ jayati.*

The *Obv.* bears in numerals the date 100+20+4=Gupta year 124=A.D. 443. Other specimens of this variety bear the dates 118, 119 and 122 of the Gupta year (D.C. Sircar, *Select Inscriptions* p. 208).

Class V comprises coins which are silver-plated and have a core of copper, showing debased issue of the silver coins called for by financial stringency. These coins have been found only in particular locality, though in large numbers, round the ancient city of Valabhī.

Their *Obv.* shows head r. with traces of Greek letters, and the *Rev.* Garuḍa crudely executed.

The legend is *Paramabhāgavata-Rājādhirāja-Śrī-Kumāragupta-Mahendrādityaḥ*.

Copper Coins. Only two specimens of the copper coins of Kumāra Gupta I are known so far, and they present two types. Type I shows on *Obv.* king standing l. wearing waist-cloth and jewellery, l. hand on hip, apparently throwing incense on altar with r. hand. The *Rev.* shows Garuḍa with outstretched wings standing facing and the legend *Kumāraguptaḥ*.

The Type II specimen shows on *Obv.* an altar with the legend *Śrī-Ku* below it. Its *Rev.* shows goddess (Lakshmī) seated on lion couchant r., facing, holding cornucopia in l. arm., and lotus in r. hand.

CHAPTER VII

SKANDA GUPTA VIKRAMĀDITYA

(*c.* A.D. 455-467)

Dates. The date A.D. 455 for Skanda Gupta's accession to sovereignty may be taken from the fact that he was the immediate successor of his father Kumāra Gupta I on the Gupta throne. This fact we know from the definite statement contained in the Bhitarī Stone Pillar inscription of Skanda Gupta to the effect that he succeeded him as his son (*suta*) on the ground of both his fidelity to his father ('adhering to the feet of his father like the bee to the lotus'), and his superior military qualifications as 'the only hero of the Gupta family' (*Guptavaṃśaikavīraḥ*) who had even as Crown-Prince, as we shall see, to fight his father's battles against the many enemies of the Gupta empire and had to continue that fight after he became emperor. Thus his succession to his father's throne was immediate and did not permit any interval or delay. The earliest inscription of Skanda Gupta, that of Junāgaḍh Rock, also furnishes three dates of his reign, the years 136, 137 and 138. This inscription also shows that the Gupta hold on Surāshṭra and Kathiawar was quite strong in the time of Skanda Gupta, showing also that he was the immediate successor of his father. The next dated inscription of his reign is the Kahaum Stone Pillar inscription of the year 141=A.D. 460, found in a village in the Gorakhpur district. The third dated inscription of his reign is that of the copper-plate found at Indrapura in the *Vishaya* or Province of Antaravedī. It bears the date 146= A.D. 465. The last dated inscription of his reign is the Gadhwa Stone inscription (Fleet No. 66) of the year 148=A.D. 467, which does not mention that it was issued in the reign of Skanda Gupta, but this may be taken as proved from the fact that the exact words used in the Indor Copper-plate inscription in relation to the reign of Skanda Gupta are also used here (*pravardhamānavijaya-rājya*). In this connexion, mention may also be made of another inscription found at Kosam (Kauśāmbī) on the pedestal of a sculpture showing Śiva and Pārvatī standing, and bearing the date 139 which falls within the chronological limits of Skanda Gupta's reign. It is stated to have been issued by Mahārāja Bhīmavarman who may be taken to have been a local chief owning allegiance to Skanda Gupta, 'Mahārājādhirāja,' as the paramount sovereign.

Lastly, his silver coins also bear dates which have been read by Vincent Smith as 144, 145 and 148=A.D. 467 (*IA*. 1902 f. 266). Thus his reign may be dated A.D. 455-467.

Succession. The epigraphic evidence as to succession has been already mentioned above. We may add to it the evidence of the Junāgaḍh Rock inscription stating that Lakshmī, the Goddess of Fortune, 'after examining by turns with due deliberation and seriously reflecting on the roots of all his virtues and foibles, fixed Her choice upon him and rejected all other sons of the sovereign.' This shows that, in accordance with the previous practice, the succession to the Gupta throne was regulated by merit rather than birth, the father choosing the best of his sons to succeed him. The epigraphic evidence is corroborated by a piece of literary evidence indicated in a verse contained in the work *Ārya-Mañju-Śrī-Mūla-kalpa* giving the following succession list of kings, viz., Samudra, Vikrama, Mahendra, and Devaraja, corresponding to the kings Samudra Gupta, Chandra Gupta II Vikramāditya, Kumāra Gupta Mahendrāditya, and Skanda Gupta. Skanda Gupta is described in this passage as *sakārādya*, i.e., as one whose name begins with '*sa*', but is also given a new name not mentioned in the inscriptions, viz., the name Devarāja. As we know, the name Devarāja was also assumed by his grandfather Chandra Gupta II whose title Vikramāditya is also assumed by Skanda Gupta. It may be further noted that Devarāja is the name of god Indra whose other name, Mahendra, is assumed by his father, Kumāra Gupta I. The comparison of these Gupta kings to Indra is first made in the case of Samudra Gupta whom the Allahabad Pillar inscription describes as the equal of Indra among other gods, while the Kahaum Stone inscription of ?.fi. 460 describes Skanda Gupta himself as resembling god Śakra (*Śakropama*). It is no wonder that Kumāra Gupta, the father of *Śakropama* Skanda Gupta is called *Śakrāditya*, by Yuan-Chwang on the basis of this epigraphic tradition, instead of the numismatic designation of *Mahendrāditya*.

History. There is an important document for the history of Skanda Gupta's reign, the Bhitarī inscription (Fleet No. 13). This inscription records the career of Skanda Gupta both as Crown Prince and as king.

As Crown Prince, he was deputed as 'the sole hero of the Gupta dynasty (*guptavaṁśaikavīraḥ*) to deal with the enemies bent on conquest (*vijigīshā-prodyatānāṁ pareshāṁ*), the Pushyamitras, who had gathered all their strength and resources (*samuditabalakoshān*). These he subdued (*jitvā*) and was then trying (*udyatena*) to reinstate the Goddess of Fortune of his dynasty shaken by them (*vichalita kula-Lakshmī*).

As king, after his father had died (*pitari divamupete*), when Gupta fortune was overwhelmed (*viplutāṁ*), he restored it by his own conquests which he reported to his mother who listened with tears of joy in her eyes, as Kṛishṇa reported his victories to his mother Devakī.

Besides restoring the former Gupta power, he increased it by fresh conquests of the earth and showed mercy to the vanquished in distress (*avaniṁ vijitvā* and *jiteshvārteshu kṛitvā dayām*).

He shook the earth (*dharā kampitā*) in subduing the mighty Hūṇas with whom he came into close conflict (*Hūṇairyyasya samāgatasya samare*).

His history is also related in another inscription, Junāgaḍh Rock inscription of A.D. 455 (Fleet No. 14) which gives it as follows: He set against the hostile kings who were like "so many serpents, lifting up their hoods in pride and arrogance, the authority of his local representatives like so many Garuḍas" (*narapatibhujagānāṁ mānadarpotphaṇānāṁ pratikṛiti Garuḍājñāṁ nirvvisho chāvakartā*). "When his father had died (*pitari surasakahitvam prāptavati*) he, by his own prowess (*ātmaśaktyā*), humbled his enemies (*avanatāriḥ*) and made subject to himself the earth bounded by the four oceans and flourishing countries (*chaturudadhi jalāntām sphita paryanta deśāṁ avaniṁ*).

"Nest, he also (*apicha*) destroyed at its roots the pride of his enemies (*āmūlabhagnadarpā*) in the Mlechchha countries and made them announce that 'victory has been achieved by him (*jitamiva*')."

Hence he was selected for the throne, discarding (*vyapetya*) all other princes, after fully weighing the grounds of their virtues and failings, by the Goddess of Fortune.

"Having thus conquered the whole earth and the pride of his enemies, he set about organizing his empire by appointing Governors in all the Provinces (*sarveshu deśeshu vidhāya goptṛīn*) and had to spend much thought (*sañchintayāmāsa bahu-prakāram*) to find out among his Officers (Provincial Governors) (*sarveshu bhṛityeshu saṁhateshu*) the most competent of them who could shoulder the burden (*bhārasya udvahane samarthaḥ*) of administering the whole of the Surāshṭra countries newly acquired (*praśishyām nikhilān Surāshṭrān*).

"Many a day and night did the king spend on this thought till he appointed Parṇadatta to rule over the Saurāshṭra region. Posting Parṇadatta on the west quarter, the king was easy at heart, just as the gods were by appointing Varuṇa as the guardian of the western quarter."

These epigraphic data help us to construct the political history of the times. It is evident that, during the later days of Kumāra Gupta, I, the Gupta empire had to face a number of enemies, among whom are mentioned the Pushyamitras. It had, in fact, to face a coalition of enemies pooling all their resources. These Skanda Gupta, as Crown Prince, was able to subdue, but, unfortunately, his

PLATE VIII

COINS OF SKANDA GUPTA

1. Bow and Arrow Type

2. King and Lakshmi Type

3. Silver Coin

father died before the fallen fortune of the family was restored by him by his conquests. Kumāra Gupta saw *kula-Lakshmī* both shaken (*vichalita*) and overwhelmed (*vipluta*).

Skanda Gupta did not stop by merely conquering his enemies. His military spirit thus roused drove him towards *digvijaya*. But it was also a *dharmavijaya*, for he showed mercy to the vanquished by reinstating them in their kingdoms.

In the course of his conquests, he had also to subdue the Hūṇas, and also the Mlechchha countries.

The result of these conquests was that he extended the territory of the Gupta empire up to the limits of the four oceans and annexed to it many flourishing countries.

His conquest in different directions was complete, for he is said to have destroyed the very roots of the power of his enemies who themselves announced that victory was his. In the Kahaum Stone Pillar inscription (Fleet No. 15), 'the result of his conquests is described by the heads of hundred kings falling at his feet in tendering their homage at his Darbar-hall (*Upasthāna*)'. It also describes Skanda Gupta as the Lord of Hundred Kings (*Kshitipaśatapatiḥ*), as the equal of Indra (*Śakropama*), and as one whose reign was tranquil (*śānta*), being free from all troubles.

His conquests were also consolidated by his administration. He was quite a realist in politics and perceived how the Gupta empire was encircled by a ring of enemies in its outlying parts, who were ready to rise against it at the slightest opportunity. Therefore, he appointed efficient local governors who, like so many Garuḍas, might eat up the serpents as they lifted their hoods for attack. A fruitful and constant source of trouble was the old Śaka kingdom of Surāshṭra newly annexed to the Gupta empire. There he appointed as Governor (*Goptā*) the best of his provincial governors, Parṇadatta by name. While he was the Governor of the Province, his son, Chakrapālita, was placed in charge of its capital named Girinagara.

There is a theory that the enemies mentioned in these inscriptions were his brothers whom Skanda Gupta fought for the throne, but the theory seems untenable on several grounds. The many enemies that Skanda Gupta had to conquer are clearly described in the inscriptions not as the internal but as the external enemies of the Gupta dynasty. They made its fortune totter. Such a description cannot apply to its scions.

The inscriptions also do not make room for any internal fratricidal war for the throne. The process of defeating the enemies of the Gupta empire is described as a continuous and prolonged process in which Skanda Gupta was engaged as Crown Prince by his father. He had to continue it even as king. Over and above this, the significant term *amalātmā*, 'of soul pure and unsullied,' as applied to him in the inscription, should rule out the supposition that he could shed the blood of his brothers for the sake of the throne.

It is also urged that Skanda Gupta was not the immediate or legitimate heir to the throne on the ground that his mother is not mentioned in the Bihar and Bhitari Stone Pillar inscriptions, while the mother of his brother, Pura Gupta, is mentioned in the Bhitarī Seal inscription (*JASB*, 1889, pp. 84-105) as Mahādevī Anantadevī. But the epigraphic practice on the point is not uniform or conclusive.

Administration. The inscriptions of the time of Skanda Gupta give some interesting details regarding administration. The empire was made up of provinces under governors. The term for a Province is *Deśa*. There are also other terms used such as *Avaṁ* and *Vishaya*. The Governor is called *Goptā* and district officer *Vishayapati*. Parṇadatta is called the *Goptā* of *Surāshtra Avaṁ*. Śarvanāga is mentioned as the District Magistrate of Antaravedī *Vishaya*. A feudatory was also sometimes appointed as the Governor of a Province, e.g. Mahārāja Bhīmavarman of Kosam (Kauśāmbī), as is mentioned in the Stone Image inscription of that place of A.D. 458.

The administration of a *Vishya* or District was carried on by officers put in charge of different departments. Some of these are mentioned in the Bihar Stone Pillar inscription (Fleet No. 12), such as *Āgrahārika*, *Śaulkika* (in charge of collections of toll or customs), *Gaulmika* (in charge of forests).

The cities were placed in charge of executive officers. Thus, Chakrapālita was the Mayor (*Nagararakshaka*) of the city called Girinagara which was the provincial capital of Saurāshṭra. Āja is the name of a *paura* or city in another *Vishaya* (Fleet No. 12). Similarly, Kakubha is the name of what is called a jewel of a village, famous (*khyāta*) as being hallowed (*pūta*) by its association with saints (*sādhusaṁsarga*). Indrapura is a city in the *Vishaya* of Antaravedī (Fleet No. 16).

The administration of the difficult city of Girinagara, the capital of the country of the Surāshṭras, has been described in detail in the inscription (Fleet No. 14). The province itself was also a difficult charge. Its governance was a problem for the emperor who exercised his mind on it for 'many days and nights' till he thought of Parṇadatta as the only man (*ekaḥ*) who was able to shoulder the burden (*bhārasya-udvahane*) of that administration (*praśishyāt*). But Parṇadatta was himself so modest (*vinīta*), upright (*satya*), straightforward (*ārjava*) and above all temptations (*viśuddha*), that the king was able to make him accept that exalted office only after a good deal of entreaties and persuasion. By appointing him to the charge of the western regions, the king was easy of heart, like the gods securing Varuṇa as the guardian of the western quarter.

Parṇadatta on his part was hard put to it to find a fit administrator for the capital of that troubled province. He selected his son Chakrapālita after testing (*parīkshya*) in person his qualities before appointing him Mayor of the city which he administered better than his predecessors. By his benign administration of the city, Chakrapālita made all people feel quite at ease, but at the same time kept under control its mischievous characters. The inscription singles out some of the administrative qualities which make a successful Mayor of a city. He must be free from debts (*anṛiṇyaṁ*), so that he may be above the financial temptations of his office, above bribery and corruption. He must be possessed of eloquence (*vākya*), so that he may be able to carry with him the votes of the Municipal Council. He must be civil in manners (*dākshiṇyaṁ*), smiling and cheerful at speaking (*pūrvasmitābhāshaṇa*), and possessed of charity (*dāna*). He must show honour (*māna*), where it is due. Mayor Chakrapālita was futher possessed of the very useful habit of making social calls on his fellow citizens by paying visits to their houses (*gṛihapraveśa*) in a free and unceremonious manner (*niryantraṇa*), while he further added to his popularity (*saṁvarddhita-prīti*) by holding receptions at his own residence (*gṛihopachāraiḥ*).

The efficiency of Chakrapālita's municipal administration was soon put to a severe strain and test. Owing to excessive rains, the lake Sudarśana which served the city suddenly burst (*bibheda*) in Gupta year 136=A.D. 455, with the result that all the rivers like Palāśinī, and Suvarnasikatā which took their rise from the neighbouring hills such as Ūrjjayat or Raivataka, and were received into the lake within which they remained confined (*chirabandhana-ushitāḥ*), found their way into the ocean (*samudra*). The lake Sudarśana, which was like a veritable ocean (*nidhitulya*), drained of its waters, became *Durdarśana*, belying its name. The citizens in despair (*vishāda*), were unable to decide what they should do when Chakrapālita came to their rescue in a true civic spirit, full of regard for the welfare of his city (*hitārtham-nagarasacha*) and for his king, had the breach repaired and the embankment renewed by an unlimited expenditure of wealth which he found out of his privy purse within the short period of two months. The embankment was 100 cubits long, 68 broad and of 7 men's height, a great masonry work (*samyak-ghaṭita-upalena*), so that the reservoir (*taṭāka*) might last for all time (*śāśvat-kalpa-kālaṁ*). Thus was brought about the renovation (*saṁskāra*) of lake (*taṭāka*) Sudarśana.

Chakrapālita crowned his public work by the construction of the temple of god, Chakrabhṛit, consecrating his life to the sacred feet of Lord Govinda and the lotus feet of Vishṇu carrying the discus (*chakra*).

Religion. Skanda Gupta was known for his policy of religious toleration which gave free scope to private philanthrophy creating endowments in favour of different religions then prevailing in the country. Chakrapālita's endowment of a temple has been mentioned above. The Kahaum Stone Pillar inscription records an endowment in favour of Jainism, the fashioning of five stone images of Ādikartṛis or Tirthaṁkaras (Ādinātha, Śāntinātha, Neminātha, Pārśva, and Mahāvira) in the niches of a pillar of stone (*śailastambha*) looking like the summit of a hill, and planted in the ground. The Indore Copper-plate inscription (Fleet No. 16) records a gift in aid of a temple of the Sun (*Savitā*). The temple was established by two Kshattriyas named Achalavarman and Bhrukuṇṭhasiṁha, who are also described as following the unusual occupation of merchants (*vaṇik*). For this temple, the provision for a lamp was made by a Brāhmaṇa named Devavishṇu, a *Chaturvedī* Brahmin (of Rāṇāyaṇīya *śākhā* and Varshagaṇa *gotra*). The Bihar Stone Pillar inscription of Skanda Gupta describes the erection of a *yūpa* or pillar and the construction of a group of temples (*devaniketanamaṇḍalaṁ*) dedicated to gods headed by god Skanda (*Skandapradhānaiḥ*) and also to the Divine Mothers (*Mātṛibhiścha*). The Divine Mothers were thus listed :

Brāhmī Māheśvarī chaiva Kaumārī Vaishṇavī tathā |
Māhendrī chaiva Vārāhī Chāmuṇḍā saptamātaraḥ ||

There is another list of eight Mothers.

Brāhmī Māheśvarī Chaṇḍī Vārāhī Vaishṇavī tathā |
Kaumārī chaiva Chāmuṇḍā Charchchiketyashṭamātaraḥ ||

The village where these works were constructed is called Skanda-Gupta-*baṭa* named after either the god Skanda or the emperor Skanda Gupta. Besides these Divine Mothers, the inscription also mentions goddess Bhadrāryā, also named Bhadrāryakā, who may be taken to be Pārvatī (Āryā=, wife of Bhadra=Śiva) [D.C. Sircar, *Select Inscriptions*, I. 317-19].

Economic Conditions : Glimpses of economic life and organization of the times are given in some inscriptions. We have already seen that the engineers of the Gupta empire were able enough to construct a reservoir of the magnitude of lake Sudarśana by damming up rivers by means of embankments of solid masonry work. Industry seems to have been organized under *Śreṇis* or

Guilds, of the working of which some details are given in the Indor Copper-plate inscription of G.E. 146=A.D. 465. It states that the city called Indrapura was the abode (*nivāsa*) of a *Tailika-Śreṇī*, a Guild of Oilmen. The foreman of the Guild (*Pravara*) is named *Jīvanta*. A Brahmin makes over to the Guild a donation of money (*mūlya*) to be held by it in perpetuity (*ājasrikam*). Out of this fund and its interest was to be provided a quantity of oil, two *palas* by weight (*taulyena*), to be applied to the maintenance of a lamp (*dīpopayojyam*). The supply of this quantity of oil was not to be interrupted (*abhagnayogam*). The fund was also to be kept intact by the Guild without any diminution from its original value (*prathamārthā-avachchhinnasaṁstham*). That the guild was well-organized and prosperous as a corporation is shown by the fact that it was trusted with a permanent fund although it might change its place, provided such a change of place did not affect its stability (*yathāsthirāyaḥ*). The guild also acted like a Bank in receiving a deposit to be held in perpetuity for a purpose prescribed by the donor. It was to maintain intact the corpus of the donation which the Bank could invest for profit which would enable it to pay the cost of oil required to feed a lamp to light a temple. The donor of the deposit and the bank were bound by a regular contract which was registered (*dāyamimaṁ nibaddham*). The violation (*vyakramaṇa*) of this stipulation was condemned as the greatest of sins (*mahāpātaka*). Thus the Guild acted as a Bank in receiving a deposit on stipulated terms. It could also like a Bank invest the deposit and earn an income from the investment. Like a Bank, it also paid interest on the deposit out of the profit earned on it. But in this case, the interest was to be paid to the beneficiary to whom it was assigned by the donor. The beneficiary in this transaction was a temple. Thus this particular obligation agreed to by the Bank was very helpful in stimulating public benefactions. A philanthropist was not at pains to find out how he could best dispose of his charities so that they might be permanently secured against loss. Gifts are not forthcoming where their security, amount, and purpose are not guaranteed. This local Bank of a Guild by acting as an administrator of trust-properties contributed very largely to the cultural life of the community by taking charge of donations for its purposes. The Bihar Stone Pillar inscription of Skanda Gupta also records the gift of a permanent religious endowment aptly called *akshayanīvī* created in the town of Ajapuraka, but the name of the corporation to whom the donation is entrusted is not traceable in the inscription.

Coins. Skanda Gupta's gold coins are not marked by the variety of types issued by his predecessors. His gold coinage shows only two or probably three types as described below:

I. *Gold*: (1) **Archer type**: *Obv.* shows king holding bow and arrow with *garuḍadhvaja* to his r.; legend: *Skanda* and '*Jayati mahītalam*' and '*Jayati divaṁ Śrī Kramādityaḥ*' and the interesting epithet *Sudhanvī*, skilled bowman.

Rev. shows '*Śrī Skandaguptaḥ*' or *Kramādityaḥ*' with Lakshmī on lotus.

(2) **King and Lakshmī type**: *Obv.* shows king with bow and arrow, and a female not to be taken as the queen but Lakshmī, and Garuḍa between them.

Rev. shows a female with lotus in 1. hand (to be taken as Lakshmī); in celebration of Lakshmī invoked in the Inscription No. 14 (Junāgaḍh). The prominence given in this type to Lakshmī is due to the king's gratitude to his tutelary deity or *Kula-Lakshmī* in helping him to restore the fallen fourtunes of his family.

The majority of the gold coins of Skanda Gupta are of the Archer type but this type divides itself into two very distinct classes by weight and also by legends. Thus the first class was struck on a standard of about 132 grains of good gold. They must have been struck earlier in his reign, as they correspond in weight to his predecessor's coins.

The second class under the Archer type comprises coins which are struck on a standard of 144.6 grains. This higher weight is coupled with a baser metal. The majority of these coins came from the Kalighat hoard and might have been in circulation in the eastern parts of the empire, and in the later years of his reign.

The difference in legends is pointed out above.

With regard to the 'King and Lakshmī' type, some numismatists call it 'King and Queen' type on the ground of its resemblance to the Chandra Gupta I type of Samudra Gupta. But the resemblance is superficial. As has been noted above, the king on the *Obv.* does not wear the Kushān dress shown on the Archer type but wears only waist-cloth and jewellery, nor is he nimbate, while there is a Garuḍa standard in front of him. On the right is a standing female figure supposed to be Skanda Gupta's queen. But this supposition is unlikely. The lotus flower in her l. hand, with the plant shooting up behind her rather makes her out to be goddess Lakshmī. She also resembles the Lakshmī on the reverse of some specimens of Chandra Gupta II's Chhatra type. A queen is appropriate on the Aśvamedha type for the part she has to take in the sacrifice and is marked out by the regal *chowrie* which is not found here. The coin also gives expression to what Skanda Gupta owes to goddess Lakshmī in retrieving the lost glory of his family, as stated in the Junāgaḍh inscription.

(3) **Horseman type**: Only one specimen of this type is known

and kept in the Bodleian collection. Its weight of 140.5 grains connects it with Skanda Gupta, as well as its *Rev.* legend, '*Kramādityaḥ*'.

I. *Silver:* Skanda Gupta's silver coins were issued both in the western and central provinces of the empire and thus fall naturally into two classes.

Western Issues: These present three *Rev.* types, viz., Garuḍa, Bull (*Nandī*) and Altar. The *Obv.* has the king's bust in common. The Garuḍa type shows on *Rev.* Garuḍa standing with outstretched wings and legend '*Paramabhāgavata Mahārājādhirāja Śrī Skandagupta-Kramādityaḥ*'.

The Bull type is represented by a small series of coins of very base metal.

The Altar types shows on *Rev.* burning altar in centre with legend '*Paramabhāgavata Śrī Vikramādityaḥ Skandaguptaḥ*' or '*Kramādityaḥ*', or without *Āditya* title.

It is to be noted that the Garuḍa type is comparatively scarce and does not also show variety of fabric, as compared with Kumāra Gupta's Garuḍa type. These facts suggest the conclusion that Skanda Gupta's hold on western territories was lost later, and that he probably did not hold the district where Kumāra Gupta's coins show such a variety of fabric.

As regards the Bull type, its specimens were found in Kathiawar, pointing to Gupta dominion in Valabhī whose *Senāpatis* adopted the badge of a Bull.

The Altar Type is the commonest, mis-shapen, and of rude fabric, in circulation in Cutch where the coins were found. They show different legends, viz., '*Vikramāditya*' or absence of '*Āditya*' title.

Central Provinces Issues: These coins do not show any alteration from those of Kumāra Gupta. They show two classes bearing the two following legends:

(1) *Vijitāvanir avanipatir jayati divaṁ Skandaguptoyam.*

(2) *Vijitāvanir avanipatiḥ Śrī-Skandagupto divam jayati.*

Extent of the Empire. It will thus appear on the basis of both epigraphic and numismatic evidence that at the zenith of his power Skanda Gupta ruled over an extensive empire which included practically the whole of northern India from Kathiawad in the west to Bengal in the east. Towards the west, the empire included regions like Surāshṭra, districts of Cambay, and the contiguous parts of Gujarat and Malwa. The Junagadh inscription proves his hold on Surāshṭra and his Bull type of coins over the Cambay coast, as the Altar type points to his hold over Cutch. It also appears that Bhaṭṭārka, the founder of the Maitraka dynasty of Valabhī, was originally a *Senāpati* who must have helped Skanda Gupta in his administration in Kathiawad. The third Maitraka ruler is Droṇa Siṁha who lived about A.D. 502, the year 183 mentioned in his Bhamodra Mohotta Copper-plate inscription. In that inscription, he still acknowledges his loyalty to a paramount sovereign referred to as *Paramabhaṭṭāraka-pādānudhyāta*. In another inscription, Droṇa Siṁha refers to his paramount sovereign who personally attended and accomplished his coronation. The inscription states that the supreme (*Paramasvāmī*) and sole (*Ekasvāmī*) lord of the entire territory himself personally attended and had the ceremony of his consecration properly executed (*svayamupahita rājyābhi-shekaḥ*). If the date of Droṇa Siṁha is A.D. 502, the date of his grandfather Bhaṭṭārka must be about 40 or 50 years earlier, so as to belong to the reign of Skanda Gupta. Bhaṭṭārka must have materially helped Skanda Gupta in maintaining his sway over these remote western regions, which were not even then free from troubles evidently caused by the Hūṇas against whom the defence of Surāshṭra was a matter of great concern to the Gupta emperor who, as stated in the Junagadh inscription, had to spend several anxious days and nights to find out a proper governor for the province till his choice fell upon Parṇadatta. It will appear that Parṇadatta and Bhaṭṭārka were contemporaries and probably divided between them the civil and military administration of the province. That is why Bhaṭṭārka is called a *Senāpati* of his paramount sovereign. Later on, probably after Parṇadatta, the military as usual got the better of the civil administration, so that ultimately Bhaṭṭārka became both the civil and military governor of Surāshṭra. This change is indicated in one of his Valabhī Copper-plates, using the expression *Maulibhṛitamitra-śreṇibalāvāpta-rājyaśrīḥ*, 'equipped with the military strength derived from an army recruited from various classes called *Maula*, *Bhṛita*, *Mitra* and *Śreṇī*, and also with the glory of kingship'. This clearly shows the union of both civil (*rājya*) and military (*bala*) functions in the provincial governor. As the higher offices in the Gupta administration were hereditary, Bhaṭṭārka was succeeded in his position in Surāshṭra by his son, Dharasena I, followed by his grandson Droṇa Siṁha. The inscriptions show that while Bhaṭṭārka and Dharasena I had each the title of *Senāpati*, Droṇa Siṁha assumed the title of *Mahārāja*, although he still acknowledged his loyalty to the Gupta overlord. But who exactly was this Gupta overlord in A.D. 502, it is difficult to ascertain.

There were other able governors of Skanda Gupta to help him to maintain his imperial sovereignty of northern India, such as Śarvanāga, who was in charge of the territory between the Kālindī and Narmadā, and Bhīmavarman in charge of the Kauśāmbī region.

CHAPTER VIII

PŪRU GUPTA VIKRAMA-PRAKĀŚĀDITYA

(C. A.D. 467-469)

Succession. The immediate successor of Skanda Gupta seems to have been Pūru Gupta who was his brother. This we know from the Bhitarī Seal inscription of Kumāra Gupta (III) which states that 'Mahārājādhirāja Śrī Pūru Gupta was the son (*putra*) of Mahārājādhirāja Śrī Kumāra Gupta by his wife and queen Mahādevī,' and 'one who was meditating on the feet of his father in devoted loyalty to him (*tat pādānudhyāta*)'.

It will be noticed that this inscription mentions Pūru Gupta immediately after Kumāra Gupta and does not mention Skanda Gupta. This had led some scholars to suppose that Pūru Gupta was not the successor of Skanda Gupta but his rival who was not on friendly terms with him. But the epigraphic practice on the point does not warrant this supposition. 'The name of Pulakeśin II is omitted in an inscription of his brother and *Yuvarāja*, Vishṇuvardhana (Satara grant, *Ind. Ant.* 1890, pp. 22 f.). The name of Bhoja II of the Imperial Pratihāra dynasty is not mentioned in the Partabgarh inscription of his nephew Mahendrapāla II, but it is mentioned in an inscription of his brother, Vināyakapāla, the father of Mahendrapāla. Besides, there was no custom prohibiting the mention of the name of a rival uncle or brother. Mangaleśa and Govinda II are mentioned in the inscriptions of their rivals and their descendants. On the other hand, even an ancestor of a reigning king was sometimes omitted, e.g., Rudrasena II is omitted in one Ajaṇṭā inscription, Dharapaṭṭa is omitted in his son's inscription (Kielhorn *N. Ins.*, No. 464).'[1]

The mention in the inscription of Pūru Gupta immediately after Kumāra Gupta and his description as *tat-pādānudhyāta* are taken by some scholars to prove that Pūru Gupta was the immediate successor of his father. But on this point again epigraphic practice is not conclusive. There are several inscriptions where the omission of an immediate successor of his father is made. For instance, the term *Śrī Rāmapāla-Deva-pādānudhyāta* is applied to Madanapāla in the Manahali grant, although he was not the immediate successor of his father, being preceded by his elder brother Kumārapāla Again, in Kielhorn's Northern inscription No. 39, the son Vijayapāla

1. H. C. Raychaudhuri, *Political History of Ancient India*, p. 496, footnote 2.

is described as the successor of his father, though his immediate successor was his brother Devapāla (*Ib.* 495).

Indeed, considering both the epigraphic and numismatic evidence as to the extent of Skanda Gupta's empire, the possibility is shut out of there being any rival ruler of his in any part of northern India including its eastern parts like Bihar and Bengal where his gold coins of depreciated metal were current, as stated above, e.g. at places like Gayā, Hugli, Midnapur (King and Lakshmī type), Faridpur and Jessore.

It will also appear that as Skanda Gupta lived long, his brother and successor, Pūru Gupta, came to the throne as an old man. Thus he did not reign long and died before A.D. 473 when his son Kumāra Gupta was ruling. In A.D. 455 Skanda Gupta was a full grown adult and quite mature in years to be able to carry on an arduous and protracted war against the many enemies of the Gupta empire and bring it to a triumphant conclusion.

History. We have already seen that numismatic evidence points to the position that Skanda Gupta's hold on the Western Provinces of the empire was not very secure. The absence of silver coins of his successors points to the fact that theirs was a more restricted dominion which did not include Western India at all. In fact, the decline and fall of the Gupta empire may be taken to date from the end of Skanda Gupta's reign, though the process was checked for a time by Budha Gupta. There is a scarcity of gold coins issued by his successors, coupled with their lack of variety, which cannot but indicate that their dominion was limited in extent, and that Gupta Imperial power, which held sway all over India, was now on the wane. There is an important literary source regarding Pūru Gupta. Paramārtha in his *Life of Vasubandhu* relates that a king named Vikramāditya whose capital was Ayodhyā became a patron of Buddhism through the influence of Vasubandhu whom he also appointed as the tutor of his Queen and the Crown Prince who is named Bālāditya. He further states that when Bālāditya became king, he invited Vasubandhu to come to Ayodhyā. Paramārtha's statement is corroborated by the evidence of coins from which we learn that Pūru Gupta's son Narasiṁha Gupta calls himself Bālāditya on these coins. We also learn from the coins of Pūru Gupta that he assumed the title of *Śrī Vikrama*, which suggests the full title of *Vikramāditya* on the analogy that King Chandra Gupta II calls himself *Śrī Vikramaḥ* on his Archer type of coins and *Vikramādityaḥ* on his Chhatra type.

On the basis of this finding, it may be assumed that the successors of Chandra Gupta II set up their capital at Ayodhyā. It also appears from the Sarnath Stone inscription of Prakaṭāditya (Fleet, No. 79) that they had another capital at Kāśī.

Coins. Pūru Gupta's gold coins are all of the Archer type and correspond very closely in style to Skanda Gupta's heavier issues, weighing 142.7 and 141.4 grs. There are two varieties of this type: one with name *Pura* in field on *Obv.* coupled with the legend *Śrī Vikramaḥ*, on *Rev.*; the second variety is without *Pura.* But on some specimens the legend *Pura* is read as *Budha* by S. K. Sarasvatī (*I.C.*, April, 1935). In that case, those may have been the coins of Budha Gupta.

There are some interesting coins which on *Rev.* name a king called *Śrī Prakāśāditya* and on *Obv.* bear the legend '*Vijitya vasudhāṁ divaṁ jayati*'. These coins are of the Horseman type and show on *Obv.* 'king to right on horseback, slaying with sword in r. hand lion which leaps at him; bow round his body, with string over l. shoulder. Garuḍa standard on r.' Allan conjectures that this *Prakāśāditya* may have been another name of Pūru Gupta. According to the Bhitarī Seal inscription of Kumāra Gupta III, Pūru Gupta's queen was Mahādevī Śrī Chandradevī.

CHAPTER IX

SUCCESSORS OF PŪRU GUPTA

A new light is thrown on the vexed problem of the kings coming after Pūru Gupta by inscriptions on seals of Vishṇu Gupta and Budha Gupta recently discovered at Nālandā. The Vishṇu Gupta seal traces the genealogy of the Gupta kings as follows:

Pūru Gupta
|
son Narasiṁha Gupta
|
son Kumāra Gupta
|
son Vishṇu Gupta

According to the reading of the inscription borne by the seal of Budha Gupta, the Gupta genealogy is as follows:

|
Mahārāja Śrī Gupta
|
son Mahārāja Śrī Ghaṭotkacha
|
son Mahārājādhirāja Śrī Chandra Gupta I
m. Mahādevī Kumāradevī
|
son Lichchhavi-dauhitra Mahārājādhirāja
Samudra Gupa *m*. Dattadevī
|
Apratiratha—Paramabhāgavata—
Mahārājādhirāja—Śrī—Chandra Gupta II
m. Mahādevī Dhruvadevī
|
son Mahārājādhirāja—Śrī—Kumāra Gupta (I)
m. Mahādevī Anantadevī
|
son Mahārājādhirāja—Śrī—Pūru Gupta
m. Mahādevī Chandradevī
|
son Paramabhāgavata Mahārājādhirāja
Śrī Budha Gupta

The only point to be settled about this genealogy is the succession after Budha Gupta. It may be solved by a study of three relevant inscriptions, viz., those on the Sarnath Buddha Stone Image of A.D. 473 and the inscriptions on the Bhitarī and Nālandā seals. It is possible to take the Kumāra Gupta of the Sarnath inscription to be different from the Kumāra Gupta of the seal without any violence to history or chronology, and to treat the Kumāra Gupta of the seal to be Kumāra Gupta III. In that case, the genealogy will stand as follows:

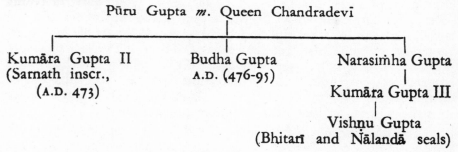

Pūru Gupta *m*. Queen Chandradevī

Kumāra Gupta II (Sarnath inscr., (A.D. 473)

Budha Gupta A.D. (476-95)

Narasiṁha Gupta
→ Kumāra Gupta III
→ Vishṇu Gupta (Bhitarī and Nālandā seals)

The Nālandā seal of Budha Gupta makes him definitely the son of Pūru Gupta, while that of Narasiṁha Gupta also makes him a son of Pūru Gupta and of queen Chandradevī.

There is again a seal of Kumāra Gupta III who is the son of Narsiṁha Gupta and of Mahādevī-Śrī-Mitradevī.

The genealogy as suggested above obviates the location of too many kings between the year A.D. 467, the last known date of Skanda Gupta and 476, the earliest known date of Budha Gupta. According to the prevailing view, Pūru Gupta, Narasiṁha Gupta, Kumāra Gupta II and Vishṇu Gupta, came one after the other within the short space of 9 years. The year A.D. 476, must have seen Vishṇu Gupta too young to be king. He must have been then only a child. The point may be argued thus: Skanda Gupta who became king in A.D. 455 had to fight many a battle against powerful enemies and could not have been very old at the time. If we take him then to be 55, he should have been born in A.D. 400 and Pūru Gupta born a little later, say, A.D. 403. Vishṇu Gupta, as his great grandson, could not have been born earlier than A.D. 475 and was, therefore, too young for the throne when it fell vacant after Kumāra Gupta II. For this reason the succession should be taken as given above so as to make the Kumāra Gupta of Sarnath inscription as Kumāra Gupta II and succeeding Pūru Gupta in A.D. 473, while he in turn was succeeded by his brother, Budha Gupta, who reigned between A.D. 476 and 495. If Narasiṁha Gupta came after Budha Gupta, he would be placed in time for contact and conflict with the Hūṇas, as stated by Yuan-chwang.

The Nālandā seal, besides helping towards the identification of Narasiṁha Gupta Bālāditya of the inscriptions and coins with king Bālāditya mentioned by Yuan-chwang, also helps us towards the historicity of another king mentioned by him as the last of the series, viz., Vajra. He may be identified with king Vainya Gupta mentioned in the inscription on a seal found at Nālandā and also on a copper-plate found at Gunaighar in the district of Tipperah. The inscription on the seal describes him as *Śrī-Paramabhāgavato-Mahārājādhirāja-Śrī-Vainya Guptaḥ*, while that on the copper-plate mentions the year 188=A.D. 508 as a date of his reign. The date helps his location in Gupta history. It was a time when northern India and the Gupta empire were fighting the aggression of the Hūṇas until they were overcome by Yaśodharman of Malwa. The fact probably was that Gupta supremacy was gradually retreating from the west towards eastern India held by the Gupta kings of Magadha and of Bengal as separate ruling families. Mahārājādhirāja Vainya Gupta must have been an independent Gupta king of Bengal.

The identification of Vainya with Vajra is supported by deriving the word *Vainya* from *Vena*. Vainya is a patronymic from *Vena* which is a name of Indra who is also known for his *Vajra* or thunderbolt. Therefore, *Vajra* may be taken to be the same as *Vainya*.

Summary. To sum up the position regarding the perplexing problem of succession after Pūru Gupta : the succession is differently stated in different inscriptions. Thus Pūru Gupta is succeeded by (1) Narasiṁha Gupta according to Bhitarī Seal inscription of Kumāra Gupta III and the Nālandā Seal inscription of Vishṇu Gupta ; (2) Budha Gupta according to Nālandā Seal inscription and (3) Kumāra Gupta II on the basis of his date of A.D. 473 as given in the Sarnath Buddha Stone Image inscription. These differences among the inscriptions are due to the fact that they only mention the successor but *not* the *immediate* successor of the previous king. The differences may be reconciled and the true genealogy constructed in the light of the data given in two *dated* inscriptions, viz., the Sarnath Buddha Stone Image inscriptions of Kumāra Gupta and of Budha Gupta. The first mentions A.D. 473 as the date of Kumāra Gupta who must, therefore, be taken as Kumāra Gupta II and the second mentions A.D. 476 as the date of Budha Gupta. These two dates thus point to the irresistible conclusion that Pūru Gupta was immediately succeeded in A.D. 473 by Kumāra Gupta II after a short reign of 4 years from A.D. 467, the last date of his immediate predecessor, Skanda Gupta, while Kumāra Gupta II in his turn was immediately succeeded after a shorter reign of only 3 years by Budha Gupta in A.D. 476.[1]

1. I owe the genealogy and succession presented here to the suggestions first made by Mr. A. Ghosh, M.A. of the Archaeological Department in the *I.H.Q.*, Vol. XIX, pp. 119-125.

CHAPTER X

KUMĀRA GUPTA II KRAMĀDITYA

(*c.* A.D. 473-476)

Kumāra Gupta II. As has been indicated above, Kumāra Gupta II was the immediate successor of Pūru Gupta. The date of his accession is given in the Sarnath Buddha Stone Image inscription which records the date, Gupta year 154 (*Varshaśate Guptānāṁ sachatuḥ pañchāśaduttare*), 'when Kumāra Gupta was protecting the earth (*bhūmiṁ rakshati Kumāragupte*)'.

Inscription. This inscription records the only event known in the reign of Kumāra Gupta II. It records that the Buddhist ascetic (*yati*) named Abhayamitra prompted by a mind disciplined (*āvarjjita*) by devotion caused to be constructed an image (*pratimā*), showing unparalleled workmanship (*aparā*), of the teacher (*śāstā*) of whom there is no equal in merits (*guṇaiḥ apratimasya*), for purposes of worship *pūjārthaṁ*). 'Let this donor who is the abode of virtue (*satvakāya*), by this religious merit thus acquired, obtain, along with his mother, father, preceptor, and ancestors, release from earthly desire and existence, "a consummation devoutly to be wished for" (*abhimatam*)'.

The appreciation of the artistic quality attributed to the sculptor in the inscription is amply borne out by a sight of the sculpture showing one of the best portraits of the Buddha in stone. The location of the sculpture is also very appropriate at a place like Sarnath as a centre of Buddhism.

Coins. The other point to be noticed about Kumāra Gupta II is his coinage. Some eighteen gold coins of his are in the British Museum and two in the Indian Museum. The coins are of the Archer type showing on *Obv.* 'King nimbate, standing l., holding bow in l. hand and arrow in r. Garuḍa standard on l., *Ku* with crescent above beneath l. arm;' and on *Rev.* 'Goddess (Lakshmī), nimbate, seated facing on lotus, holding fillet in r. hand and lotus in l., symbol on l.'

On r. occurs the legend *Kramādityaḥ*.

There are some coins of ruder fabric, showing on *Obv.* the word *go* or the word *jā* between king's feet and the legend around to the following effect: *Mahārājādhirāja-Śrī-Kumāragupta-Kramādityaḥ*.

The *Rev.* bears the legend *Śrī-Kramādityaḥ*.

These coin-legends testify to the status of Kumāra Gupta II as a regular emperor of the Gupta dynasty.

Imperial Status. His imperial status is further borne out by the Khoh Copper-plate inscription of Parivrājaka Mahārāja Hastin issued in the Gupta year 156 (*shatpañchāsottarābdaśate*) = A.D. 475 which belongs to the reign of Kumāra Gupta II, the time when, as stated in the inscription, 'the Gupta kings were in the enjoyment of sovereignty' (*Gupta-nṛipa-rājya-bhuktam*). This expression shows that Hastin was his feudatory. Indeed, he was one of his most important feudatories who 'gave away thousands of cows, elephants, horses, and gold coins, and also many lands, as a religious devotee (*bhakta*) and achieved victories in many hundreds of battles.'

Grant of Land. The inscription records the gift of a village named Vasuntarashaṇḍika made to a Brahmin named Gopasvāmin of Vājasaneya-Mādhyandina *Sākhā* and Kautsa *Gotra* and to a few others named with him. The village had its boundaries fixed by trenches dug on all sides (*samantād garttāḥ*) and the gift carried with it the incomes derived from taxes known as *udraṅga*, the share of the produce due to the State, and *uparikara*, tax levied on cultivators who do not own the land they cultivate, together with the privilege that it should not be visited by the irregular or regular troops so as to be free from their exactions (*a-chāṭa-bhaṭa-prāveśya*). These exactions proved to be burdensome taxation on the villagers in the form of forced contributions of money or provisions for the troops on march through the villages. Such inroads of the military on the rural civil population of the countryside with the financial levies they meant were thus not permitted in a village dedicated to a religious purpose. The village was also protected against disturbances (*vyāghāta*) from the royal family and its dependents (*pādapiṇḍopajīvī*). The grant, however, did not carry with it the income derived from fines imposed on thieves (*chora-varjjam* = *chora-daṇḍa-varjjaṁ* occurring in the Khoh grant of Mahārāja Jayanātha of the year 177). The *chowkidari* tax or police cess was an integral part of the revenue-resources of the entire kingdom whose main function was the maintenance of its Law and Order and so the revenue derived from crimes could not be alienated.

The inscription describes Hastin himself as a sovereign who had feudatories of his own (*pāda-piṇḍopajīvinaḥ*), 'subsisting on homage to the royal feet.'

Officers. The inscription further mentions the interesting detail that this grant or charter (*śāsana*) was written or engraved (*likhita*) by Sūryadatta, a descendant of an *amātya* or counsellor, and of a *Bhogika*, the officer in charge of a division of a province or *bhukti*. It also mentions an officer called *Dūtaka* whose duty was that of a messenger to carry the king's sanction and order to the local officials who would then have the grant or charter drawn up and delivered to the grantee.

Mandasor Inscription. Another event of the reign of Kumāra Gupta II is indicated in the Mandasor inscription (No. 18 of Fleet) stating, as already noticed, how a Sun-temple which was built by a guild of silk-weavers, who were immigrants from Lāta Vishaya, at the city of Daśapura under the popular rule of Bandhuvarman in Mālava year 493=A.D. 436, was renovated by the same guild in the year 529=A.D. 472. The repair of the temple thus took place in the reign of Kumāra Gupta II. As stated in the inscription, it was the time 'when Kumāra Gupta was ruling over the earth' (*Kumāragupte pṛithivīṁ praśāsati*).

The inscription thus also testifies to the imperial status of Kumāra Gupta II whose paramount sovereignty was recognized in Malwa and whose court was adorned by the great poet, Vatsabhaṭṭi, the author of this inscription which is a masterpiece of literary composition.

CHAPTER XI

BUDHA GUPTA

(*c.* A.D 476-495)

Budha Gupta. There are several inscriptions which are valuable sources of the history of Budha Gupta's reign.

Sarnath Inscriptions. Two inscriptions appear with practically the same text on two images in stone of the Buddha found at Sārnāth. The first bears the date Gupta year 154=A.D. 473 and mentions Kumāra Gupta (II) as then reigning (*bhūmiṁ rakshati Kumāragupte*), while the latter mentions the date Gupta year 157 (*Guptānāṁ samatikkrānte sapta-paṁchāśaduttare śate*, 'when of the Guptas, 100 years increased by 57 had passed away') and Budha Gupta as 'ruling the earth, (*pṛithivīṁ Budhagupte praśāsati*). The Gupta year 157=A.D. 476.

Images of the Buddha. The first of these images is that of standing Buddha with two attendant *chaurī*-bearing figures (probably Bodhisattvas), placed on pedestal bearing the inscription, and two kneeling figures, one of which is that of a monk and the other holds a censer.

The second image is that of the Buddha seated in *abhayamudrā*.

Both the images show fine workmanship and justify their description in the text of the inscription stating that the *Śākya-bhikshu* Abhayamitra had caused to be made this divine (*divya*) image (*pratimā*) of the Buddha, 'with the gods as his disciples or sons' (*Devaputravato*), with uplifted hand (*uddhasta*) (as a symbol of *abhayamudrā*), with umbrella (*sachhatra*), and seated cross-legged in contemplation (*padmāsana*), and 'decorated with all the art of the sculptor.' The gift of this statue, and also of the earlier one bearing the inscription of the time of previous king, Kumāra Gupta II, was made by the Buddhist monk named Abhayamitra who records his noble prayer that whatever religious merit (*puṇya*) he may have earned (*bhṛitam*) by this sacred undertaking is offered by him to his mother, father, preceptor, ancestors (*pūrviḥ*) and all his fellowmen (*lokasya*), as an aid to their attainment of final beatitude (*samāptaye*) (*Arch. S. Report*, 1914-15, pp. 99, 125).

It will thus appear from these inscribed statues that Sarnath or Benares continued to be an important place in the Gupta empire under Budha Gupta, as it was in the reign of his predecessor.

Damodarpur No. 2 Copper-Plate Inscription. The next inscription of the time of Budha Gupta is that found on a copper-plate at Damodarpur, a village in Dinajpur district, and dated in the Gupta year 163 = A.D. 482 when "*Paramadaivata* ('of resplendent glory'), *Paramabhaṭṭāraka* ('His Most Worshipful Majesty'), *Mahārājādhirāja* ('the Lord of Lords'), *Śrī* ('His Majesty of abounding wealth and prosperity') Budhagupta was the ruler of the earth (*pṛithivīpati.*)"

Administrative Details. This inscription, like the inscriptions on the other two Damodarpur Copper-plates of the time of Kumāra Gupta I, records a grant of land, and repeats most of the details and words of the first two plates.

As has been already noticed, these inscriptions throw great light upon the system of local government in the Gupta empire. They show how the district magistrate (*Vishayapati*) was helped in his administration (*saṁvyavaharati*) by an Advisory Council of four members representative of the different interests of the locality, viz., (1) *Nagaraśreshṭhī*, 'the President of the Chambers of Commerce or Bankers in the city', whose name was Dhṛitipāla; (2) *Prathama-kulika*, 'the foreman of the Guild of Artisans', who is named Dhṛitimitra; (3) *Sārthavāha*, who represented the merchants of the city and is named Bandhumitra; and (4) *Prathama-kāyastha* who was the chief secretary to the administrative council, whose name in the present case is Śāmbapāla.

As has been already stated, these inscriptions are especially concerned with the administrative machinery and procedure prescribed for grants of land for public purposes, charitable or religious. The machinery is first set in motion by the application of a private person for grant of such land; but the alienation of such land by the State should not mean any loss of revenue to it. Accordingly, such land is required to be (a) *aprada*, that which is not yet settled, (b) *aprahata*, that which is not yet ploughed or cultivated, and (c) *khilakshetra* which is uncultivated land. It may be noted that in the *Rigveda* separate plots are called *kshetras* and they are separated from one another by what are called *khilyas* or *khilas*. The *khila* was no man's land, the grass-land, separating one plot from another, and used as village common for purposes of pasture for cattle.

In the present case, the applicant for the grant of land was a Brahmin named Kārpaṭika, and the public purpose for which he wanted the grant is stated to be facilities for the performance of the *agnihotra* rites (*agnihotropayogāya*).

It may be noted that though the land to be granted was not cultivated land yielding income, but uncultivated waste land, yet the State insisted on a price being paid for it. The customary price stated in the inscription is at the rate of 3 *dīnāras* for each *kulyavāpa*. The term *kulyavāpa* means that amount of land on which one *kulya* of seeds could be sown, one *kulya* weighing 8 *droṇas*.

Lastly, the grant by government of land thus applied for depended upon the recommendation of the local record-keepers called *Pustapālas*. These formed a Committee of three who are named Ṛishidatta, Jayanandin, and Vibhudatta. Perhaps to prevent corruption, one record-keeper was not depended upon for such transactions.

The purpose of the grant of land in the inscription on Plate 2 is stated to be the performance of the five daily sacrifices (*Pañchamahāyajña-pravartana*).

Damodarpur No. 3 Copper-Plate Inscription. In the Budha Gupta inscription on Plate 3 which is dated Gupta year 163 = A.D. 482, some additional details of administration are given.

Brahmadatta is named as emperor Budha Gupta's Provincial Governor called *Uparika-mahārāja*.

It also refers to the Council of non-officials associated with local administration, made up of four classes of members: (1) the village elders called *Mahattaras*; (2) the *Ashṭakulādhikaraṇas* who were officers in charge of groups of eight households in the locality; (3) the heads of villages (*Grāmikas*); and (4) the householders (*Kuṭumbinaḥ*).

In the case of this inscription, the application for grant of land is made by a person named Nābhaka belonging to the village called Chaṇḍagrāma. The purpose stated in the application is that he wished to settle in the village some good Brahmins (*ārya*) for the *puṇya* of his parents. On the receipt of this application, the local Advisory Council sent it on from its official headquarters named Palāśavṛindaka, which was the centre of a Union of villages, for its consideration by the leading men of the village among its Brahmins, citizens (*akshudra-prakṛiti*, lit., important subjects) and householders. These then asked the record-keeper named Patradāsa to report on the application. On Patradāsa reporting that the application was a proper one (*yuktaṁ*) and conformed to the prevailing conditions and customs relating to sale (*vikraya-maryādā*), the land was inspected (*pratyavekshya*) by the above village Council who then got it severed (*apaviñchhya*) or separated from other plots by the measurement of 8×9 reeds (*ashṭaka-navaka-nalābhyām*).

Damodarpur No. 4 Copper-Plate Inscription. There is another inscription found on Plate No. 4 at Damodarpur which is not dated but is referred to the reign of Budha Gupta. It states that the Provincial Governor of Puṇḍravardhana-*bhukti* under Budha Gupta was the *Uparika-Mahārāja* Jayadatta. Jayadatta appointed Śaṇḍaka as the officer in charge of the district (*Vishya*) named Koṭivarsha, the District Office being called *Adhishṭhāna*. The Advisory Council for the district then included (1) Ṛibhupāla as *Nagaraśreshṭhī*, (2) Vasumitra as *Sārthavāha*, (3) Varadatta as *Prathama-kulika*, and (4) Viprapāla as *Prathama-kāyastha*.

The inscription locates village Doṇagrāma where lands were granted on Himavachchhikara i.e. 'on Himalayan Peaks'. The same village Doṇagrāma is also mentioned in the earlier Damodarpur record of year 124=A.D. 443 of the time of Kumāra Gupta I.

Again, the later Damodarpur record of year 224=A.D. 543 refers to the temple (*Devakula*) of God Śvetavarāhasvāmī as located in a forest (*araṇya*) and calling for repairs for which it records provision made by a further grant of land and also for worship of the Deity by supply of its materials such as flowers, incense, lamp, and oblations.

The difficulty arises as to the exact location of these Temples. The lands that were granted for them may be taken to have been situated in the neighbourhood of Damodarpur, a village in the Balurghat Sub-division of Dinajpur district. But the Temples concerned are stated to be on the Himalayas.

The *Brahma Purāṇa* (Ch. 219, 229) mentions Kokāmukha-Tīrtha, the river Kokā, and the Varāha-Vishṇu Temple, as being located on the Himalayas, without mentioning the exact place of their location.

The *Varāha Purāṇa* (Ch. 140) mentions Kokāmukha-Tīrtha and its 20 sacred spots and their association with the two rivers, Kokā and Kauśikī, and their confluence. Kauśikī may be taken to be modern Kuśī flowing from Nepal through Purnea district. A Varāha (or Kokāmukha)-Kshetra is a known place of pilgrimage in Nepal, together with the rivers, Sun, Kuśī, and Kokā-Kola (from *Kulyā*, a small stream).

The holy places of Nepal have always attracted pilgrims from Bihar and Bengal. At the time of Budha Gupta, pilgrims from North Bengal used to visit the Varāha (Kokāmukha) Kshetra of Nepal. One such pilgrim was Ṛibhupāla who carried home his devotion to God Kokāmukha Varāha by constructing at his native place near Damodarpur two Temples where were installed the images of Gods Śvetavarāha and Kokāmukha in imitation of their original (*ādya*) shrines in distant Nepal. Thus Ṛibhupāla was able to provide for worship at these Temples by his gift of lands for it, while, about half a century later, one Amṛitadeva added to the endowment of the Śvetavarāha Temple by making further grants of land to it. It may be noted that the last epigraphic record locates the Temple in a forest (*araṇya*) of the District (*Vishaya*) of Koṭivarsha, and not on the Himalayas.

It is on the basis of the above assumptions that we can correctly locate the Temples at a place close to the lands granted to them for their maintenance [Dr. D. C. Sircar in *IHQ*, XXI, 56].

Procedure for Land-Grant. In the present case, the applicant for grant of land is Ṛibhupāla himself. He states in his application: 'In Doṇgā-*grāma* in Himavachchhikara (*lit.* the summit of the Himalaya), 4 *kulyavāpas* of *apradā* land were formerly given by me to Kokāmukha-svāmin and 7 *kulyavāpas* to Śvetavarāha-svāmin, in the hope of benefit to myself (and) for the sake of increasing religious merit. Now in the neighbourhood of these cultivated lands, I wish to build two temples and their two store-rooms for those supreme gods Kokāmukha-svāmin and Śvetavarāha-svāmin (and?) one *Nāmaliṅgaṁ* (?).'

As usual, the application was referred for report to a Committee of three *Pustapālas* named Vishṇudatta, Vijayanandin, and Sthāṇunandin, who thus reported: 'It is a fact that by him were given in *Himavachchhikara* 11 *kulyavāpas* of *apradā* lands to Kokāmukha-svāmin and Śvetavarāha-svāmin, and so the application has been properly made (by him) for *vāstu* land to be given to him in the neighbourhood of those cultivated lands for the purpose of building temples and store-rooms.'

It may be noticed that this inscription gives a new detail. It records an application not merely for land for cultivation but also land for building (*vāstu*).

Paharpur Copper-Plate Inscription. Another inscription of the time of Budha Gupta is the Paharpur Copper-Plate inscription dated G.E. 159 = A.D. 479. It may be noted that Paharpur is situated in the eastern part of the Province of Puṇḍravardhana and thus shows the eastern limits of the Gupta empire.

A Brahmin's Gift to a Jaina Vihāra. The Government order for grant of land was issued by the *Āyuktakas* of Puṇḍravardhana jointly with the city Municipal Council (*Adhishṭhāna-adhikaraṇa*) headed by (*puroga*) the Mayor of the city (*Ārya-nagaraśreshṭhī*).

This inscription brings to light new units of settlement and administration, arranged in the following ascending order: (1) *Grāma*, (2) *Pārśvd*, (3) *Maṇḍala* and (4) *Vīthī* (part of a district or *Vishaya*).

The proprietory right to a village is indicated by the technical term *Prāveśya* (right to revenue).

The government order on the subject is communicated as usual to the Village Council consisting of the elders among Brahmins (*Brāhmaṇottaras*), leading villagers (*Mahattaras*), and householders (*Kuṭumbinaḥ*).

The applicants for land were husband and wife, and Brahmins.

They make the donation in favour of a Jaina Vihāra belonging to the *Pañchastūpa* Sect (*Nikāya*) founded by the Nigrantha Śramaṇāchārya Guhanandi of Benares. This shows the religious toleration of the times. The gift was made for provision of scent, incense, flowers, and light for worship of the divine Arhats. This indicates that this Jaina sect might have been the Śvetāmbaras, and not the Digambaras who do not permit worship with flowers bringing in insects which may be killed.

Procedure. The inscription describes the usual procedure laid down for such land-transactions. The application is made to both the district officers and city Municipal Council who refer it to the Board of *Pustapālas* or record-keepers consisting of one head record-keeper (*Prathama Pustapāla*) and at least five others named.

It will appear that the Faridpur and Damodarpur grants also mention more than one but less than five record-keepers. The record-keepers, after making necessary inquiries, recommend the transaction as bringing some revenue to the State (*arthopachaya*).

Akshaya-Nīvī-dharma. The administrative authorities then sanction (*avadhāraṇa*) the transfer of land and ask the elders of the respective villages to make out the (*apaviñchhya*) boundaries of the lands thus granted. The gift was to conform to the Code called *Akshaya-nīvī-dharma*, implying that the land given was to be inalienable and irrevocable.

The applicants wanted 1½ *kulyavāpas* of land distributed among four villages for the double purpose of the provision of aforesaid worship and construction of a resting-place for the *Vihāra* (*talavāṭaka*).

Khila- and Vāstu-Lands. This inscription does not differentiate between the rates for two classes of land, *khila* and *vāstu*. But the land required for *vāstu* or building was naturally less in quantity, viz., only 1½ *droṇavāpas* in the present case. More land was needed if it was for cultivation the produce from which was to meet the cost of worship. A larger area of land was required for cultivation than for building.

The total quantity of 1½ *kulyavāpas* of land was made up of the four following plots located at four villages, viz., 1½ *droṇavāpas* of *vāstu* land + 4 *droṇavāpas* in one village + 4 *droṇavāpas* in another village + 2½ *droṇavāpas* in the fourth village = total 12 *droṇavāpas* equated in the inscription with 1½ *kulyavāpas* as stated above. This shows that quantitatively 1 *kulyavāpa* = 8 *droṇavāpas*.

The price paid for the total 1½ *kulyavāpas* = 3 *dīnāras* at the rate of 2 *dīnāras* for 1 *kulyavāpa*.

Their Prices. Grants of land are described in detail in most of the Bengal Copper-plate inscriptions such as those of Dhānāi-daha, Damodarpur, Faridpur or Ghugrāhāṭi. The rate of land is 3 *dīnāras* per *kulyavāpa* in Damodarpur and 4 in Faridpur as against 2 of the present grant. No. 2 Damodarpur, for instance, mentions 2 *dīnāras* being paid for 5 *droṇavāpas=roughly 2/3 kulyavāpa*, so that the rate is 3 *dīnāras* for a *kulyavāpa*. Apparently, land was cheaper at Paharpur.

Eran Inscription. To the reign of Budha Gupta also belongs an inscription on Eran Stone Pillar bearing the date G.E. 165=A.D. 484. This inscription refers to Mahārāja Suraśmichandra as the feudatory of Budha Gupta and administering (*pālayati*) the country lying between the river Kālindī or Jumna and the Narmadā. It records the erection of a pillar called a *dhvaja-stambha* or flag-staff of God Vishṇu under the name Janārdana by a Mahārāja named Māṭṛi Vishṇu and his younger brother, Dhanya Vishṇu.

Nandapur Copper-Plate Inscription. Another inscription of the time of Budha Gupta is that of Nandapur Copper-plate dated Gupta year 169=A.D. 488. Nandapur is a village in the district of Monghyr. Unfortunately, the inscription does not make any reference to the Gupta emperor of the time. The seal attached to the plate might have borne the name which, however, is worn out. Its script, and its contents and wording establish its affinity with the other inscriptions associated with northern Bengal.

Details of Land-transaction. The details and data which the inscription records regarding the land-transactions of the time are worth noting, although they repeat most of those given in other inscriptions of North Bengal.

A district officer (*Vishayapati*) here applies to his fellow-officers (*Ayuktakas*) for land. The *Āyuktakas* then intimate and write (*bodhayanti likhanti cha*) to the District Office (*Adhikaraṇa*) as well as to the Brahmins, the chief officers and others (*uttarānsaṁvya-vahāryādi*) and also householders, to that effect. The applicant wants to buy 4 *kulyavāpas* of fallow land (*khila-kshetra*) and give it to a Brahmin/belonging to an *Agrahāra of* Nanda-*vīthī* (sub-division of a district) to enable him to perform the five Great Sacrifices (*Bali*, *Charu*, *Vaiśvadeva*, *Agnihotra*, and *Atithi*) (*pañcha-Mahāyajña-pravarttanāya*).

The sale was effected according to the established system of the district (*Vishaya*) by which land that was lying fallow (*khila*), devoid of vegetation (*astamba*), and not yielding any revenue to the State (*samudayabāhya*), might be sold provided it was for purposes of a permanent endowment (*akshaya-nīvyāḥ*), and the customary price was paid at the rate of 2 *dīnāras* for, *kulyavāpa* of such land.

The local Board of Record-keepers (*Pustapālas*) was then to ascertain (*avadhṛitam*) by enquiry (*avadhāraṇā*) that the transaction conformed to the above conditions.

And then the last consideration was that there would be no loss of revenue to the Crown from the sale of such revenue-free (*utprati-kara*) fallow land but, on the contrary, some gain to the king in the shape of *dharma*.

Therefore the order was : *Tad-dīyatāmiti*.

The order ran thus : 'You should give away the plot situated in an area where it may not affect the cultivation of settled peasants (*kuṭumbināṁ karshaṇāvirodhi-sthāne*), after measuring it by the standard unit of 8×8 reeds (*nala*), and then demarcate (*apaviñ-chchhya*) it by permanent marks of ash, charcoal, etc. (*tushāṅgārādi-chihnaiḥ*).

Thus the last condition of the grant was that it should not cause loss to the local agriculturists by effecting any change in the areas of the plots settled on them. The land granted must be in an isolated area of waste-land in the village, and must not be made up by piecing together slices taken from the settled lands already under cultivation.

Feudatories. There are some inscriptions issued by the feudatories of emperor Budha Gupta. The Parivrājaka Mahārāja Hastin, for instance, issued two inscriptions on copper-plates found at a village Khoh in modern Nagod State and dated G.E. 156=A.D. 476 and G.E. 163=A.D. 482. Of these, the first may be dated to A.D. 475, in which case it belongs to the reign of the previous king, Kumāra Gupta II. Both these inscriptions refer to the enjoyment of sovereignty by the Gupta kings (*Gupta-nṛipa-rājyabhuktau*). They both refer to the high status of Hastin who was practically the ruler of his territory, described 'as the victor in many hundreds of battles, and the giver of thousands of cows, elephants, horses, and gold pieces, and also of many lands.'

The second inscription records a grant made by him of an *agra-hāra* situated in a *paṭṭa* with the usual immunities from the taxes *udraṅga* and *uparikara*, and freedom from molestation by the military.

The inscription is interesting for its social data showing the strength of Brahmanism in those days. The following Brahmin *gotras* are mentioned: *Bharadvāja*, *Kautsa*, *Bhārgava*, *Vāsula*; and the following Vedic *Śakhās*, *Vājasaneya* and *Kaṭha*.

Political History. These inscriptions also throw light upon the political history of the reign of Budha Gupta. They point to the indisputable fact that Puṇḍravardhana or northern Bengal was an integral part of the Gupta empire under Budha Gupta. Budha Gupta's authority was also acknowledged in the region of Benares, as proved by the Sārnāth Buddha Image inscriptions. The Eran Stone Pillar inscription shows that the empire included the kingdom of Malwa or rather the extensive tract of land between the Kālindī and the Narmadā. It may be assumed that the position of Mahārāja Suraśmichandra, as the Governor of this region, was similar to that of the *Uparika-Mahārājas*, Brahmadatta, and Jayadatta, the Governors of the province of Puṇḍravardhana, while the position of the *Āyuktaka* Śaṇḍaka, in charge of the district or *Vishaya* of Koṭivarsha, is comparable to that of Mahārāja Matṛi Vishṇu as *Vishayapati* under the provincial Governor Suraśmichandra. This fact is furtherborne out by the Eran Stone Boar inscription of Toramāṇa's time (No. 36 of Fleet) stating that in the first year of that Hūṇa chief's rule in the portion of Āryavārta (Malwa), Dhanya Vishṇu, younger brother of Matṛi Vishṇu, who was then not living (*svargagata*), built a temple in which was enshrined the Boar-incarnation of Vishṇu, 'in his own *Vishaya* of Airikiṇi'. It thus stands to reason that Dhanya Vishṇu's elder brother Matṛi Vishṇu was the officer-in-charge of the *Vishaya* of Airikiṇi when Suraśmichandra was Budha Gupta's Governor in Malwa and the adjoining tracts. From these facts it is thus clear that the Gupta empire under Budha Gupta did not at all shrink in size, but extended from Malwa to northern Bengal, from the Kālindī to the Gaṅgā.

It will thus appear that the empire under Budha Gupta recovered its position and prestige after the dark days following the death of Skanda Gupta.

Budha Gupta issued silver coinage of the Central India type on which his own name has been inscribed together with his title *Avanipati*. The Bharsar hoard of coins points to a king called Prakāśāditya coming after Skanda Gupta. The *Mañju-Śrī-Mūla-Kalpa* states that *Śrīmān U* succeeded Kumāra Gupta II. It is interesting to note that the same letter *U* is to be found below the king's image on the coins of Prakāśāditya. Therefore, it may be concluded that Śrīman *U*, Prakāśāditya, and Budha Gupta are one and the same person.

It is also to be noted that of the three specimens of Budha Gupta's coins of the Central India type kept at the British Museum, one bears the date G.E. 175=A.D. 494, the last known date of Budha Gupta.

CHAPTER XII

NARASIMHA GUPTA BĀLĀDITYA

Narasimha Gupta. As has been already shown, the Bhitarī and Nālandā Seal inscriptions of Kumāra Gupta III make it quite clear that Narasiṁha Gupta must be taken as the successor of Budha Gupta. That he had from his predecessor the legacy of a large empire and paramount sovereignty is indicated in the literary text, *Ārya-Mañju-Śrī-Mūla-Kalpa*. It describes the empire of Bālāditya as *nissapatnam* and *akaṇṭakam*, an empire free from rivals and enemies. The larger number and heavier types of gold coins prove the truth of this statement.

His Coins. All his coins are of the Archer type. The obverse shows: 'King nimbate, standing l., wearing waist-cloth with long sash and jewellery, holding bow in l., and arrow in r. hand. Garuḍa standard on l.' It also shows the word *Nara* beneath left arm and an incomplete legend ending with *jayati Narasiṁhaguptaḥ*.

The *Rev.* shows: 'Goddess (Lakshmī) mimbate, seated facing on lotus, holding fillet and lotus.' It also bears the legend '*Bālādityaḥ*'.

Hūṇa Invasions. It was not, however, for long that his empire remained *akaṇṭaka*. Very soon it had a difficult *kaṇṭaka* or thorn on its side. He was not fated to have any smooth sailing in the troublous waters created by the successive waves of Hūṇa onslaught on the empire. It may be useful at this stage to sum up the available evidence in regard to this fateful struggle between the Gupta empire and the Hūṇas. We have already seen from the first Eran Pillar inscription of Budha Gupta dated A.D. 484 that the region of eastern Malwa was under the suzerainty of Budha Gupta who had, as his feudatories, the two brothers, Matṛi Vishṇu and Dhanya Vishṇu. There is a second inscription of Eran which records the building of a temple enshrining the *Varāha* (Boar) incarnation of Vishṇu. The figure of the Boar is decorated with sculptures representing *ṛishis* and saints clinging to its mane and bristles, and the Earth as a woman hanging on to its right tusk. The breast of the Boar bears an inscription stating that the temple was constructed by Dhanya Vishṇu (brother of the deceased Matṛi Vishṇu of the first inscription) in the first year of the reign of Toramāṇa.

Bhānu Gupta. Over and above this, we have to consider the light thrown upon the events of the times by the Eran Stone Pillar inscription of A.D. 510. It mentions a king named Bhānu Gupta, 'the bravest on earth (*jayati pravīro*), a mighty king (*rājā mahān*), the equal of Pārtha (*Pārtha-samo*), who was followed by a valiant chief named Goparāja who fell fighting in a very famous battle (*yuddhaṁ sumahat prakāśaṁ*) and was followed to death by his devoted wife.'

His Status. It is to be noted that this inscription calls Bhānu Gupta merely as a *Rājā* and does not apply to him even the title *Mahārāja*, nor the higher imperial title of *Mahārājadhirāja*, and the like. Therefore, it stands to reason that the proper way to locate Bhānu Gupta in Gupta history would be to treat him as the Governor of Malwa under emperor Narasiṁha Gupta in my scheme of Gupta genealogy. The position, therefore, would be that it was left to the ruler (*Rājā*) of Malwa as the western outpost of the Gupta empire to defend it against the incursions of the Hūṇas, the brunt of whose attack fell upon it. In that defence, Bhānu Gupta's military lieutenant, Goparaja, famous for his prowess (*vikhyāta-paurusha*) fell fighting, leaving the way clear for the further advance of the Hūṇas towards Magadha. Bhānu Gupta is not heard of after he lost this fateful battle.

Toramāṇa. It will thus appear that Toramāṇa was leading the Hūṇas and achieved victory over the provincial Gupta Chief, Bhānu Gupta, and his feudatory, Goparāja, in the battle of Eran in A.D. 510, after which year dates Toramāṇa's supremacy in Malwa. Thus the Gupta empire lost Malwa after Budha Gupta. Therefore, the Eran Boar Image inscription dated in the first year of Toramāṇa must be later than A.D. 510.

Literary Evidence. Some light is thrown on the turmoil of the times by the literary work named *Mañju-Śrī-Mūla-Kalpa*. It states that 'after the death of Budha Gupta, two kings in the Gupta line were crowned, one in Magadha and another in Gauḍa.' The Gupta king crowned in Magadha must refer to Narasiṁha Gupta Bālāditya. The work further states that after Bhānu Gupta had lost Malwa, Toramāṇa carried on his expedition up to Magadha and compelled Bālāditya to retreat to Bengal. He also crowned one Prakaṭāditya as king at Benares in place of the absconding Gupta emperor. Toramāṇa, however, died at Benares while returning westward. This Prakaṭāditya is also stated to have been a son of Bālāditya. This shows that the power of Narasiṁha Gupta was still felt in that region and was not completely extinguished and so it was able to assert itself again.

Mihirakula. After Toramāṇa, the Hūṇas were led by his worthy son Mihirakula whose inscription at Gwalior dated year 15 of his reign, which may be taken to be A.D. 528 (on the assumption that Toramāṇa died in A.D. 513) records that on a hill called Gopa a Sun Temple was constructed by one Mātṛicheṭa. Gopa is a hill in Malwa and so this inscription shows that Mihirakula ruled in Malwa up to at least A.D. 528.

Yaśodharman Vishṇuvardhana. About this time, we have to consider the evidence of two important inscriptions, the Mandasor Stone Pillar inscription of Yaśodharman and another Mandasor inscription associated with two kings, Yaśodharman and Vishṇuvardhana. The first inscription, which is not dated, attributes to Yaśodharman conquest of countries which 'not even the Guptas or Hūṇas could ever conquer, and to whose feet homage was paid even by Mihirakula.' Though not dated, the inscription definitely establishes the fact that it was left to Yaśodharman to achieve the credit of conquering the Hūṇas and winning an empire 'from the Brahmaputra to the Western Ocean and from Himālayas to Mahendragiri.' The second Mandasor inscription which is dated A.D. 532 (M.E. 589) describes Yaśodharman as *Janendra*, the 'Lord of his people', and also refers to another king (*narādhipati*) named Vishṇuvardhana to whom are applied the titles *Rājādhirāja* and *Parameśvara*. The context of the inscription seems to indicate, as supposed by Fleet, that, in spite of his imperial titles, he seems to have acknowledged to some extent the supremacy of Yaśodharman. Yaśodharman is once again described in this inscription as 'achieving victory' (*jayati*), 'plunging into the army of his enemies (*śatru-sainyaṁ vigāhya*), bending down the fame of all heroes (*vīra-kīrti-vinamya*), with his body decorated all over with battle-scars'. It is possible that the two Yaśodharmans of these two inscriptions are one and the same person. The two inscriptions record almost the same exploits. They both repeat the sovereignty of the king over *prāchī* ('eastern India') and north (Kashmīr). Yaśodharman and Vishṇuvardhana may also be taken to be identical from the words, '*sa-eva*', used in the second inscription to introduce Vishṇuvardhana. This inscription also records the construction of a large well by a person named Daksha, a younger brother of Dharmadosha, a Minister of Vishṇuvardhana. This shows that Malwa and western India were placed under the governorship of Dharmadosha by his paramount sovereign Yaśodharman Vishṇuvardhana. It may be noted that this inscription gives an interesting genealogy of this family of Ministers and mentions Bhānu Guptā, the wife of Daksha's grandfather, Ravikīrri. The name Bhānu Guptā points to some connexion between her and king Bhānu Gupta from whom she was removed by one generation, Daksha coming one generation after Bhānu Gupta.

CHAPTER XIII

VAINYA GUPTA

Vainya Gupta. We have thus seen that Imperial Gupta history after Budha Gupta is somewhat uncertain, obscure, and confused. It can be traced only in fragments through names of certain kings associated with it in some of the records of the times. Kings like Bhānu Gupta and Yaśodharman-Vishṇuvardhana and Kumāra Gupta III have to be assigned their places in that history. We have also to add to these names one more name, that of Vainya Gupta. This name is brought to light in the Guṇaigarh Copper-plate inscription found in Comilla in eastern Bengal. This inscription records that Vainya Gupta granted from his victorious camp at Kripura to his feudatory, Mahārāja Rudradatta, some lands in a village in Uttara-maṇḍala for maintaining a Buddhist Vihāra. The reference to a feudatory indicates his somewhat independent status. The inscription further mentions the fact that Vijayasena was his Governor of the *Bhukti* of Uttaramaṇḍala situated in Samataṭa. It also mentions a number of *Kumārāmātyas* serving as his *Vishayapatis*. The inscription is dated G.E. 188=A.D. 507. This inscription throws light on what was happening in eastern India just as the Eran inscriptions do for western India.

His Coins. To add to this epigraphic evidence, there is some amount of numismatic evidence supposed to have a bearing on Vainya Gupta. Three gold coins of the Archer type have been discovered bearing a name read by Allan as *Chandra* but by others as *Vainya* and also the *Āditya*-title *Dvādaśāditya*. The name *Chandra* would need the addition of Chandra Gupta III to the list of Gupta kings, a name not known from any other source, whereas the name *Vainya* is attested by epigraphic evidence.

It is, however, doubtful how far Vainya Gupta, who is associated with eastern Bengal, can be rightly regarded as belonging to the direct line of the imperial Guptas.

His Guṇaigaṛh Inscription. We may now consider in detail the interesting contents of an inscription on a copper-plate found at the aforesaid Guṇaigarh. The village is named in the inscription as *Guṇekāgrahāra*. To the copper-plate is soldered the royal seal bearing the legend '*Mahārāja Śrī Vainya Guptaḥ*.'

The date of the inscription is given both in numerals and words (*Varttamānāshṭāśītyuttara-śaka saṁvatsare*) i.e., current (*varttamāna*) Gupta year 188=A.D. 507. Vainya Gupta thus lived in the time of Bālāditya, the Gupta emperor. The inscription refers to Vainya Gupta's camp of victory described in the usual terms: 'The camp full of big ships (*mahānau*), elephants, and horses, located at Kripura.'

Unlike the Gupta emperors who were worshippers of Vishṇu, Vainya Gupta is described as a worshipper of Mahādeva or Śiva.

It records the gift of 5 plots of land in a village in Uttaramaṇḍala, apparently a province ruled by a Governor, Mahārāja Rudradatta, who is described as a *pādadāsa* or a vassal of Mahārāja Vainya Gupta. At the request of Rudradatta, the royal gift was made in the form of an *agrahāra* in absolute possession (*sarvato bhogena*). It was made in favour of a particular Saṁgha of Mahāyāna Buddhist monks (Śākya-Bhikshu). This Saṁgha was originally established by the great Mahāyāna teacher, Āchārya Śāntideva, and housed in a monastery called *Āśrama-vihāra* which was consecrated to Avalokiteśvara. This *Vihāra* was thus an earlier establishment in that locality. The inscription states that an earlier gift was made by the same Rudradatta to provide the Saṁgha with its necessaries in the shape of clothing (*chīvara*), food (*piṇḍapāta*), beds (*śayana*), seats (*āsana*) and medicines for the sick, and the like, and also the means of its maintenance by repairing all breaches (*khaṇḍa*) and cracks (*phuṭṭa*) in the *Vihāra*.

The inscription also mentions the king's messenger (*Dūtaka*) who was the great frontier king, Mahāsāmanta Mahārāja Śrī Vijayasena. Vijayasena combined in himself several offices such as those of the High Chamberlain (*Mahāpratīhāra*), the Commander of Elephant-Forces (*Mahā-pīlupati*), President of the Board of Five Adhikaraṇas (the chief of five officers of the district) and President of the Board of City-Mayors (*Purapāla-Uparika*).

The *Dūtaka* communicated the royal gift to three *Kumārāmātyas* concerned, showing that his official position was superior to that of the *Kumārāmātya*.

The inscription also gives a high status to its scribe called *Karaṇa Kāyastha* Naradatta who also held the office of the Minister for Peace and War.

The inscription gives a concrete detail regarding the gift of land. It was divided into 5 plots measuring a total of 11 *pāṭakas* of uncultivated (*khila*) lands. It also gives the areas of the plots in terms of *droṇas*, on the basis of which we arrive at the equation, 1 *pāṭaka* = 40 *droṇavāpas*.

The inscription is the earliest record of a Hindu king making a gift to a Buddhist monastery.

Vainya Gupta a king in Eastern Bengal. The inscription is significant as showing the part of Bengal where Vainya Gupta held sway as sovereign. His headquarters were located in South Tippera, and Uttaramaṇḍala must have formed the northern limit of his kingdom. Thus the sphere of his authority lay in remote eastern Bengal away from Puṇḍravardhana and Magadha as parts of the Central Gupta empire.

CHAPTER XIV

KUMĀRA GUPTA III

Kumāra Gupta III. The Damodarpur No. 5 Copper-plate inscription bears the date Gupta year 214=A.D. 533. It is also read as 224=A.D. 543. A seal is soldered to it and bears the inscription '*Koṭivarshādhishṭhānādhi (kārṇa) sya*', 'of the office or court of the *adhishṭhāna* (headquarters) of *Koṭivarsha*.'

The inscription mentions the Gupta emperor of the time, to whom it applies the following epithet: *Paramadaivata Paramabhaṭṭāraka-Mahārājādhirāja*, but, unfortunately, only the second part of his name 'Gupta' is legible in the inscription, and not its first or personal part. Only one of its letters is traced and read as '*Ku*', which is taken to indicate Kumāra Gupta. From the date of the inscription, this Kumāra Gupta is to be taken as Kumāra Gupta III who must then figure as the last of the imperial Guptas. The emperor is described as *Pṛithivī-pati*, 'Ruler of the Earth', indicating that there is no diminution in the extent of the Gupta empire at that time. But this description is merely conventional, and need not be taken literally.

An interesting fact stated in the inscription is that the Governor of the *Bhukti* of Puṇḍravardhana was a son of the emperor, *Rājaputra-Deva-Bhaṭṭāraka*, bearing the title *Uparika-Mahārāja* and 'tendering his homage to the king.'

It also states that the province was very prosperous under the rule of the royal Viceroy with 'an adequate military force of elephants, cavalry and infantry.'

It mentions a particular district or *Vishaya* of the province named Koṭivarsha. The district magistrate (*Vishayapati*) is named Svayaṁbhūdeva.

There was an Advisory Council associated with the District Magistrate in his administration of the district. The district office is called *adhishṭhānādhikaraṇa*.

The Advisory Council of the District was constituted by four members representing its different interests, viz., (1) The Mayor of the city (*Nagara-śreshṭhī*); (2) Representative of Trade-Guilds (*Sārthavāha*); (3) President of Craft-Guilds (*Prathama Kulika*); (4) President of the Writers' Union (*Prathama Kāyastha*), who must have been an expert in dealing with documents and conveyancing.

An application for a grant of land was made to the district officer by a nobleman who belonged to Ayodhyā. This shows that the Gupta empire then included both Ayodhyā and Puṇḍravardhana.

The purpose of the grant was to make provision for the repairs of the temple of God *Śvetavarāhasvāmī*, of its breaches (*khaṇḍa*) and cracks (*phuṭṭa*), and also for the offering of *Bali*, *Charu*, *Satra*, supply of cow's milk (*gavya*), incense (*dhūpa*), flowers (*pushpa*), *madhuparka*, lamp (*dīpa*), etc., required for worship.

The land that was needed for this provision measured 5 *kulyavāpas* of *khila* (fallow) along with *vāstu* (homestead) land. The land was not found within one village. It was made up of portions derived from four or five villages named. This was because it was difficult to find a large plot of unsettled or surplus land in one village. All available land in every village was under the plough and intensive cultivation.

The condition on which land was to be granted by government to a private person was that it should be by way of a permanent and inalienable gift (*apradādharmeṇa*). The State could only encourage the permanent charities of private persons.

The application was then referred to a Board of three Record-keepers (*Pustapālas*) under a Chief (*Prathama*) who had to ascertain (*avadhāraṇa*) if it was in order (*yukta*), or if there was any objection (*virodha*) to it.

The transaction was effected after the applicant's payment of the price of the land at the customary rate which is stated to be 3 *dīnāras* for 1 *kulyavāpa* of uncultivated (*aprahata*, 'whose sods were not turned up by the plough)', waste (*khila*) land (*kshetra*); which was thus not productive of any revenue or income (*samudaya-bāhya*) to the State.

The deed for the transaction was in the form of a copper-plate upon which the order for the grant of land was inscribed.

CHAPTER XV

LOCAL KINGS

Local Kings of Eastern India: Gopachandra. The *Arya-Mañju-Śrī-Mūla-Kalpa* refers to the rule of a king called '*Va*' and of his successor called '*Dha*'. '*Va*' may be taken to point to Vainya Gupta and '*Dha*' *to Dharmāditya.* This work also mentions Gopa as a king of the east.

Faridpur Copper-Plate Inscription of the year 18. The *Gopa* of this literary text may be taken to be king Gopachandra mentioned in this inscription. He carved out an independent kingdom in Bengal after the downfall of the imperial Guptas. It included a wide area comprising the Faridpur district in eastern Bengal and Burdwan in western Bengal.

It also repeats the name of the District Office (*Vishayādhikaraṇa*) of Vārakamaṇḍala.

It describes Gopachandra as *Mahārājādhirāja*, *Apratiratha*, and as *Bhaṭṭāraka*. At that time, Nāgadeva was administering the province of Navyāvakaśika and held several offices as *Mahāpratīhāra*, *Kumārapādīya*, *Amātya*, and *Uparika*. He appointed under him Vatsapāla as the Magistrate of the district Vārakamaṇḍala.

Mallasarul Copper-Plate Inscription. This inscription was found in a village near Galsi in Burdwan district. To its plate is soldered a seal bearing the figure of a standing Deity with a *chakra* (wheel of Law) behind. Below the figure is the legend *Mahārāja Vījayasenasya*.

Though it is not dated, palaeographically its script resembles that of the Faridpur plates of Dharmāditya and Gopachandra assigned to the sixth century A.D.

The inscription invokes God Lokanātha, and the Buddhist saints (*santaḥ*).

It mentions the time of Mahārājādhirāja Gopachandra (*Gopachandre praśāsati*).

It also mentions Vardhamāna *Bhukti* and its officers, viz., (1) *Kārttākṛitika*, Head of Executive; (2) *Kumārāmātya*, Minister in attendance on the Prince; (3) *Chauroddharaṇika*, Chief of Police; (4) *Uparika*, Governor; (5) *Audraṅgika*, Collector of *Udraṅga* Tax; (6) *Āgrahārika*, Superintendent of *Agrahāras;* (7) *Aurṇasthānika*, Superintendent of Silk Factories; (8) *Bhogapatika*, Officer-in-charge of a *Bhoga* or a Division; (9) *Vishayapati*, District Magistrate; (10) *Taddyuktaka*, Treasury Officer; (11) *Hiraṇyasāmudāyika*, Currency Officer; (12) *Pattalaka*, Officer in charge of a *Pattala;* (13) *Āvasathika*, Superintendent of *Dharmaśālās*. Next follows a list of the village elders (*Mahattaras*) and other important persons concerned with the land transaction. Some of these are described as *Agrahārins*, *Bhaṭṭas*, *Khāḍgis*, and *Vāhanāyakas*.

The inscription records a gift of land to a Brahmin for performing the Five Great Sacrifices. It measured 8 *kulyavāpas*. It is situated in a *Grāma* registered as belonging to a *Vīthī*, in the *Bhukti* of Vardhamāna.

The plot is marked out by pegs (*kīlaka*) bearing the device of a string of lotus seeds (*kamalākshamālā*).

As usual, Vijayasena applied for the land to the elders and other leaders of the villages concerned and also the district office (*vīthī-adhikaraṇa* or collectorate). These held their enquiry into the matter and signified their approval. Then the applicant paid the price of land in *dīnāras* to the Collectorate. Then the sale-proceeds of the land were distributed among the different villages and credited to the account of each by the *Vāra* officers, (*Vārakṛitaiḥ*, officers appointed by turn or in a place called *Vāra*). This class of officers is supposed to carry out the apportionment of the price paid for the total land purchased at the *Vīthī* office among the villages concerned.

A new condition for the sale is mentioned, viz., that the usual dues in respect of the land to be sold would be borne by the buyer and credited to the revenues of the *Vīthī* (*Vīthī-samudaya-eva praṇāyya*). Thus the land that is sold in the present case yielded revenue and was not *khila* or waste land. Having in this manner obtained the right of ownership of the land, he transferred it to the Brāhmaṇa Vatsasvāmin by executing a copper-plate charter (*tāmrapaṭṭa*). The attending *Pustapāla* had the copper-plate heated (*tāpita*).

Vijayasena. The historical value of the inscription may now be noted. Gopachandra may be identified with Gopachandra of Faridpur copper-plates and Vijayasena who is mentioned as his vassal is to be identified with Vijayasena of the Guṇaigaṛh Plate inscription of Vainya Gupta of A.D. 507. In Vainya Gupta's inscription, the status of Vijayasena was lower, that of a mere *Dūtaka*. In the present inscription, Vijayasena issues a charter under his own seal showing that he was in a position of greater dignity and authority. Therefore, this inscription may be considered to be later than that of Vainya Gupta.

It is also to be noted that Vainya Gupta in the Guṇaigaṛh inscription is not called Mahārājādhirāja but only a Mahārāja. Probably he was a local chief posted in eastern Bengal by his paramount sovereign Gopachandra. It seems that King Gopachandra was ruling over a large part of Bengal, western and eastern, when it included Vardhamāna *Bhukti*, the present Burdwan division. The fact seems to be that Bengal, by the middle of the sixth century, was lost to the Guptas of Magadha and was ruled by the local princes in different tracts, until it was absorbed in the empire of Harsha.

Dharmāditya. Besides Dharmāditya of Faridpur plates and Gopachandra of this plate, another Faridpur plate (the Ghugrāhāti plate) mentions a third independent ruler of Bengal named Samāchāradeva.

Faridpur Copper-Plate Inscription of Dharmāditya. A seal joined to the plate bears the legend '*Vārakamaṇḍala Vishayādhikaraṇasya*'=from the office of the *Vishaya* or district called Vārakamaṇḍala (in modern Goalunda and Gopalagunj sub-divisions of Faridpur district).

The inscription refers to Dharmāditya as the invincible Ruler of the Earth (*Pṛithivyāmapratirathaḥ*) who had as his vassal (*Tatprasādalabdhāspada*) Mahārāja Sthāṇudatta in charge (*adhyāsana*) of a privince. He appointed (*tadviniyuktaka*) Jajāva as the *Vishayapati* of Vārakamaṇḍala. Sthāṇudatta was apparently Dhārmāditya's Viceroy of the province called Navyāvakāśika.

The inscription refers to an officer named Sādhanika who had something to do with the realization of debts and fines (*sādhana*), and hence was a judicial officer.

As the land concerned in the transaction recorded here bordered on the sea, it followed the custom of that region aptly called *Prākṣamudra-maryādā*, i.e., custom prevailing in the countries bordering the eastern sea (Bay of Bengal). Here the price of 1 *kulyavāpa* = 4 *dīnāras*. But it was not *khila* or *aprahata* but cultivated land (*vāpa kshetra*). Hence it price is higher. The separated plot is called a *khaṇḍala* marked out by boundaries (*kṛita-kalana* = *kṛita-chihnāṅka*, also called *Sīmāliṅgāni*), which were visible at first sight (*dṛishṭimātra prabandhena*).

Another Faridpur Copper-Plate Inscription of Dharmāditya. This inscription also mentions Dharmaditya as *Māhārājadhirāja* and *Bhaṭṭāraka*, and his *Uparika* or Viceroy posted in the region called *Navyāvakāśika*. The name suggests its derivation from a canal (=*avakāśa* or opening). Nāgadeva who bears the title of *Mahāpratīhāra* and *Uparika* appoints under his administration (*adhyāsana*) Gopālasvāmī in charge of the district (*Vishaya*) named Vārakamaṇḍala.

CHAPTER XVI

MATERIAL AND MORAL PROGRESS

Political Achievement. Much of the material and moral progress of the country was ultimately the outcome of its stabilized political conditions. The Gupta Empire was a well-organized State which achieved the political unification of a large part of India under the umbrella of its paramount sovereignty, establishing a sphere of influence which was much wider than that of its direct dominion and administration. Samudra Gupta was the first to set before himself the imperial ideal as stated in the expression *dharaṇībandha* used in his Allahabad Pillar inscription. It indicates his programme of *digvijaya*, of conquests in different directions, by which the *dharaṇī* or India could be bound (*bandha*) together as a unit.

Greater India. The empire's sphere of influence is indicated in the Allahabad Pillar inscription, as we have already seen. It contains the earliest reference to the oversea relations cultivated by Samudra Gupta. It states how he cultivated these relations with 'Siṁhala and other islands' that were bound to him in ties of friendly political relationship 'by offering him various gifts, applying to him for charters recognizing their sovereignty and, finally, by tendering their personal loyalty (*ātma-nivedanam*).' This reference in the inscription gives the earliest inkling into the beginnings of India's expansion beyond her borders so as to form a sort of Greater India as an empire of Indian thought. Another piece of evidence of India's oversea intercouse is furnished by the account of the despatch by king Meghavarṇa of Ceylon (A.D. 350-380) to Emperor Samudra Gupta of an Embassy with gifts and a request to him for permission to build a *Vihāra* at Bodh-Gayā for the benefit of the pilgrims from Ceylon to that holy place. Such international outlook, and colonial activities are the product of a condition of equilibrium whereby the Mother Country, enjoying peace at home and the blessings of an ordered government, not troubled by political unrest or unsettlement, became a live self-conscious unit, expressing itself in a variety of political and creative movements, economic and cultural.

Evidence of Fa-Hien. We find that Greater India had already made a good start from the evidence of Fa-Hien, that cultured Chinese pilgrim who has left us such a detached and valuable view of India's civilization as he saw it in the time of Chandra Gupta II. We see from his record how centres and outposts of Indian culture had already sprung up in several countries outside the northern boundaries of the country.

Foreign Centres of Indian Culture. The first of these centres seen by Fa-Hien was *Shan-shan* where he saw, as already stated, more than 4,000 Hīnayāna Buddhist monks, while its common people also 'practised the religion of India.' In several *Tartar* countries he found many ascetics who studied 'Indian books and the Indian spoken language.' In the country of *Kara-shahr*, he found Buddhist Hīnayāna monks numbering over 4,000. In *Khotan*, he found several tens of thousands of Mahāyāna Buddhists and a monastery known by the name of *Gomatī* where, at the sound of a gong 3,000 Buddhist monks 'assembled to eat'. Khotan had 14 such large monasteries. In the neighbourhood, he found another monastery 'which was 250 feet high, overlaid with gold and silver, and took 20 years to build and the reigns of three kings'. In *Kashgar*, he found 1,000 Hīnayāna monks, and its king was a Buddhist. In *Darel* was another centre of Hīnayāna Buddhism.

Religion. This spread of Indian culture to foreign countries testifies to its high degree of development in the Mother Country. It was marked by a revival of Brahmanical religion or Hinduism. Ample evidence of this has been already cited in connexion with the reign of each Gupta emperor. We may sum up here some of the facts of this religious revival.

Vedic Religion. It was represented in its Sacrifices. The great Vedic imperial Sacrifice known as *Aśvamedha* was revived by Samudra Gupta and Kumāra Gupta I. The Poona Copper-plate inscription of Prabhāvatiguptā describes Samudra Gupta as 'a performer of many a horse-sacrifice'. A minister of Kumāra Gupta I set up a *yūpa* or sacrificial pillar at Bihar (No. 12). Similarly, Mahārāja Vishṇu Vardhana, a local king, erected a *yūpa* after performing the *Puṇḍarīka* sacrifice (No. 59). This sacrifice was undertaken to obtain, in terms of Vedic vocabulary, religious objectives like *Śrī-Yajña-Dharma-Śreya-Abhyudaya-Yaśa-Kula-Vaṁśa-Bhāga-Bhoga*. Some Vākāṭaka kings are stated in their inscriptions (Nos. 55 and 56) to have performed four and ten horse-sacrifices, as well as several other sacrifices named *Agnishṭoma*, *Aptoryāma*, *Ukthya*, *Shoḍaśin*, *Ātirātra*, *Vājapeya*, *Bṛihaspatisava*, and *Sādyaskra*, and are also described as the devotees of *Śiva*, *Maheśvara* (*Śambhu*), or *Svāmī Mahābhairava*. These inscriptions also refer to the gift of a village to a community of 1,000 Brahmins of various *gotras* and *charaṇas* named. The inscriptions also refer to the performance of other Vedic sacrifices like *Agnihotra* and the *Pañcha-mahāyajñas* (Nos. 16, 25, 29, 40 and 80).

Vaishṇavism. Most of the Gupta emperors and the local kings of the times called themselves *Parama-bhāgavatas*, i.e., worshippers of *Bhāgavata* or *Vāsudeva*. An inscription of Parivrājaka-Mahārāja, Saṁkshobha, opens with the prayer: '*Oṁ Namo Bhagavate*

Vāsudevāya' (No. 25). As worshippers of Vishṇu, the Gupta emperors introduced His *Vāhana*, Garuḍa, on the obverse of their coins and goddess Lakshmī, His Consort, on the reverse and also *Chakra*, Vishṇu's Wheel.

God Vishṇu is worshipped under various names: *Ātmabhū* (No. 51), *Chakrabhṛit* (No. 14), *Chakradhara* (Nos. 17 and 47), *Gadādhara* (No. 17), *Chakrapāṇi* (No. 55), *Chitrakūṭasvāmin* (No. 66) *Govinda* (No. 15), *Janārdana* (No. 19), *Muradvish* (No. 79), *Mādhava* (No. 42), *Madhusūdana* (No. 17), *Nārāyaṇa* (No. 36), *Varāhāvatāra* (No. 36), *Śvetavarāhasvāmin*, *Dāmodara* (No. 42), *Śāriṅgapāṇi* (No. 33), and *Vāsudeva* (No. 25).

A temple of Vishṇu is called a *Vishṇu-sthāna* (No. 17). Skanda Gupta's officer Chakrapālita, as a devotee of God Govinda and Chakradhara, constructed a temple of Chakrabhṛit. Bhāgavata temples are referred to in inscriptions numbered 27 and 28. Those numbered 25, 29, and 31 refer to a Deity called Pishṭapuri or Pishṭapurikādevī, probably another name of Lakshmī. Sometimes, a flagstaff or *dhvaja-stambha* was erected as a symbol of worship (No. 19). The famous Iron Pillar inscription at Meharauli calls the pillar as a *Vishṇu-dhvaja*. A Vaishṇava cave was constructed at Udayagiri in A.D. 401 by a Sanakānika chief who also had it decorated with sculptures showing four-armed Vishṇu and twelve-armed Lakshmī. Skanda Gupta's special devotion to Lakshmī is expressed in his coins of the 'King and Lakshmī type' and in his inscriptions mentioning *Kula-Lakshmī* as the tutelary Deity of the Gupta family. Inscription No. 66 found on a *Daśāvatāra* temple names Vishṇu and Anantasvāmī and Chitrakūṭasvāmī. A Damodarpur inscription refers to the temple of Vishṇu named Śvetavarāhasvāmī. Nos. 3 and 17 refer to the Vaishṇava festival of *Śayana-ekādaśī*.

Śaivism. The prevalence of worship of Śiva is testified to in many inscriptions referring to His worship under various names indicative of the different aspects of His divinity installed in appropriate shrines. Probably, the earliest *Śiva-Liṅga* is that bearing an inscription dated A.D. 436, and found at Karamadāṇḍā in Fyzabad. The God Śiva was also taken out in a procession called *Devadroṇī* in this inscription. It is curious that two Ministers of the Vaishṇava emperor, Chandra Gupta II, were worshippers of Śiva named Śambhu and Mahādeva-Pṛithivīśvara-Śaileśvarasvāmī, the former constructing a cave (No. 6) and the latter granting land for His worship. The inscriptions mention the worship of Śiva under the following names: *Īśa* (No. 18), *Mahābhairava* (Nos. 55, and 57), *Bhūtapati* (No. 49), *Hara* (No. 49), *Īśvara* (No. 39), *Jayeśvara* (No. 39), *Kapāleśvara* (No. 80), *Kokāmukhasvāmin*, *Mahādeva* (No. 39),

Maheśvara (Nos. 38, 39, 46 and 55), *Mihireśvara* (No. 80), *Paśupati* (No. 39), *Pṛithiviśvara, Pinākin* (No. 35), *Śambhu* (Nos. 6, 35, 55 and 56), *Śarva* (No. 37), *Śiva* (Nos. 55 and 56), *Śaileśvara, Sthāṇu* (No. 34), *Śūlapāṇi* (Nos. 33, 34 and 79), *Śūrabhogeśvara* (No. 39), *Tripurāntaka* (No. 80), *Ardhanārīśvara* (No. 49), and *Bhavasṛij* (No. 35). Mahārāja Hastin was a Śaiva (Nos. 21-23). So also was another feudatory chief, Mahārāja Bhīmavarman, who had inscribed his name on a pedestal bearing standing figures of Śiva-Pārvatī. The inscription was found at Kosam and is dated G.E. 139=A.D. 458, the time of Skanda Gupta. The emperor Skanda Gupta restruck the silver coins of the previous rulers, which were in circulation in western and central provinces of the empire, and these western issues show on *Rev.* the figure of a *Bull* which must have been Śiva's bull, *Nandi*. This Bull-type of coins is attributed to the Valabhī *Senāpatis* or rulers whose emblem was the Bull. The Śaiva sect of *Māheśavaras* was flourishing in Mathurā in the time of Chandra Gupta II, as stated in an inscription already cited.

Worship of Śakti. *Śakti* also is worshiped under different names as *Bhagvatī* (Nos. 25, 29, 31), *Bhavānī* (No. 50), *Devī* (Nos. 49 and 50), *Gaurī* (No. 79), *Kātyāyanī* (No. 50), *Pārvatī* (No. 33). Inscription No. 17 records how a Minister of a local king named Viśvavarman, a feudatory of Kumāra Gupta I, constructed a temple for the worship of the Divine Mothers (*Mātṛis*), 'a very terrible abode, filled full of *Dākinīs* or ghosts who utter loud and tremendous shouts in joy and stir up the very oceans with the mighty winds rising from the performance of *tāntrika* rites.' Along with the images of the Seven Mothers, the temple also bears an image of *Śakti* as *Mahishamardinī*. The Bihar Stone Pillar inscription of Skanda Gupta also refers to the construction of a group of temples (*Devaniketanamaṇḍalaṁ*) dedicated to the Divine Mothers including goddess *Bhadrāryā*, also named *Bhadrāryakā*, who may be taken to be Pārvatī (*Āryā*), wife of Bhadra (Śiva).

Some of the Gupta imperial coins show on *Rev.* goddess Durgā as *Siṁhavāhanā*, seated on lion, as on Chandra Gupta I coins, or Lion-slayer type of coins of Chandra Gupta II.

The Tiger-type of coins of Samudra Gupta introduces goddess Gangā as *Makara-vāhanā*, on *Rev.*, and the Lyrist-type, goddess Sarasvatī as Goddess of Music associated with the *viṇā* shown on *Obv.*

Several other goddesses are also mentioned in the inscriptions as being worshipped in those days, e.g.: *Devakī* (No. 13); *Jāhnavī* (Nos. 38, 39); *Jāmbavatī* (No. 67); *Lakshmī* (Nos. 14 and 79); *Vaishṇavī* (No. 40); *Paulomī* (No. 49); *Śachi* (No. 49); and *Sarasvatī* (No. 42).

Kārtikeya. The worship of Kārtikeya, the God of War, is mentioned in several inscriptions. The Bilsad inscription of the time of Kumara Gupta I [A.D. 415, (No. 10)] refers to a temple (*āyatana*) for worship of *Svāmi-Mahāsena* also named god *Brahmaṇya*, in honour of whose worship the temple was equipped by a devotee named Dhruvaśarman with (1) a *pratoli* or gateway with a flight of steps to reach up to its height; (2) a *muni-vasati*, 'rest-house for saints'; (3) a *dharma-sattra*, or free feeding or alms-house; and (4) a lofty pillar (*stambha*). The flight of steps is called *svargasopāna*, 'steps leading to heaven', showing that the temple was very high, and its way marked by an equally high pillar. Dhruvaśarman for his piety was honoured by the Committee of the temple (*pārshada-mānita*).

Sūrya. Worship of the Sun was also popular. It was left to a Guild of Silk-Weavers to construct at Daśapura a temple of the Sun, *Dīpta-raśmi*, and to carry out its repairs on a magnificent scale, so that 'the *gṛiha* of *Bhānumān*' was rendered the best of the city's buildings (*bhavana-vara*), as is stated in inscription No. 18. In the time of Skanda Gupta, a temple of god *Savitā* was founded by two Kshatriya merchants in Antarvedi-*Vishaya* (No. 16). Inscription No. 28 of A.D. 512 records the grant made by Mahārāja Śarvanātha of Uchchakalpa for the repairs of a shrine for the worship of god *Āditya-Bhaṭṭāraka*.

Other Deities. Most of the deities of the Hindu Pantheon were known and find mention in the Gupta inscriptions. These are: the God of Wealth called *Kubera* (Nos. 1 and 2) or *Dhanada* (Nos. 1, 3, 4 etc.), or *Dhaneśa* (Nos. 38 and 39); *Varuṇa*, God of Justice (Nos. 1, 4, 10-13, etc.); *Indra* God of Gods (No. 1) or *Śakra* (No. 15); *Yama*, the God Invincible, or *Antaka* (Nos. 1, 3, 4 etc.) or *Kṛitānta* (Nos. 4, 10, 12 etc.); *Hanumat* (No. 42); *Rāma* (No. 17); *Kāmadeva* (Nos. 18, 35); *Lokapāla* (Nos. 19, 57); *Meghavān* (No. 35); *Bṛihaspati*, God of Wisdom (No. 1); *Vidyādhara* (Nos. 17, 18 and 42); *Nara* (No. 18); *Kinnara* (No. 18); *Gandharva* (No. 18); *Mahishāsura* (No. 50); and *Nandi* (No. 33), as *demi-gods*.

Buddhism. Although the Gupta emperors were orthodox Hindus or followers of Brahminical religion, they were catholic enough not to have enforced their personal religion as the official religion of the empire. They encouraged equally the promotion of all religions, including Buddhism and Jainism. Sāñchī continued to be a great centre of Buddhism. An inscription (No. 5) dated G.E. 92 = A.D. 412 records the gift of a village to the *Āryasaṁgha* of Kākanādaboṭa-*vihāra* (Sāñchī), governed by its *Pañchamaṇḍalī*, and also of 25 *dīnāras*, the interest of which was to feed five *Bhikshus* and a lamp. This *Mahāvihāra* is described as the 'abode' (*āvasatha*) of the most pious *Śramaṇas*. No. 11 of the year 129=A.D. 448 of the time of Kumāra Gupta I records the installation of the image (*pratimā*) of the Perfectly Enlightened One of irrefutable doctrines, Buddha *Bhagavān* (*samyak-sambuddha*). No. 62 of the year 131=A.D. 450 of the time of Kumāra Gupta I records the grant by a lady, possibly out of her own *strīdhana*, of certain sums of money to the *Ārya-saṁgha* at the *Mahāvihāra* of Kākanādaboṭa for the spiritual merit of her own parents. It also refers to four images of the Buddha previously installed in the *Vihāra*, Like Sāñchī, Sārnāth was another centre of Buddhism and noted for the two famous images of the Buddha bearing inscriptions of the time of Kumāra Gupta II and Budha Gupta. The Buddha is here called *Śāstā*. He is called *Sugata* in No. 52.

Jainism. The Udayagiri Cave inscription of the year 126=A.D. 445 and hence of the reign of Kumāra Gupta I mentions the construction of an image (*ākṛiti*) of *Jinavara* Pārśva. Another inscription records the installation of a Jain image at Mathura in the year A.D. 423. The Kahāum Stone Pillar inscription of the time of Skanda Gupta records an endowment in favour of Jainism, the fashioning of five stone-images of *Ādikartṛis* or *Tīrthaṅkaras* in the niches of a pillar of stone 'as high as a hill'.

Thus the Buddhist and Jain *Vihāras* were as familiar as the Brahminical *Deva-kula* and *Deva-sabhā* (No. 18).

Worship of Teachers and Texts. Along with the worship of deities, there was also a custom of offering worship to the teachers and founders of religions whose images and statues were installed in shrines (*gurvāyatana*), as stated in the Mathurā Pillar inscription of the time of Chandra Gupta II. Fa-Hien also noted how Buddhist teachers and sacred Buddhist texts were worshipped in shrines specially constructed for the purpose.

Endowments. All these religions were promoted by public benefactions which usually took the form of gifts made in both cash and kind. The gifts of cash were not usually spent, but kept as a permanent fund (*akshaya-nīvī*), the interest of which only was to be spent on their purposes, as stated in No. 62. Gifts in kind were generally grants of land in the shape of an *agrahāra* or village to learned Brahmins in furtherance of their religious pursuits. These endowments were also made for the supply of requisites of worship such as scent, incense, flowers, or oil for lights, besides construction of alms-houses (*sattras* or *vihāras*). The Guṇaigaṛh inscription of Vainya Gupta records the gift to a Mahāyāna *Saṁgha* of Śākya-Bhikshus for provision for their *Chīvara* (clothing), *piṇḍapāta* (food) *śayana* (bedding), *āsana* (seating) and medicines. It was followed by another gift of an *Agrahāra* to the same *Saṁgha* then housed in a *Vihāra* called *Āśrama-vihāra* which was consecrated to Avalokiteśvara.

Social Service. There were also endowments of social service and works of public utility. Fa-Hien saw more of these specially in what he calls the Middle Kingdom. Rest-houses were constructed with 'supply of beds and mattresses, food and clothes'. While travelling through the U.P., Fa-Hien noticed, built along even 'out of the way roads, houses of charity providing for shelter with beds, food and drink', though one could not stay there indefinitely. Fa-Hien further reports how these endowments were made in the shape of gifts of 'lands, houses, and gardens, with men and bullocks for cultivation, on the basis of binding title-deeds which were written out and which no subsequent kings dared disregard.' Educational benefactions of those days were made in the form of grants of lands which could be profitably cultivated to produce the income required to maintain them. This meant that these schools were equipped with efficient agricultural departments and staffs to look after their landed estates, their villages, their paddy fields, orchards, and also dairy-farms, as testified to by the later Chinese pilgrims, Yuan Chwang, and I-Tsing in respect of Nālandā University. Fa-Hien also refers to public benefactions endowing *free* hospitals for poor patients, 'orphans, widowers, and cripples.' 'They are well taken care of under an attending physician and are given their prescribed food and medicine and are discharged when they are cured.'

Education and Learning. This religious and cultural revival points to a sound system of education and adequate progress of learning. Teachers are mentioned in inscriptions by the titles of *Āchāryā* and *Upādhyāya* and the pupils were called *Śishyas*. The *Upādhyāya* is a sub-teacher who is well up only in a part of the Veda or in grammar and in the other Vedāṅgas (see Nos. 56, 61, 71). Besides *Śishyas*, disciples were also called *Brahmachāris* (Nos. 22, 23, 39 and 60).

Learned Brahmin teachers were honoured by the title of *Bhaṭṭas* (Nos. 12, 39 and 81). Villages consecrated to the use of religious students (*Brahmachāris*) were called *Agrahāras* (No. 60). Religious students were grouped under *Sākhās* and *Charaṇas* (No. 55). These were names of Vedic Schools following a particular recension of one of the Vedas. In the inscriptions, the following Vedic recensions are mentioned, namely, *Aupamanyava* (No. 41), *Bahvṛicha* (Nos. 40 and 60), *Chhandoga-Kauthuma* (No. 23), *Kaṭha* (No. 22), *Maitrāyaṇīya* (Nos. 19 and 36), *Nārāyaṇīya* (No. 16), *Taittirīya* (No. 56), *Vājasaneya-Mādhyandina* (Nos. 21, 26 and 81) and *Vājasaneya-Kaṇva* (No. 38).

The three Vedas are called *Trayī* (No. 39). There is a reference to *Paramarshi* Veda-Vyāsa as the arranger of the Vedas (No. 21). A Brahmin acquainted with all the four Vedas is called a *Chaturvedin* (Nos. 16, 39 and 55). There were also Brahmins who specialized in one Veda, e.g., *Sāmavedī* Brahmin. Vedas are not mentioned individually in the inscriptions except Atharva Veda (No. 80).

The interpreter of Vedic quotations and words is called *Naigama* (No. 35).

As regards the subjects of study other than the Vedas, we have reference to the 14 *Vidyās* (No. 25) comprising 4 *Vedas*, 6 *Vedāṅgas*, the *Purāṇas*, *Mīmāṁsā*, *Nyāya* and *Dharma* or Law; to Sanskrit and Prākṛit poets (No. 33); to the grammar of Pāṇini called *Śālāturīya* (No. 39); to Atharva Veda in which there was specialized study (No. 80); to *Vyāsa*, the arranger of the Vedas, and son of *Parāśara* (No. 31); to the *Mahābhārata* (Nos. 26, 27, 28 and 31) and to its *Śatasāhasrī-saṁhitā* (edition of 100,000 *ślokas*) [*ibid*].

Some of the characters of the *Mahābhārata* are also referred to as being popularly known, viz., Yudhishṭhira (No. 38) called Dharmarāja, Vidura (No. 35), Vainya famous for hereditary virtue (*abhijāti-guṇena*) (No. 17), Uddhava (No. 35), Sagara, whose 60,000 sons dug out the bed of the ocean (*ibid*), Bhagīratha (No. 17), Pṛithu (No. 2), Rāghava (*ibid*), Pārtha (Nos. 18 and 20), Māndhātā (No. 33), Manu, Bharata and Alarka (*ibid*), and Anu son of Yayāti (No. 49).

Method of learning. All this learning was imparted orally by the teacher to his pupil. The subjects of study were not reduced to writing, and instruction had to be received by the pupil directly from the lips of the teacher uttering its words. There was hardly available in the country any written literature which could be copied and conserved and carried in manuscripts. As Fa-Hien states on the basis of his personal observation, the teacher's words had to be 'heard, pondered over, and contemplated' (as *Śruti*) by his pupils. In fact, lessons and literature had all to be *heard*. He further states that in the various countries of northern India through which he travelled, he always found that sacred works were handed down orally from one teacher to another, so that he could hardly find any written volume which he could copy. He found an exception only at one place, at the Mahāyāna monastery at Pāṭaliputra, where he found a copy of the 'Disciplines', some extracts from the *Abhidhamma* and complete copies of two *Sūtras*. To copy out these works, Fa-Hien was compelled to stay here for 3 years in having to learn to write and to speak Sanskrit. There were thus no libraries in those days where knowledge could be stored up in MSS. The teachers were themselves the living and walking libraries, and custodians of the nation's heritage and stock of learning.

Popularity of Sanskrit. The medium of higher instruction and the language of the cultured classes must have been Sanskrit in those days. All the Gupta inscriptions are written in Sanskrit, replacing Prākṛit or Pālī of the earlier inscriptions. Very probably, while in the earlier times the inscriptions were written in Prākṛit which was then read by the people at large, Sanskrit, in the time of the Gupta emperors, displaced Prākṛit as the popular language, for it may be assumed that epigraphic records are meant to be read by the public.

Its Cultivation by Kings. The spread of Sanskrit learning was mainly due to its patronage by the kings some of whom became known as distinguished Sanskritists themselves. For instance, Samudra Gupta was himself a poet, the author of a large volume of poetry (*bahukavitā*), upon whom is bestowed the extinct title of *Kavirāja*, 'the prince of poets', by Harishena. His poetical output was known both for its quantity (*aneka-kāvya-kriyābhiḥ*) and quality. Many a poet could have earned his living from poetry like his (*vidvajjanopajīvya*). For his poetry was not obscure but clear (*sphuṭa*) in its meaning and hence was popular, and won him much fame (*kirti*).

But he was not merely a poet. He was well-versed in the Vedas and Śāstras whose inner meaning (*tattva*) he understood and upheld (*bharttā*). He was a 'path-finder', a pioneer, in the study of the sacred Ṛigvedic hymns (*sukta-mārggaḥ*). By his versatile learning, he ruled in the realm of letters (*vidvalloke*), as he ruled in the realm of politics, and won for himself a new kingdom of fame (*kīrti-rājya*). He was the protector of religion whose limits (*prāchīra*) he would not permit anyone to transgress. His learning penetrated into the deepest truth of religion (*vaidushyam tattvabhedi*). By his spirituality, he was worthy of the company of the sages.

Literary Conferences. He made another contribution to learning by upholding its standard. He used to convene Conferences of literary critics (*budha-guṇita*) to judge of true poetry (*satkāvya*) and weed out (*ūhata*) that which would violate (*viruddha*) its dignity (*śrī*).

Samudra Gupta as a Musician. Samudra Gupta was also a devotee of other fine arts besides poetry. He was like a *Nārada* and *Tumburu* in choral skill and musical accomplishments (*gandharva-lalita*). He Lyrist-type of coinage celebrates his skill in instrumental music and playing on the *vīṇā*.

Śāba Vīra-sena. Among other learned noblemen is mentioned Śāba Vīra-sena, the Minister (*Sachiva*) of that saintly emperor, *Rājādhirājarshi* Chandra Gupta II. He is described as a poet (*kavi*) who was also proficient in other scientific subjects like Etymology (*Śabdārtha*), Logic (*Nyāya*), and State-craft (*Lokajña*) (No. 6).

Skanda Gupta. No 13 describes the accomplisments of emperor Skanda Gupta 'of spotless soul' (*amalātmā*), who was well-versed in the knowledge of different tunes (*tāna*) of music.

Learned Chiefs. Mātṛi Vishṇu was a local chief who was a Ṛishi of a Brahmin (*Viprarshi*) who completed his Vedic study, and was given to the performance of Vedic sacrifices (*Kratu-yājī*) (No. 19).

The local chief Visvavarman is described as the equal of Śakra and Bṛihaspati (No. 18).

Learning among Silk-Weavers. This inscription also describes how even the members of an industrial guild, a Guild of Silk-weavers (*Paṭṭavāya Śreṇi*), showed great aptitude for general cultural subjects, along with technical topics. Some acquired proficiency in Military Science (*Dhanurvidyā*), some in Stories (*Kathāvids*), and some in Astrology (*Jyotisha*).

Literary Value of Inscriptions. The Allahabad *Praśasti* as a literary composition is creditable to its author, Harisheṇa. The Meharauli inscription is also a good piece of poetry. The Mandasor Stone inscription of Kumāra Gupta I and Bandhuvarman is the composition of the poet, Vatsabhaṭṭi.

Centres of Learning. We owe to Fa-Hien an account of the residential colleges or *Vihāras* of those days.

Udyāna. When he first crossed over to India he saw in the country called Udyāna Buddhism very flourishing and Sanskrit as the language of the country.

Gandhāra. His next move was towards Gandhāra and its cities of Takshaśilā and Peshāwar, all full of monuments enshrining the relics of the Buddha or incidents of his life.

Punjab. In passing through the Punjab, he saw many monasteries accommodating in all 10,000 monks.

Mathurā. Next, he came to Mathurā where he found 20 monasteries with some 3,000 monks, along the banks of the Jumna.

Middle Kingdom. South of the Jumna began the Middle Kingdom, the region of Brahminism, with its high standard of culture and refinement. 'Throughout the country, no one kllls any living thing, nor drinks, wine, nor eats onions or garlic. The people do not keep pigs or fowls. There are no dealings in cattle, no butchers' shops, or distilleries in the market-places.'

This Middle Kingdom was the heart of the Gupta empire, and its Brahminical culture based upon non-violence, refined manners, customs, and dietary, must have greatly impressed the Buddhist pilgrim.

Sankīśa. At Sankīśa, he saw a *Vihāra* of 1,000 monks.

Śravastī. Śrāvastī was a famous centre of Buddhism, full of its antiquities and remains. It was also a strong centre of Brahminical culture. Fa-Hien saw this region intellectually very active. There were as many as 96 Schools of Brahminical Doctrine and Philosophy, each with its own ascetic followers who begged their food, but did not carry alms-bowls like the Buddhist monks.

Pāṭaliputra. The next important centre of culture was Pāṭaliputra where Fa-Hien saw Aśoka's palace 'still in existence', but the manner of his reference shows that Pāṭaliputra did not occupy the same position in the Gupta empire as it did in the Maurya empire.

Its Learned Teacher. Fa-Hien found at Pāṭaliputra one Mahāyāna and another Hīnayāna monastery. The former monastery was noted for a prodigy of learning, the Brahmin Buddhist teacher named Raivata to whom the whole country looked up as the highest authority in Mahāyāna. He had as his associate another Brahmin teacher named Mañju Srī who was equally learned.

Magadha. The civilization of Magadha impressed Fa-Hien very much, with its large cities, rich and prosperous people, who vied with one another 'in practising charity of heart and duty to one's neighbour'. At their religious processions of images carried in 'four-wheeled cars of five storeys', the Brahmins 'come to invite the Buddha', showing their complete catholicity.

Tāmluk. In the country of Tāmluk, there were 24 monasteries in one of which he stayed for 2 years, 'copying out *Sūtras* and drawing pictures of images'.

Art of Coinage. A good deal of the artistic achievements of the age is exhibited in the delicate workmanship of Gupta coinage in its various types. The variety of designs shown in the types of coinage gave great scope to art. The general scheme followed in the fashioning of this coinage is to exhibit on the *Obverse* the portrait of the king concerned and on the *Reverse* an appropriate goddess together with the corresponding accompaniments of associated symbols.

The king is shown in a variety of positions, shooting a tiger or a lion, playing on lyre, seated on high-backed couch, riding a horse or an elephant, feeding a peacock, holding a standard, or bow and arrow, or battle-axe. Among the accompaniments are well-executed figures of Altar or Tulasi plant, Garuḍa, or Dwarf.

The *Reverse* is reserved generally for the figure of the goddess, the deity worshipped by the king, *Lakshmī* in most cases, or *Gaṅgā-makara-vāhanā*, to go with the Tiger on *Obverse* as symbolizing the conquest of the forested regions of which the Tiger is a native; or *Durgā-siṁha-vāhanā*, *Śakti*, to whose blessings the king owed his conquests; or *Kulā-Lakshmī*, the tutelary deity, the Goddess of Fortune to favour the royal family; or *Sarasvatī*, as the Goddess of the softer arts of Peace going with the *Vīṇā* on *Obverse*.

There are departures from this general design in some coin-types. The Aśvamedha types of both Samudra Gupta and Kumāra Gupta I omit the king on *Obverse* but insert in his place the figure of the doomed *horse* standing before and tied to the *yūpa*, with a brick shown to symbolize the altar, while the *Reverse* brings forward the Queen who is indispensable for the sacrifice, as well as the ceremonial spear. The Chandra Gupta I type shows a variety, the figures of both King and Queen on *Obverse*. The Kācha type introduces a new element on *Obverse*, the standrad surmounted by the wheel or *chakra* of Vishṇu. The Chhatra type of Chandra Gupta II introduces on the *Obverse* the typical symbol of royal authority, the umbrella which is appropriately held on his head by the dwarf. Specimens of his Lion-slayer type show a great variety in depicting the king hunting down the lion in all possible positions. One shows him striking at the heart with the sword at close quarters. His Horseman type declares his paramount sovereignty symbolized by the victorious career and return of the horse, an embodiment of *ajitavikrama*. His silver coins for western provinces are adapted to the local conditions of newly-conquered territories. They show on *Obverse* the bust of the king and not his full length, but on *Reverse* the Garuḍa as token of Gupta sovereignty and not the usual goddess of Śaka coins. The craftsmen were quite good at executing these adaptations. These coins introduce for the first time the royal titles of *Vikramāditya* and *Vikramāṅka* earned by the king at the zenith of his conquering career as a *Śakāri*, the conqueror of the Śakas, pushing the limits of his empire up to the western seas. His copper coins show two new features : Garuḍa eating up snake, and flower-vase (*kalaśa*) on *Reverse*. The Horseman type of Kumāra Gupta I has a variety in its legend, *Ajita-Mahendraḥ*, but the word *ajita* is retained as going with the invincible prowess symbolized by the horse. Kumāra Gupta I as the ruler of both western and eastern India issued both the Lion and the Tiger types of coinage recalling those two regions. His Peacock type is an innovation. Its *Reverse* represents a God and not a Goddess, the God of War, Kārtikeya as *Śakti-dhara* and *Mayūra-vāhana*, with the appropriate legend *Mahendra-kumāraḥ* expressive of the king's devotion to both these gods. His Pratāpa type is unique in that it brings on the *Obverse* three figures, two females with the king between, and legend *Śrī-Pratāpaḥ* on *Reverse*. His silver coins for the western provinces declare in their legend the king's religion more emphatically before the conquered Śakas than the coins of his predecessor, though they agree on Garuḍa as its symbol on *Reverse*. The leged uses with vengeance the expression *Parama-bhāgavata* while it replaces *Vikramāditya* by *Mahendrāditya*. The silver issued for the central provinces have the figure of peacock on *Reverse*, as the copper coins show Garuḍa. Skanda Gupta's Archer type introduces the appropriate legend *Sudhanvī*, 'the skilled bowman', on *Obverse*. His King-and-Lakshmī type is singular. It brings on *Obverse* both king, and the deity he worships, Lakshmī, whose figure is reproduced on *Reverse*, too, to emphasize his devotion to Her as *Kula-Lakshmī* to Whom he owes the restoration of the fallen fortunes of his family. His silver western issues continue the legend of his predecessor on *Obverse*, and on *Reverse* Garuḍa with outspread wings. They introduce two innovations, the figures of Bull and Altar on *Reverse*, and the titles *Vikramāditya* and *Kramāditya* on the *Reverse* of the Altar type.

The execution of all this numismatic variety in designs and devices shows the originality, resourcefulness, and adapting capacity of the craftsmen concerned in translating thought in terms of metal.

Sculptures and Structures. Besides Coins, Gupta Art receives adequate expression in Monuments and Sculptures. These are all connected with one or other of the different religions them prevailing in the country and are meant to serve their interests. Only their most typical examples may be considered here.

Śaiva Sculptures. The temple of Bhitargaon in the Kanpur district is profusely decorated with carved brick-work, and brilliant terra-cotta panels, illustrating Śaiva themes. The structure is of the sixth century A.D. Of the same time is the famous temple at Deogaṛh in the Lalitpur sub-division of the Jhansi district, which is decorated with sculptures and panels showing a high standard of art. One of these, representing *Śiva as a yogī*, is one of the masterpieces of Indian Art in the opinion of V.A. Smith. In Kosam in the Allahabad district has been found a very artistic sculpture of *Śiva* and *Pārvatī* with an inscription dated 458 A.D. Some Śaiva images have been found at Kaman in Ajmer, e.g., the *liṅga* bearing faces of *Brahmā*, *Vishṇu*, *Śiva* and *Sūrya*, and a sculpture depicting the marriage of *Śiva* and *Pārvatī*. *Eka-mukha liṅgas* have been discovered at Khoh and Bhumra. The Khoh specimen is a masterpiece of art.

Kṛishṇa Sculptures. The worship of Vishṇu is also represented in many a monument. One of the cave-temples in the Udayagiri Hills, bearing an inscription of A.D. 401, has some fine sculptures representing the incarnation of Vishṇu as *Varāha* and also the goddesses *Gaṅgā* and *Yamunā*, standing respectively on *makara* and *kachchhapa*. In the same neighbourhood, at a place called Pathāri, is found a temple containing a massive relief on the nativity of Kṛishṇa, showing how the new-born babe lies by the side of the Mother, watched by five attendants. It has been considered as the finest and largest piece of Indian sculpture by Beglar. The Deogarh temple also has a panel representing Vishṇu reclining on Ananta, the Serpent, the symbol of eternity. At Mandor near Jodhpur have been found fragmentary sculptures of the fourth century A.D., depicting beautiful Krishṇa-scenes including the raising of Mount Govardhana.

Sūrya Sculptures. The Bhūmra temple shows an image of Sūrya dressed like the famous Kanishka statue at Mathurā Museum. He is not shown with his horses. But seven horses appear in the sculpture of Kaman (Ajmer).

Buddhist Sculptures. Buddhism has inspired some of the best examples of Gupta Art in the form of images. The Mankuwar Stone Image of the Buddha bearing an inscription dated A.D. 448 is supposed to be an example of Kushan Art, but is of the Gupta age. The Mathurā Jain Image, which is dated 113 = A.D. 432 in its inscription, also corresponds to the Kushān type. These examples show how cultural history outlives political history.

Some of the best examples of Gupta Art are found at Sārnāth. In these images Gupta Art has achieved its complete emancipation from foreign influence, and a synthesis of different artistic elements and traditions. As pointed out by Dr. Vogel, the Buddha Image of the period exhibits a new and purely national development, and, indeed, represents a new type which in artistic merit is infinitely superior to its predecessor (the Kushān Image). Some of the Buddha statues of this period, by their wonderful expression of calm repose and mild serenity, give a beautiful rendering of the Buddhist ideal. The indications of the drapery having been almost wholly discarded, the monastic robes are merely marked in outlines. On the contrary, the halo encircling the head of the Master becomes lavishly decorated with floral and foliated ornament. Evidently the real significance of this 'Circle of Light' (*prabhāmaṇḍala*) was completely forgotten. The Gupta sculptors thus succeeded in their effort to eliminate or modify those features which in the Kushan period still indicated the foreign origin of the Buddha image (*Sārnāth Museum Catalogue*).

The Sārnāth seated image of the Buddha in the act of his preaching the first sermon is considered as one of the masterpieces of Indian Art, and of its Gupta style marked by its symbolism. Thus the wheel and the two deer carved on its pedestal indicate respectively the *Dharma Chakra*, and the *Mṛigadāva*, where the wheel was first turned. His hands are shown in the position known as *Dharma-Chakra-pravartana-mudrā*. Indeed, there was a great development in the *mudrās* in the Buddhist Iconography of the time.

We also see in these Gupta Buddhist sculptures more importance being given to the figure of the Buddha, as compared with other figures which, though associated with Him in life, are now much reduced in size, and subordinated in position.

While early Buddhism banned the direct portraiture of the Buddha, Gupta Art was not trammelled by such restrictions and was free to fashion His figure in large numbers and in a variety of forms. Images of the Buddha were installed in the monasteries in their cells, in their special chapels and temples, and even in their outer niches and relic-towers.

Another marked feature of the Gupta Buddhist sculpture is that it is dominated by the cult of the Bodhisattvas, which is now very pronounced.

We have many an image not merely of Maitreya, but also, and in particular, of Avalokiteśvara.

The Sārnāth excavations have also brought to light certain other features of Indian Art of the times. There is introduced into Buddhist Art the figuring of numerous deities derived from the Brahminical pantheon, such as Vaiśravaṇa, the God of Wealth, the Goddess of Fertility, Vasudhārā, the Goddess of Plenty, Tārā, Marīchī and the like.

The expansion of the Buddhist pantheon and multiplication of images of new deities naturally resulted in a decrease in the production of sculptures directly bearing on the life of the Buddha. In this respect, Gupta Art differentiates itself from the Graeco-Buddhist Art of Gandhāra which addressed itself so much to the task of representing in stone and sculptures every possible incident in the life of the Buddha. For the same reason it is seen that while the earlier Art of Bharhut and Sāñchī was so much inspired by the *Jātakas*, Gupta Art has drawn upon other sources such as Brahminical.

Schools of Art. It will thus be seen that the Art of the Gupta Age is represented in the main by two Schools, those of Mathurā and of Benares. Mathurā was the older School which continued the traditions of Kushan-Gandhāra Art and penetrated into distant parts where its products were in request. That is why its product like the Buddha Stone Image is found so far from Mathurā at Mankuwar in Karchana in Allahabad district. Mathurā work is known from its material of mottled red stone quarried at Karri in Mathurā district, and also by its foreign features. The product of the Benares School is also declared by its material of Chunār sandstone, and its artistic features which are free of foreign influence. It also produced a new type of Buddhist stelae which are used to depict in the old Gandhāra style the incidents in the Buddha's life, typical eight or four incidents, and, in some cases, even one incident elaborated in detail.

Metal Images : Pāṭaliputra School. Gupta Art is also seen in some singular metal images of which the best examples are the

Buddha Image found at Nālandā and the collosal Buddha Image found at Sultanganj in Bhagalpur district. These examples are taken to point to a third School of Gupta Art, called by R. D. Banerji the Pāṭaliputra School, which culminated in a separate Eastern India School with its own style and technique.

Other Centres. Besides these centres, there are other minor centres of Gupta Art at places like Udayagiri, Bhilsā, Eran, Deogarh, Daśapura or Mandasor. For instance, we have already seen how at Deogaṛh, Brahminical subjects are introduced for the first time into reliefs.

National Awakening. Post-Maurya and pre-Gupta Art of northern India was shaped to a great extent by Hellenic influence and Mahāyāna Buddhism. As we have seen, Gupta Art has been mainly influenced by Brahminical religion or Hinduism, the popular religion of the country. The political conditions of the Gupta empire were favourable for creative cultural movements. The whole country was politically unified and felt the stirrings of a new life. A newly roused national spirit expressed itself in different spheres of thought and action. Its effects were seen in the field of Art and Architecture. Art acquired a new structural procedure. From imitative, Art became creative, abandoning the servile copyings, of meaningless foreign forms, and reaching out to more rational principles of architectural composition.

The First Temple. The outstanding innovation introduced in the field of Architecture was the use for the first time of dressed stone-masonry as an important step taken in the technique of building construction. Architecture, composed of stone-masonry, was first seen in the emergence of the Hindu temple.

In this connexion, it may be useful to note that Brahminical thought did not for long favour an elaborate architecture. For instance, the *Śatapatha Brāhmaṇa* describes a Hindu shrine as consisting of two sheds, 'formed of pots and beams, and covered with reeds and mats'. This kind of simple construction is seen in the bas-reliefs of Bharhut and Sāñchī, showing fire-altars and shrines which were practically unroofed, so that religious service and rituals were performed in the open air. Perhaps the earliest example of a Brahminical stone-structure is the Vishṇu shrine at Besnagar near the Heliodorus Pillar, and hence of the second century B.C. Brahminical religion insisted on the contemplation of the Formless, in which Art could not originate. For the object of Art is to render and present the Infinite and Formless in terms of the Finite and Form. Art arose from the irrespressible popular craving for worship of God in a visible form. So the deity had to be enshrined, and structutal shrines came into being.

Growth of Temple Architecture. We may trace the evolution of the structure of the Hindu temple in its different stages: (1) a leafy bower, (2) a hut of reed, (3) a cella of wood and bricks. Eventually emerged in the Gupta period the sanctum of stone: the *garbha-gṛiha*, a small cell with only one door-way so as not to intrude upon the inner darkness conducive to contemplation. Within was enshrined the effigy of the deity. The walls of the interior were naturally devoid of ornament but not so was the exterior of the temple. The outer side of the door-way came to be richly carved, and to the door was added a porch for shelter, which appeared as a pillared portico in the later Gupta examples.

These smaller Hindu sanctuaries were not yet glorified into regular temples. They were only shrines or chapels. Along with these stone-built structures there appeared excavated chambers, with attached structural porticos as seen in the Udayagiri caves.

Scope for Elaboration. The evolution of Gupta temple-architecture had these small beginnings marked by a flat roof and pillared portico. They gave room for artistic elaboration in regard to the following features, viz. (1) the shape of the pillar and its capital, (2) the treatment of inter-columniation, (3) the continuation of the architecture as a string-course round the entire building, (4) the design of the door-way.

Examples. The elaboration of these features may be seen in the following typical examples: (1) The temple at Tigawa in Jabbalpur district, (2) The Narasiṃgha and other shrines at Eran, north-east of Bhilsā, (3) A temple at Sāñchī, (4) The famous temple at Bhūmara in Nagod State, (5) A temple at Nachna in the Ajaigarh State, (6) A group of rock-out sanctuaries at Udayagiri near Sāñchī.

Tigawa Temple. Of these examples, the most typical is the Vishṇu temple at Tigawa. It keeps up the small size of the sanctum and the cella. The arrangement of the portico-pillars and the inter-columniation leaves a wider interval in the middle than on either side. The design of the pillar is typically and strictly Gupta. It consists of the following parts: (1) a massive abacus surmounted by a device of lions; (2) a capital resembling a vase or *kalaśa* (or inverted lotus); (3) a short shaft of many sides; (4) a plain square pedestal.

The design of the pillar takes after the famous *Garuḍahavaja* of Besnagar, while the lion is a link with the Aśokan capital.

The other new feature of Tigawa temple is the shape and decoration of its door-way. The upper angle of the door-way departs from the older Buddhist device of a dryad embracing a tree or a *Yakshī*. Instead, it shows on one side *Yamunā* on tortoise and on the other side *Gaṅgā* on crocodile. This feature becomes very prominent on the door-ways of later Gupta temples, and is carved on the base of the door-post.

The most important feature of the Gupta capital is the *Pūrṇa-kalaśa*, 'the Bowl of Plenty', typifying a renewed faith, suggesting the '*vase-and-flower*' motif, one of the most graceful forms in the whole range of Indian Architecture.

Temples at Bhūmara and Nachna. The Siva temple at Bhūmara and the Pārvatī temple at Nachna, which are probably to be dated earlier than A.D. 500, add a new feature, a processional path which is open in one case and roofed in the other. In each case, the door-ways show typical Gupta design, with their over-hanging lintels, figure-panels in the upper corner, and general ornate treatment. The spirited floral scrolls and crisp modelling, the chiselled patterns on lintels, recall the brush forms of the Ajantā frescoes in their artistic workmanship. The Bhūmara temple, indeed, is noted for its ornamental sculptures, decorated gateways, fine arabesque medallions, *Kīrtimukhas*, and ceiling decorated with figures of foliage, creepers, and breakers. It has also fine *Chaitya*-windows with medallions bearing the figures of *Gaṇeśa*, *Brahmā*, *Yama*, *Kubera*, *Kārtikeya*, *Śiva* dancing on Bull, *Sūrya*, *Kāma*, and *Mahishāsura-mardinī*.

Deogaṛh Temple. The Deogaṛh temple adds a pyramidial tower over the sanctum (the first appearance of the *śikhara*), and also four porticos supported on a row of four pillars to each of the four sides of the temple. The door-way is also charged with abundance of decorative additions.

Pillars. Besides these temples, Gupta Art is also represented in several free-standing pillars such as the Budha Gupta Monolithic Pillar at Eran dated A.D. 484, and the earlier more famous Iron Pillar at Delhi. The shaft of the former is surmounted by a lion-abacus. It supports at the top a statuette of good Vishṇu. The pillar is 43 feet high. The Iron Pillar at Delhi was removed to its present site from its original site at Mathurā or a hill near the Beas. It was presumably fashioned to the order of emperor Kumāra Gupta I about A.D. 415, because the inscription it bears describes the exploits of his father Chandra Gupta II. Its height is 23 feet and 8 inches. It is composed of pure malleable iron and is over six tons in weight. It is a remarkable testimony to metallurgical skill and to the capacity of the foundry to have forged such a piece of iron.

The temples of the times were constituted into Corporations which issued their own Seals Such Seals have been discovered at places like Gayā, Vaiśālī and Bhīṭā. One bears the legend '*Śrī-Vishṇu-pāda-Svamī-Nārāyaṇa*' and was issued by the *Vishṇupāda* temple at Gayā.

The upper part of the seal bears figures of Vishṇu's symbols such as mace, conch, and wheel, together with symbols of Śiva, Sūrya, and Chandra. A Vaiśālī seal bears the legend '*Bhagavato Ādityasya*', and was issued by the temple of the Sun. Its upper part bears the figure of an altar as symbol of the Sun. Some seals figuring the fire-altar have also been found at Bhīṭā.

Varṇāśrama-dharma. Social life was based upon the orthodox Hindu system designated as *Varṇāśrama-dharma*, the system marked by division of society into *Varṇas* or Castes and of life into graduated stages known as *Āśramas*. It was the duty of the sovereign to uphold the social order and prevent confusion and unlawful mixture of castes. Abhayadatta, Governor (*Rājasthānīya*) of a Province, is described as 'the protector of castes' (*varṇāḥ*) and his successor Dharmadosha as preventing the mixture of castes (*Varṇa-saṅkara*) (No. 35).

The Brahmins as the highest caste represented the highest standard of intellectual and moral life to merit social respect. They produced *Yogīs* intent on concentrated contemplation (*dhyāna-ekāgrapara*) for achievement of *siddhi* (self-fulfilment) and *moksha* (salvation), and also *Munis* who with devotion (*bhakti*) gave themselves up to total and extreme (*tīvra*) penance as their only concern in life (*topodhana*) (No. 18). In the Karamadāṇḍā inscription of the reign of Kumāra Gupta I (*EI*, X, 72), the Brahmins are noted for their penance (*tapaḥ*), Vedic study (*svādhyāya*), and proficiency in the *Mantras*, *Sūtras*, *Bhāshyas*, and *Pravachanas*. They won the respect of the King. Mahārāja Hastin is described as 'extremely (*atyanta*) devoted to gods and Brāhmaṇas' (No. 21). As we have seen, the inscriptions are full of grants of lands and *agrahāras* to Brahmins to help them in their life of learning and religion and performance of expensive Vedic ceremonies like *Agnihotra* and *Pañcha-mahāyajñas*. Brahmins were respected for their piety by followers of all religions. For instance, a village is described as a holy place for its association with saints (*sādhu-saṁsarga-pūta*), while a Jain nobleman named Madra takes credit to himself in his inscription (No. 15) for his attachment (*prīti*) to *dvija-guru-yati*, 'Brahmins, religious preceptors, and ascetics.' A royal family had its own preceptor or *āchārya*. Queen Prabhāvatī Guptā made a gift of a village to her family-*guru*, Āchārya Chaṇāla Svāmī, a member of a Brahmin colony (*agrahāra*) of *Chāturvidyas* (those who are learned in the four *vidyās*) [*EI*, *XV*. 39]. A city is spoken of as being purged of its sins and infirmities by the singing of prayers by hundreds of Brahmins engaged for the purpose by its Mayor (No. 14). Mātṛi Vishṇu is a rare example of a Brahmin king 'who was like a Ṛishi (*viprarshi*), devoted to the duties of his order (*svakarmābhirata*), and performance of Vedic Sacrifices (*Kratu-yājī*), well-read in the Sāstras and Vedas' (No. 19).

A Brahmin was assigned to the *Gotra* or lineage by which he was known. The inscriptions tell of the following *Gotras* as being then prevalent: *Ātreya* (No. 56); *Aupamanyava* (No. 23); *Bharadvāja* (Nos. 56, 60, 81); *Bhārgava* (No. 22); *Gautama* (No. 26); *Gotama* (No. 67); *Kāṇva* (No. 20); *Kāśyapa* (No. 56); *Kauṇḍinya* (Nos. 41, 51, 56); *Kautsa* (Nos. 6, 21, 22); *Maudgalya* (No. 56); *Pārāśarya* (*Ibid*); *Śāṇḍilya* (*Imid*); *Śarkarāksha* (No. 39); *Śāśataneya* (No. 27); *Śāṭyāyana* (No. 56); *Varshagaṇa* (No. 16); *Vāsula* (No. 22); *Vatsa* (Nos. 38 and 41); *Vātsya* (No. 56); *Vishṇu-vṛiddha* (Nos. 55 and 56); *Aśva* and *Vājī*. Brahmins were also known by the Vedas they followed, e.g., *Sāmavedī* Brahmins.

Though castes were ordinarily confined to the pursuit of their prescribed crafts, the inscriptions record some exceptions, as we have already seen. Minister Mayūra-rakshaka was a Brahmin and so also was the chief Mātṛi Vishṇu. Minister Śikharasvāmī was also a Brahmin of the class called Chhāndogas whose *Gotras* were *Aśva* and *Vājin* (Karamadāṇḍā inscription). Kshatriyas also figure as traders (No. 16).

There are also on record cases of inter-caste marriage. Brahmin Ravikīrti is married to a Kshatriya named Bhānuguptā (No. 35).

Kings were given to polygamy, e.g., Chandra Gupta II, and Kumāra Gupta I, as already shown. But the chief Queen was possessed of a high constitutional status so as to figure on coins as participating in the King's *aśvamedha*. A woman had her *strīdhana* out of which she makes a charitable grant (No. 62). *Satī* was known (No. 20).

Economic Conditions. The facts and data of economic life and organization have been already dealt with in the account of the reign of each particular king. We may here give a general view and summary of these.

The outstanding fact of the economy of those times is the organization of industry or handicrafts under Guilds called *Śreṇīs*. Their corporate character is brought out by the seals which were issued by them. The abundance of seals found at only one city like Vaiśālī shows to what extent these Guilds played their part in the economic life of the country. These Vaiśālī (Basāṛh) seals bring to light the Guilds (*nigamas*) of Bankers (*śreshṭhīs*), Traders (*sārthavāhas*) and Artisans (*kulikas*). Sometimes these Guilds federated themselves into a larger Corporation, as in the legend '*Śreshṭhī-Kulika-Nigama*', i.e., the Corporation of Bankers and Artisans. 'There are again many seals testifying to the corporation formed by the federation of the three Guilds of Bankers, Traders and Artisans. One seal also has the legend *Prathama-kulika* showing that he was the President of the Guild of Artisans. As Dr. T. Bloch who discovered these Vaiśālī-seals points out: 'It looks as if during those days, something like a modern Chamber of Commerce existed in Upper India at some big trading centre, perhaps at Pāṭaliputra' (Archaeological Survey, Annual Report, 1903-4, p. 104). It will be apparent from these numerous seals that Vaiśālī in those days was a very flourishing centre of trade, banking and business.

Some of the inscriptions of the time of the Gupta emperors, as we have seen, bear sufficient testimony to the growth of these Guilds for which the established technical term is *Śreṇi*. The Indore Copper-plate inscription of A.D. 465 mentions a *Tailika-śreṇī*, Guild of Oilmen, of which the President (*Pravara*) is named Jīvanta. This Oilmen's Guild was trusted even by a Brahmin with the custody of his donation to be held by it in perpetuity (*ājasrikam*) under a contract which was registered (*nibaddha*). The Bihar Stone Pillar inscription of Skanda Gupta also records the creation of a permanent endowment aptly called *akshayanīvī* in favour of a guild of the town of Ajapuraka.

The Mandasor inscription of the reign of Kumāra Gupta II (No. 18) mentions a Guild of Silk-Weavers (*Paṭṭavāya-Śreṇī*) and its prosperous finances as shown by its construction of an unequalled temple of the Sun.

These Banking functions were sometimes undertaken by other bodies than these *Śreṇīs*. For instance, the governing body of the *Mahāvihāra* at Kākanādaboṭa (Sāñchī), the *Ārya Saṁgha* with its Executive called the *Pañchamaṇḍalī*, received a permanent donation for the benefit of its monks (No. 62). Similarly, the Temple Committees also received permanent gifts of cash or kind for perpetual supply of some of the requisites of worship such as scents, incense, flowers, or lights, as shown above.

The main point of banking involved in these transactions is that these Corporations gave facilities to private philanthropists by taking permanent custody of their gifts, the corpus of which they held intact as trust-property (*akshayanīvī*). They also allowed payment of interest on these permanent deposits and agreed to spend this income on the objects mentioned by the donors. That they were paying interest on their deposits shows that they were investing to profit these deposits on their own account. The rate of the profit must have been greater than the rate of interest paid out. Thus these Guilds, acting as Trustees, gave great stimulus to private charities by guaranteeing their security against loss, embezzlement, or misappropriation.

The Gupta empire was based upon a money-economy, as is

shown by the abundance and variety of types of coinage in gold, silver, and copper in circulation in all its parts.

A reference may also be made in this connexion to the construction of Public Works of Utility in those days. Glimpses of some of these are given in the inscriptions. The largest of such works is the *taṭāka* or the reservoir named *Sudarśana* which was originally constructed in the time of the Maurya emperor, Chandra Gupta, about 750 years back, by damming up the courses of the rivers rising from the hills near Girnar (Girinagara) by means of a rocky embankment; but this embankment, in the time of Skanda Gupta, burst as a result of continuous rain creating a breach in it. The engineers of those days were, however, efficient enough to repair the breach within two months, and by executing proper masonry work (*samyak-ghaṭita-upalena*) reconstructed the embankment, with a length of 100 cubits, breadth of 68 cubits and 7 men's height= about 40 feet.

The second reference to these engineering works occurs, as already stated, in the Gangdhar Stone inscription of Viśvavarman who endowed his city built on the bank of the Gargarā with wells for irrigation (*vāpī*), tanks (*taḍāga*), temples and halls of gods (*surasadma-sabhā*), drinking-wells (*udapāna*), parks (*upavana*) of various kinds, causeways (*saṁkrama*) and reservoirs of water (*dīrghikā*).

Similarly, the Mandasor Stone inscription describes how *Lāṭa-Vishaya* was adorned with temples (*deva-kula*), assembly halls of gods (*deva-sabhā*) and *vihāras*, with rows of storeyed mansions (*prāsāda-mālā*) like rows of aerial chariots (*vimāna-māla*) which were as high as the hills.

Political Conditions: Royal Succession. The Gupta emperors generally nominated their successors on the throne Chandra Gupta I announced his nomination of Samudra Gupta as his successor before his Council or *Sabhā*. The Ṛiddhapura inscription also hints at such nomination in the expression *tatpāda-parigṛihīta*. In the case of Chandra Gupta II, his nomination by his father is indicated in the expression *tat-parigṛihīta* (No. 4), an expression repeated in Nos 12 and 13. Inscription No. 61 prepares the way by describing him as the *satputra* of his father.

Imperial Titles. The inscriptions already dealt with mention the following titles usual for the emperor: *Paramadaivata*, *Paramabhaṭṭāraka*, *Mahārājādhirāja* and *Pṛithivīpāla* (Damodarpur Copper-plate inscriptions); *Parameśvara* (No. 36), *Samrāṭ* (No. 33), *Ekādhirāja* (No. 32), and *Chakravartin* (No. 39). The king received the homage of his subjects in the *Upasthāna* or Darbar-Hall (No. 15).

Local Kings. These are called in the inscriptions *Nṛipa*, *Nṛipat* or *Pārthiva* or *Mahārāja* (No. 18), or a *Mahāsāmanta*, a feudatory (No. 80).

The king was assisted in his administration by a Chief Minister called *Sachiva* described as 'his third eye' (*rājñaḥ tritīyameva chakshuḥ*) (No. 17).

There were also other officers attached to the royal household such as the *Mahāpratihāra* (the Chief Usher of the palace), the *Vinayasūra* (whose function seems to have been to announce and conduct visitors to the king), the *Sthapati-Samrāṭ* (probably superintendent of the attendants of the woman's departments) (No. 26), and the *Pratinartaka* (who was the Official Chronicler or Minstrel) (No. 39).

His Chief Secretary who was of the rank of a provincial governor is described on a Vaiśālī seal as *Śrī-Paramabhaṭṭārakapādīya*.

An important officer of the Palace staff was the Superintendent of the royal kitchen called *Khādyaṭapākika*.

The king as a conqueror employed special officers (*yuktapurushas*) to administer the difficult charge of restoring to the vanquished the properties seized by him (*vibhava-pratyarpaṇa*) (No. 1).

Administrative Divisions. The inscriptions indicate a hierarchy of administrative divisions from top to bottom. The empire is called a *rājya* (No. 55), a *rāshṭra*, *deśa* or *maṇḍala*. The word *pṛithivī* (Damodarpur) is also used along with the word *avanī*. Instances of these are *Sukuli-deśa* (No. 5), *Dabhāla-deśa* (No. 19), *Surāshṭra-avanī* (No. 14).

The empire or kingdom was divided into provinces. A province is called a *Bhukti* such as *Puṇḍravardhana-bhukti* (Damodarpur), *Tīra-bhukti* (Basāṛh seal), *Nagara-bhukti* (No. 46), and *Uttaramaṇḍala bhukti* (Gunaigaṛh inscription of Vainya Gupta). A province is also called a *Pradeśa*, such as *Airikiṇa-pradeśa*. It is also sometimes called a *Bhoga*, and its Governor a *Bhogika* (Nos. 21, 23, 26, 27, 29 and 30). Below the province, and a part of it was the *Vishaya* or district. We have references in the inscriptions to the following *Vishayas*: *Koṭivarsha* (Damodarpur), *Khādāpāra* (Damodarpur 1, 2 and Dhānāidaha), *Pañcha-nagarī* (Baigram Charter), *Lāṭa* (No. 18), *Vaiśālī* (seal), and *Antaravedī* (No. 14). A part of a district is called a *Vīthī* in some inscriptions (e.g. Pāhārpur). The *Vīthī* is connected with the series: *Vīthī-Maṇḍala-Pārśva-Grāma* (*ib.*). A Faridpur grant of Dharmāditya mentions the *Vishayapati* of *Vāraka-maṇḍala*. No. 39 of Fleet gives the series: *Dhāra-Paṭhaka-Grāma*. A Union of Villages is called a *Peṭhaka* (No. 25) and *Santaka* (No. 26). Smaller units or divisions of a village are called *Paṭṭa* and *Agrahāra* (No. 22).

Provincial Administration. The Head of the Province is called

Uparika-Mahārāja in the Damodarpur Copper-plate inscriptions. He is also called *Goptā* (No. 14), *Bhogika*, and *Bhogapati*. No. 35 employs a new term *Rājasthānīya*. The term is thus explained by Kshemendra in his *Lokaprakāśa*: *Prajā-pālanārthaṁ-udvahati-rakshayati cha sa rājasthānīyaḥ*, i.e., 'the officer who shoulders the burden of protecting and promoting the welfare of the subjects'; but the term is used for lower officials in Nos. 38 and 46.

Sometimes, the Governor may be the king's son (*Rājaputra Devabhaṭṭāraka* in Damodarpur Copper-plate 5). The Minister in attendance on the royal governor is called *Kumārāmātya*.

The Head of the Province was attended by a staff of private secretaries to act as intermediaries between him and the administration, and communicate his orders to them. These are called in the inscriptions *Dūtas*, *Dūtakas*, or *Ājñā-dāpakas* (No. 22). Thus these offices involved great trust and responsibility and were given only to the higher officers of the rank of a *Rājasthānīya* and a *Uparika*, as the mouthpiece of the sovereign or the Head of the administration. For instance, a great frontier king (Mahāsāmanta) figures as a *Dūtaka* who communicates the royal gift to the *Kumārāmatyas* concerned, showing that his official position was superior to that of the *Kumārāmātya*. It appears that the officer complementary to the *Dūtakas* was the scribe called *Karaṇa-Kāyastha* who put into writing the royal order and held the high office of the king's Minister for Peace and War (*Sāndhivigrahika*) (Gunaigaṛh inscription of Vainya Gupta).

The provincial administration included the following staff as Heads of Departments as mentioned in the Vaiśālī Seal inscriptions: (1) *Baḷādhikaraṇika*, the holder of the office of the head of the army or the military, (2) *Daṇḍapāśādhikaraṇika*, the Chief of the Police, (3) *Raṇabhāṇḍārika*, the Chancellor of the military exchequer, (4) *Mahādaṇḍanāyaka*, Chief-Justice, (5) *Vinaya-sthiti-sthāpaka*, Minister for Law and Order, (6) *Bhaṭāśvapati*, Commandant of infantry and cavalry. The Commandant of the elephant-force is called *Mahā-pīlupati* in Guṇaigaṛh inscription of Vainya Gupta. It also testifies to another officer who controlled five district offices, like a modern Divisional Commissioner. A Faridpur inscription of Dharmāditya mentions an officer called *Sādhanika* who had to deal with debts and fines (*sādhana*) and was hence a judicial officer.

The Allahabad Pillar inscription adds the office of *Senāpati* or Commander-in-chief.

The Mallasarul Copper-plate inscription of king Gopachandra mentions the following additional provincial officers: (1) *Kartākṛitika* (Head of the executive); (2) *Bhoga-patika* (officer-in-charge of a *bhoga* or division); (3) *Tādāyuktaka* (Treasury officer); (4) *Hiraṇya-sāmudāyika* (Currency officer); (5) *Aurṇa-sthānika* (Superintendent of silk factories); (6) *Audraṅgika* (Collector of the *udraṅga* tax); (7) *Chauroddharaṇika* (Inspector-General of Police); (8) *Āgrahārika* (Superintendent of the *agrahāras* in the province).

District Administration. The Head of the District is called *Vishayapati*. The civil station or the headquarters of the district bore the name of *Adhishṭhāna*. The office is called *Adhikaraṇa*. The City-Magistrate is also called *Drāṅgika* (No. 38). Thus a Vaiśālī seal contains an inscription '*Vaiśālī-adhishṭhāna-adhikaraṇa*'. The executive officers of the district are called by the generic names of *Sambyavahāri* (Baigram and Nandapur Copper-plate inscriptions) and *Āvuktakas* (Nandapur Copper-plate inscription). The District Magistrate was helped in his administrtion by a representative body of officers mentioned as follows: (1) *Mahattaras* (Village Elders) (2) *Ashṭakulādhikaraṇikas* (probably officers in charge of groups of 8 *kulas* or families in the local area) (3) *Grāmika* (Village-Headman) (4) *Śaulkika* (Collector of customs and tolls) (5) *Gaulmika* (in charge of forests and forts) (6) *Āgrahārika* (in charge of the *agrahāras*, settlements dedicated to gods or Brahmins) [No. 12] (7) *Dhruvādhikaraṇika* (in charge of land revenue) (No. 38) (8) *Bhāṇḍāgārādhikṛita* (Treasurer), [*EI*, XII, 75] (9) *Talāvāṭaka* (Village Accountant) [No. 46] (10) *Utkhetuyiṭa* (Collector of Taxes) [*EI*, XII, 75] and (11) *Pustupāla* (the Notary and Keeper of Records).

The District Records Office is called *Akshapaṭala* under the departmental Head called the *Mahākshapaṭalika* (Nos. 39 and 60). The Department of Records comprised clerks who had to write and copy out records and documents. These writers are called *Diviras* (No. 27) and *Lekhakas* (No. 80), while the documents are called *Karaṇas* (No. 56) and were kept in the custody of the Registrar called *Karaṇika*. The officer drafting the document is called *Kartṛi or Śāsayitṛi* (*EI*, XII, 75).

Besides these officers with specified functions, there were also employed in the district office what may be called general superintendents designated as *Sarvādhyakshas* (No. 55) under whom were employed men who were of noble lineage and called *Kulaputras*, to guard against corruption.

City Administration. The Mayor of the city is called *Purapāla* (Gunaigarh inscription), or *Nagara-Rakshaka* (No. 14). There was also a Super-Mayor who controlled the Mayors of different cities, *Purapāla-Uparika* (Gunaigarh inscription). The Mayor of Daśapura is called *Daśapura-pāla* (No. 18). A city was governed by a Municipality called *Parishat*, as in the case of the city of Udānakūpa. A city had a special officer as a Superintendent of *Dharmaśālās*, who was called *Āvasathika* (Mallasarul inscription of Gopachandra).

The Pāhāḍpur Copper-plate inscription of G.E. 159=A.D. 479

and of the time of emperor Budha Gupta gives new details regarding local administration. It refers to the executive officers of the district as *Āyuktakas* and to the city municipality [*adhishṭhāna* (=city)-*adhikaraṇa* (=municipal office)] headed by (*Puroga*) the Mayor of the city (*Ārya-nagara-śreshṭhī*). The proposals for transfer of land in the village are in the first instance referred to the standing non-official Village Council consisting of (1) leading Brahmins (*Brāhmaṇottaras*), (2) leading villagers (*Mahattaras*), and (3) representative householders (*Kuṭumbinaḥ*).

The Damodarpur Copper-plate inscription No. 2 also gives slightly different details. It composes the Village Council of 4 classes of members, viz., (1) *Mahattaras*, (2) *Ashṭa-kulādhikaraṇas*, (3) *Grāmikas*, and (4) *Kuṭumbinas* (householders).

Sources of Revenue and Taxation. These are indicated in the records of grants of land specifying the benefits and immunities which the grants carried for the beneficiaries. These are thus mentioned: (1) *Udraṅga* (probably the land-tax); (2) *Uparikara* ('a tax levied on cultivators who have no proprietory rights on soil'—Fleet); (3) *Vāta* (unexplained); (4) *Bhūta* (probably what is 'grown', as distinguished from 'withered '*vāta*') (5) *Dhānya*; (6) *Hiraṇya* (gold); (7) *Ādeya* (what is to be surrendered); (8) *Vaishṭika* (forced labour, if necessary); (9) *Daśāparādha* (Fines from Ten Offences, viz., (a) *three* offences of the body, theft, murder, and adultery; (b) *four* offences of speech, harsh words, untruthful words, libellous words and pointless words; and (*c*) *three* offences of mind, coveting others' property, thinking of wrong, and devotion to what is not true); (10) *Bhoga* (enjoyment); (11) *Bhāga* (share). No. 55 of Fleet's '*Gupta Inscriptions*' indicates very well, though negatively, the obligations imposed by the State on a village rendered free by the king's grant: 'It is *not* to pay taxes (*akaradāyī*); it is *not* to be molested by the regular troops or police (*bhaṭa*), or by outlaws (*chāṭa*); it is *not* to yield increase in its cows and bulls; *nor* in its flowers or milk, pasturage, hides, and charcoal; *nor* any taxes on salt or wet salt, on sale and purchase, or produce of mines; it is *not* to contribute forced labour or surrender its hidden treasures and deposits, the *klṛipta* and *upaklṛipta* (unexplained)'. We may also cite in this connexion the Poona Copper-plate inscription of Prabhāvatī Guptā (*EI*, XV 39) recording her grant of a village to her family *Guru*, Āchārya Chanāla Svāmī belonging to the community or *agrahāra* of Chāturvidyas. The record enumerates the following exemptions (*parihāra*) carried by the grant: 'freedom from molestation by soldiers (*bhaṭa*) and the king's umbrella-bearers (*chhātra*); *not* yielding the right to pasturage (*chārāsana*), hides (*charma*), *aṅgāra* (charcoal), the purchase (*kreṇi*) of fermenting drugs (*kiṇva*) and mines (*khānaka*), *not* yielding the right to increase of cattle; *not* to supply animals for sacrifice; *not* to give any share of flowers and milk, or hidden treasures and deposits, together with *klṛipta* and *upaklṛipta* (probably sales tax).'

Bengal Inscriptions. In conclusion, it may be noted that most of the Bengal inscriptions of the period are remarkable for the concrete details and data they contain as regards land-transactions and the light they throw upon the working of the village administration. These inscriptions may be enumerated in the chronological order as follows:—

I. Reign of Kumāra Gupta I (A.D. 415-455).

(1) Dhānāidaha Copper-plate inscription of G.E. 113=A.D. 432.
(2) Kalaikuri Inscrption of 120=A.D. 439.
(3) Damodarpur No. 1 Copper-plate inscription of G.E. 124=A.D. 443.
(4) Same No. 2 of the year G.E. 128=A.D. 447.
(5) Baigram Copper-plate inscription of G.E. 128=A.D. 448.

II. Reign of Budha Gupta (*c.* A.D. 476-495).

(6) Damodarpur No. 3 Copper-plate inscription of A.D. 476.
(7) Pāhāḍpur copper-plate inscription of G.E. 159=A.D. 479.
(8) Damodarpur No. 4 Copper-plate inscription of G.E. 163=A.D. 482.
(9) Nandapur Copper-plate inscription of G.E. 169=A.D.488.

III. Reign of Narasimha Gupta (A.D. 495-533).

(10) Gunaigaṛh Copper-plate inscription of Vainya Gupta of G.E. 188=A.D. 507.

IV. Reign of Kumāra Gupta III.

(11) Damodarpur No. 5 Copper-plate inscription of G.E. 224=A.D. 543.

V. Reign of Dharmāditya.

(12) Faridpur Copper-plate inscription No. 1 of Dharmāditya.
(13) Same No. 2.
(14) Mallasarul Copper-plate inscription of Vijayasena and Dharmāditya.

VI. Reign of Gopachandra.

(15) Faridpur-Copper-plate inscription of Gopachandra.

Land Transaction. The evidence of these inscriptions has been already considered in connexion with the reigns of the kings associated with them. It will suffice here to notice only some of its general features.

As a rule, the entire cultivable land of a village was settled and distributed into holdings among its householders (*kuṭumbinaḥ*). Land that was required for a public purpose or a charity could not be taken by government out of these settled holdings of peasant-proprietors. It had to be taken out of the fallow and unsettled land of the village without disturbing the existing holdings (*kuṭumbināṁ karshaṇā-virodhisthāne*).

Such land has been described by a variety of terms used in the different inscriptions. It should be (1) *apradā* (unsettled), (2) *aprahata* (not tilled), (3) *astamba* (devoid of vegetation), (4) *khila* (fallow), (5) *samudayabāhya* (not productive of any income or revenue), (6) *apratikara* (not yielding any revenue), (7) not causing any loss of revenue to the king by its grant or alienation by the king (*na kaśchit rājārtha-virodhaḥ*), (8) *utpratikara* (not assessed).

But such land, though uncultivated, was cultivable. It could be profitably brought under the plough and would bring additional revenue to the State (*upachaya*). That is why the State charged to its donor the customary sale-price (*vikraya-maryādā*) which it could bear. Out of its yield, the donor was also able to create an endowment to maintain his charity. It is thus called a *kshetra*, a plot that could be cultivated to profit.

Land was required as a building site, for purposes of a homestead (*vāstu*), or for digging trenches (*sthala*) and gardening (*talavāṭaka*).

The grant of these lands by the State for charitable purposes was governed by a particular rule called *nīvī-dharma* or *apradā-dharma*. The rule is that the charity must be irrevocable and a permanent one so that the land granted for it could not be given away or transferred to any other party to profit as if it were private property. It was to be treated as trust-property aptly called *akshya-nīvī*, to remain intact for all time without any diminution (*akshaya*), and inalienable.

The inscriptions also show that the unsettled land of the village was government property. When a slice was taken out of it for purposes of a charitable grant of the aforesaid description, it was done by government suspending its standing rule as to its non-transferability (*anuvritta-apradākshayanīvī*).

The government in making the grant had also to make sure that it was not to pay for the land granted any compensation due to its dispossessed proprietor (*akiñchit-pratikara*), if any. This stipulation also indicates that such land must not come out of settled plots and holdings, but out of unsettled fallow land (*khila kshetra*).

One of the Faridpur grants, however, mentions a gift of land which was not *khila*-or *aprahata*-but *vāpa-kshetra*, i.e. land which was already under cultivation, for which a higher price was also charged by the State.

Plots were marked out from one another by ash (*tusha*), charcoal and the like (*aṅgārādi*), by pegs (*kīlaka*), or by boundary signs (*sīmāliṅgāni*) which were prominently visible (*drishṭi-mātra-prabandhena*).

ADDENDA

I

THE BAYANA HOARD OF NEW IMPERIAL GUPTA COINS

Recently a vast hoard of imperial Gupta coins has been discovered at Bayana in Bharatpur State containing some new varieties of coin types as noticed by Dr. A. S. Altekar in the Journal of the Numismatic Society of India, VIII, pp. 179-184, X pp. 95-118 and later in his monograph on the subject. These are described below :—

(1) SAMUDRA GUPTA :—(a) Of the various types of coinage of Samudra Gupta, the most popular type is the Standard type of which the largest number of examples has been so far discovered as compared to those of other types. The name *Samudra* without *Gupta* is more usual on these coins.

(b) The Bayana hoard has revealed coins applying the title *Vikrama* to Samudra Gupta. But so far it was known to have been a title of Chandra Gupta II.

(c) The Archer type shows examples with the new legend *Avanīśo*.

(d) The Lyrist type shows two varieties of larger and smaller size.

(e) The legend on Aśvamedha coins restored by Venis as '*Divaṁ Jayati-Āhṛita-Vājimedhah*' is confirmed by these coins.

(f) The Kācha type shows specifically Indian features, the King wearing *dhoti* and Goddess on the reverse holding *Pāśa*.

In the prayer or Dhayāna of Durgā Daśabhujā, ten-handed, there is an enumeration of ten weapons with which she is armed by the gods as Mahishāsuramardinī, the Subduer of the Demon Mahisha. One of these weapons is mentioned as *Pāśa* in the following expression :

'*Kheṭakam Pūrṇachāpañcha Pāśamaṅkuśameva cha.*' Again, in *Śrī Chaṇḍī* of *Mārkaṇḍeya Purāṇa*, it is stated that the gods were arming the Goddess for her coming combat with the Demons with the weapons special to each. In their enumeration, Varuṇa's gift to the Goddess was his special weapon *Pāśa* or noose with which the enemy who was not to be killed was to be tied (*Sā kshiptvā tasya vai Pāśaṁ taṁ babandha Mahāsuram*) as stated in the following : '*Kāladaṇḍād Yamo daṇḍaṁ Pāśaṁ cha Ambupatirdadau*', 'Yama (the God of Death) gave his Invincible Rod and Varuṇa, the Lord of the Ocean, gave Her his Noose.'

But *Śrī Chaṇḍī* does not indicate the hand in which the Goddess holds the *Pāśa*. She is also called in this text by several names such as Śivā, Ambikā, Bhadrakālī, Bhagavatī, Chaṇḍikā, etc.

The hoard has no coins of Rāma Gupta.

(2) CHANDRA GUPTA II :—(a) Examples of Archer type of Chandra Gupta II show the king holding *Kaśā* consisting of wooden handle to which is attached a leather thong tied to it by a knot.

(b) The Bayana hoard contains the largest number of Lion-Slayer coins of Chandra Gupta II.

(c) It reveals a new type (Addendum Pl. figs. 2, 3) which may be called *Chakravikrama type*. The observe depicts the figure of Chakra looking like a halo round the deity who must be Chakrapurusha (Sudarśana personified). The god offers to the king His boon which must be the boon of *parākrama* as indicated by the appropriate legend *Chakravikrama* appearing on the reverse.

(3) KUMĀRA GUPTA I:—The coinage of Kumāra Gupta I shows a large variety of types, as many as fourteen.

(a) The Elephant-rider of this hoard shows the following complete legend: '*Kshtaripu Kumāragupta goptā rājā jayatyaniśam*' 'Rājā Kumāragupta, Protector of his people, is constantly conquering, with his enemies afflicted.' The reverse shows the complete legend '*Śrī-Mahendra-gajaḥ*' 'the elephant of Śrī Mahendra (Kumāra Gupta)', not so far read.

(b) The Elephant-rider Lion-slayer type shows on the reverse the legend '*Simhanihantā Mahendragajaḥ*.'

(c) A new coin of the Bayana hoard corresponding to the 'Pratāpa' type contains a legend on the reverse which is read by Dr. A. S. Altekar as *Apratigha*. The figures on the obverse of this coin are exactly those of the old Pratāpa type.

The following are new types of coinage of Kumāra Gupta I brought to light in the hoard: (1) Chhtra type (2) Lyrist type (3) The King and Queen type. The observe of this shows the King offering flowers to the Queen. (4) Rhino-slayer type. The obverse shows the King on a horse wearing a buttoned coat and trousers and leaning to attack the rhino by the sword (Addendum Pl. I fig. 1). The rhino stands at bay with his single horn on his head and circular spots on his body, turning back his head to attack the king. The legend reads: '*Bhartā Khadgatrātā Kumāragupto jayatyaniśam* (*Jayatyaniśam*), 'Always conquering is Lord Kumāra Gupta who saves himself from *Khaḍga* (rhino), or saves (his people) by his *Khaḍga* (Sword).

II

1. Chandra Gupta I Coinage—p. 33.

The legend on the reverse which is read as *Lichchhavayaḥ* should be interpreted to mean that the coin in question was issued by the Republican Community of Lichchhavis whose sovereignty and independence were not affected by the alliance in marriage between Chandra Gupta I and the Lichchhavi princess Kumāradevī also named on the reverse. Although the Lichchhavi republic perhaps became a part of the Gupta empire, it did not affect the local autonomy of the Lichchhavis as a republic who thus exercised their right to issue their own coins.

2. As usual the reverse figures a goddess who is taken to be Durgā as *Simhavāhanā* or seated on lion but Śrī C. Śivaramamurti has pointed out to me that the lion is also figuring along with the lotus and therefore he suggests that the lotus should point to goddess Lakshmī and the lion to her status as the Goddess of Sovereignty (Rājyalakshmī) of which the lion is the symbol.

3. The reverse also gives the figures of the 'Cornucopia,' the bowl of plenty, corresponding to the traditional Sanskrit term *Kośa* for the royal treasury, and also of the noose which stands for *Daṇḍa*, the other emblem of sovereignty. These two symbols further strengthen the supposition that the goddess Lakshmī is the sovereign goddess of the empire (Kshiti) symbolised by *Kośa* and *Daṇḍa*. Cf. Kālidāsa: *kośadaṇḍāviva kshitih*.

4. Archer type—p. 34.

This and similar legends on other coins are inspired by Kālidāsa's classical description of heaven being attained by good deeds on earth-*dyām sukritopalabdhām* and *kumudāvadātaih dyām ārjitām karmabhirāruroha* (*Raghuvaṁśa*).

5. Chandra Gupta II Couch type—p. 54.

The reverse showse the figures of the king holding a lotus in the right hand and the legend *rupākṛiti*, 'embodiment of beauty.' Kālidāsa describes a prince at the *svayaṁvara* of Indumatī flourishing a lotus to appear handsome (*Raghuvaṁśa*).

6. Chandra Gupta II Chattra type—p. 54.

The *chattra* in Hindu polity is the symbol of sole and supreme sovereignty, that of an *ekarāṭ* as described in Kalidāśa's significant lines *ekātapatraṁ jagataḥ prabhutvam* (*Raghuvaṁśa*).

7. Kumāra Gupta I Peacock type—p. 88.

Kālidāsa throws light on the appropriateness of god Kārttikeya or Skanda appearing on the reverse as the god of war, an appropriate object of worship by kings. Kings must take after Kārttikeya and Kālidāsa writes (a) *Kumārakalpaṁ sushuve kumāram* (b) *hareḥ kumāropi kumāravikramaḥ* and *bhūyishṭham āśid upameyakāntir mayūrapṛishṭhāśarayinā guhena* (*Raghuvaṁśa*). The last line is translated into the figure of the coin.

8. Kumāra Gupta I Elephant-rider type—p. 89.

According to Sanskrit tradition the king has always a state elephant as a symbol of his sovereignty of which the umbrella is also another token.

It will thus appear from the aforesaid and many other passages of Kālidāsa that the poet created the entire vocabulary and tradition which have inspired the later Imperial Gupta inscriptions and coinage. About the priority to the Gupta age of Kālidāsa whom tradition assigns to 57 B.C. we may note a remarkable piece of evidence found on coinage to support it. It is that issued by Yajña Śrī Sātakarṇi whose date is not later than 2nd century A.D. A coin of this type shows on *obverse* the bust of king whose youth is very appropriately indicated by the symbol *kākapaksha* while his widespread fame is indicated on the *reverse* by the following symbols: (a) crescent on hill, (b) crescent on Ujjain symbol, (c) zigzag line, (d) circle of dots. The meaning of these symbols is best understood in the light of the following verse of Kālidāsa (*Raghuvaṁśa*, VI, 77): *Ārūḍharmadrīn udadhīn vitīrnaṁ bhujangamānāṁ vasatiṁ pravishṭam* | *ūrddhvaṁ gataṁ yasya na chānubandhi yaśah parichchhettuṁ iyattayālam* | The king's fame ascended the mountains (symbolised by the moon on hill), crossed the oceans (figured by the four circles of the Ujjain symbol and crescent), penetrated into the subterranean abode of Vāsuki (as figured in the zigag line) and went up to the most high (as represented in the dots standing for starry heaven).

[These references to Kālidāsa are taken from Śrī C. Śivaramamurti's interesting work entitled 'Numismatic Parallels of Kālidāsa,']

PLATE IX

Framed panel of sculptures from Deogarh Temple (*c.* 5th Century A.D.) in Jhansi District, representing four-armed Vishṇu lying in *Samādhi* or *Yoga-nidrā* on the Cosmic Serpent (*Śeshaśāyī*). Above, Brahmā on lotus in the centre; on his right, Indra and Kārttikeya, and, on left, Śiva-Pārvatī on Nandi Bull, followed by an attendant. Below, five heroes and a female figure, probably the five Pāṇḍavas and Draupadī seen at the right end. Art-critics consider this sculpture as a masterpiece of Indian art, with its unique artistic setting in a frame of pilasters and architraves in which the panel is sunk to look like a false window.

PLATE X

Penance of Nara and Nārāyana (from Deogarh Temple)

PLATE XI

A sunk panel or niche in a wall of the Deogarh Temple representing the Deliverance of the Lord of Elephants (Gajendramoksha) by Krishṇa.

PLATE XII

Deogarh Temple gate-way, with its Jamb of four decorated posts showing from right to left:

(1) Door-keeper (*Pratihārī*) surmounted by foliated scroll (*Patravalli* or *Patralatā*).

(2) A female dancer surmounted by figures of amorous couples (*Mithuna*).

(3) Another female dancer with other dancers above.

(4) A Dwarf (*Pramatha*) surmounted by the Tree of Prosperity (*Srī Vṛiksha*).

PLATE XIII

Seated Buddha Image of Sarnath, admitted on all hands as a masterpiece of art.

PLATE XIV

Deogarh Temple showing the beginnings of the *Sikhara*. (as restored by B.N. Chaudhuri, B.E., A.M.I.E., M.R. San. I. (Lond). Architect, Calcutta).

PLATE XV

Restored Bhitargaon Temple of about 4th Century A.D. in Cawnpore and its restored porch (from Percy Brown's *Indian Architecture*).

PLATE XVI

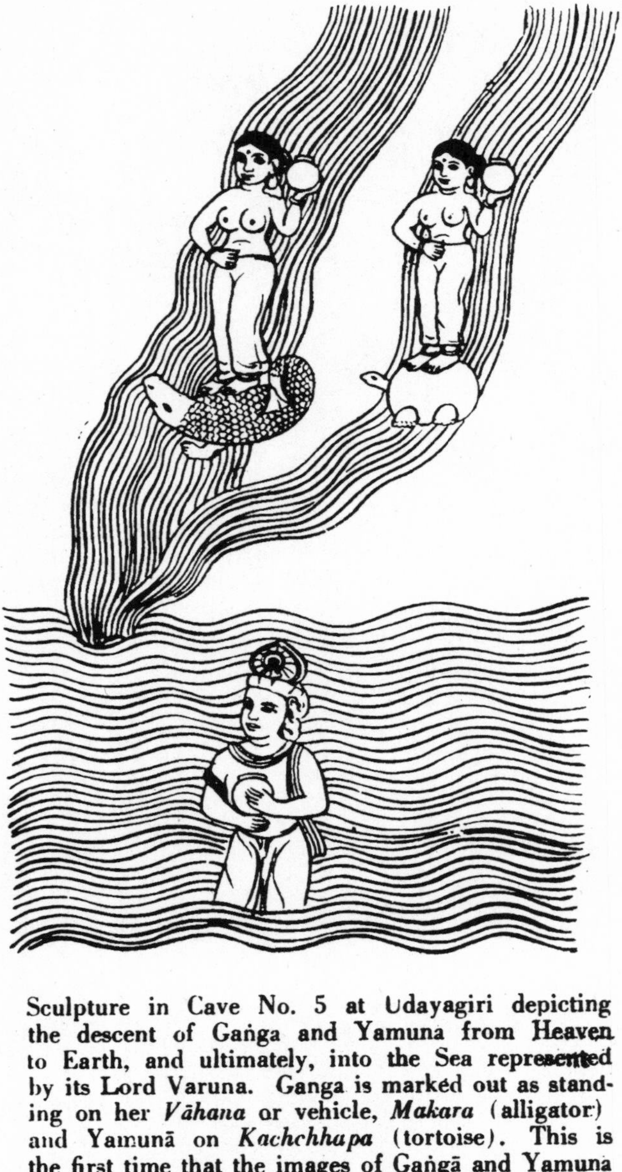

Sculpture in Cave No. 5 at Udayagiri depicting the descent of Gaṅga and Yamuna from Heaven to Earth, and ultimately, into the Sea represented by its Lord Varuna. Ganga is marked out as standing on her *Vāhana* or vehicle, ***Makara*** (alligator) and Yamunā on ***Kachchhapa*** (tortoise). This is the first time that the images of Gaṅgā and Yamuna appear in Indian sculpture with the revival of Brahmanism under the Gupta Empire, and its conquest of the countries associated with these two rivers.

PLATE XVII

Boar-Incarnation of Vishṇu from Udayagiri Cave No.5. With His right tusk the God lifts up the tiny figure of goddess Prithivī out of the floods overwhelming Her, a picture of strength and determination in carrying through His cosmic Mission of rescuing Mother Earth.

PLATE XVIII

Figure of God Sūrya as capital of a Pillar found at Pawaya (Gwalior) of Gupta times.

PLATE XIX

Fragment of lintel showing music and dance found at Pawaya: Gupta Sculpture.

INDEX OF NAMES

B

E

F

G

H

I

L

M

N

O

P

R

S

W

Y

Z